The 11 MYTHS
of MEDIA
VIOLENCE

The 11 MYTHS *of* MEDIA VIOLENCE

W. James Potter

University of California at Santa Barbara

SAGE Publications
International Educational and Professional Publisher
Thousand Oaks ■ London ■ New Delhi

For information:

Sage Publications, Inc.
2455 Teller Road
Thousand Oaks, California 91320
E-mail: order@sagepub.com

Sage Publications Ltd.
6 Bonhill Street
London EC2A 4PU
United Kingdom

Sage Publications India Pvt. Ltd.
M-32 Market
Greater Kailash I
New Delhi 110 048 India

Printed in the United States of America

Library of Congress Cataloging-in-Publication Data

Potter, W. James.
The 11 myths of media violence / W. James Potter.
    p. cm.
Includes bibliographical references and index.
ISBN 0-7619-2734-4 (hard) — ISBN 0-7619-2735-2 (pbk.)
  1. Violence in mass media. I. Title: Eleven myths of media violence.
II. Title.
P96.V5 .P678 2002
303.6—dc211

                              2002008802

02   03   04   05   10 9 8 7 6 5 4 3 2 1

Acquiring Editor:	Margaret H. Seawell
Editorial Assistant:	Alicia Carter
Production Editor:	Claudia A. Hoffman
Copy Editor:	Rachel Hile Bassett
Typesetter:	C&M Digitals (P) Ltd
Indexer:	Molly Hall
Cover Designer:	Michelle Lee

CONTENTS

PREFACE

—————•◦•—————

We are constantly flooded with violent images from the media. At the movies, we are given a choice of police officers killing dozens of people (the *Die Hard* and *Lethal Weapon* series), psychopaths killing dozens of people (the *Halloween* and *Nightmare on Elm Street* series), or teenagers killing each other (the *Scream* and *I Know What You Did Last Summer* series). When we retreat to our homes for peace and security, the evening news features crime scenes, where victims are hauled away from the bloody sidewalks in body bags. And if we ignore the news and limit our TV viewing to entertainment programs, there is more than a 60% chance that the program we choose to watch will present us with at least one violent act (National Television Violence Study [NTVS], 1999).

With these messages constantly bombarding our society, many think that the media are one of the factors responsible for the high rate of crime and violence in our country. The United States has a very high rate of crime compared with other industrialized countries. For example, among developed nations, there are 1.2 murders per million people each year; in the United States there are 65 murders per million people annually (Geen & Donnerstein, 1998). A woman reports a rape in this country every six minutes (U.S. Department of Justice, 1999). The number of aggravated assaults has increased 700% over the last five decades, starting in the early 1950s, when most American first brought televisions into their living rooms (McCain, 1998). Even relatively minor acts of aggression are increasing. On our highways, aggressive behaviors such as tailgating, weaving through busy lanes, honking or screaming at other drivers, and exchanging insults and even gunfire are a factor in nearly 28,000 traffic deaths annually; the number of such incidents is increasing at a rate of 7% a year (Wald, 1997).

Children are actively participating in this real-world violence. Gun-related violence takes the life of an American child every three hours. Every five minutes, a child is arrested for a violent crime. Should we be surprised that many children feel they must arm themselves in order to attend school safely? Every day, more than 100,000 children carry guns to school (Males, 1996).

Among adolescents, murder rates have doubled since 1990. Homicide is now the leading cause of teenage death, ahead of accidents and natural causes. Violent crime arrests have gone up 70% over the past decade; adolescents currently account for 24% of all violent crimes leading to an arrest. Depression among adolescents has increased 10-fold since the 1950s. We have more adolescents on Prozac and other antidepressants than ever before. Even so, adolescent suicide rates have tripled in the past three decades (Resnick, 1997).

There is also a huge financial cost. The U.S. Justice Department estimates the total cost of violent crime (including child abuse and domestic violence in addition to crimes such as murder, rape, and robbery) to be $500 billion per year (Butterfield, 1996). This figure is about twice the annual budget of the U.S. Department of Defense.

All things considered, the level of violence is likely to get even worse. Why? Because the emerging generation of children already appears to be more accepting of violence and more prone to act aggressively and violently. A survey of child care providers in Texas reports some startling results. Over the past five years, expressions of rage and anger in children under three years of age have increased dramatically, by 77%. For the slightly older nursery and kindergarten-age children, the child care workers reported that violent outbursts have increased 88% over the past five years. Although tradition has it that males are more prone to violence, the child care workers report that girls are almost equally as likely as boys to deal with their peers in a violent, confrontational manner (Ross, 1999).

ROLE OF MEDIA VIOLENCE

Is it a coincidence that American society has become so violent while at the same time the media—especially television—are portraying attractive characters using physical force to solve their problems? Almost all media researchers and a large percentage of the public do *not* think this is a coincidence.

Researchers have built up a base of knowledge in what some scholars estimate to be as many as 3,000 studies (Donnerstein, Slaby, & Eron, 1994) and perhaps as high as 3,500 studies (Wartella, Olivarez, & Jennings, 1998) that present ever-growing evidence that exposure to violence in the media can lead to many different negative effects. Also, since the early 1950s, public opinion has been consistently critical of the media's presentation of violence. In repeated public opinion polls on media violence, *at least* half of the American people have called for a reduction in the amount of media violence. Yet the amount of violence has remained consistently high in entertainment programs and has dramatically increased in news shows (NTVS, 1998).

Despite the half century of public criticism, congressional hearings, and research activity, the problem persists. Why? This book suggests an answer to this question by arguing that our perspective on the problem has been and continues to be faulty, because the public debate and discussion on this issue are limited by misinformation, which leads to misperceptions. We need to challenge our beliefs and the ways we look at this problem.

How did I come to this conclusion? It wasn't a sudden epiphany. Instead, it developed through a gradual accretion of experience. For more than 15 years, I had been conducting scientific studies on the content and effects of violence in the media. As the editor of the scholarly *Journal of Broadcasting & Electronic Media,* I made hundreds of judgments about the value of the research of others. Then I served as one of the principal investigators on the National Television Violence Project, which was funded by the National Cable Television Association and which analyzed the content of over 10,000 hours of television across 23 channels over three years.

During this time of reading the research, generating research of my own, listening to people in the industry and government, and reading about public opinion, I had a growing feeling that something wasn't right. It seemed that we were on a course that was leading us nowhere.

It occurred to me that there were in essence two problems. The surface problem was the proliferation of violence in the media and how it affects individuals and society. This is the more visible problem and the one that receives all the attention. The other problem is more fundamental and needs to be addressed first. This underlying problem is the lack of sharing of good information. Instead, a lot of misinformation circulates, and this serves more to help different people win arguments or defend their position than to foster a sense of understanding through cooperation.

The separation of people into four different cultures is in large part what makes this underlying condition such a persistent problem. These four cultures are the producers (writers, directors, studio heads, television programmers, etc.), who create and market the messages that contain violence; the public, who complain about the violence while at the same time supporting it with their money and attention; researchers, who generate knowledge about the forms of media violence and how they put the public at risk for negative effects; and policymakers, who try to negotiate a compromise between the public's criticism and the producers' right to artistic expression. The people in each of the groups–producers, public, researchers, and policymakers–have become entrenched. Each group has its own set of beliefs, and the unthinking adherence to these beliefs prevents people in one group from understanding the people in the other groups. As a result, the discourse about media violence is characterized by arguments designed to protect one's own way of thinking rather than an openness that allows for cooperation and a sharing of wisdom. These arguments often depend on misinformation, because the goal is to win the argument, not to increase understanding of the problem. Until we make progress on overcoming the underlying problem of misunderstanding, we have no hope for making any worthwhile contributions to address the surface problem of changing practices, such as the way producers present violence in the media, the way large numbers of the public complain about too much violence yet are still attracted to it, the way researchers have allowed their work to be marginalized in the public debate, and the way policymakers heighten expectations for change but then fail to follow through. Greater understanding is the infrastructure required for meaningful change.

CHALLENGING EXISTING BELIEFS

This book presents a challenge to a set of existing beliefs about media violence. I refer to these existing beliefs as "myths" because these beliefs are accepted by most people in a culture, despite their flaws either in reasoning or in factual evidence.

Some myths are strongly held beliefs by people within only one culture; for example, Myth 5 (Violence in the media reflects violence in society) is strongly held by most producers but not by many people in the other cultures. Other myths cut across cultures and are believed by people in several different cultures; for example, Myth 4 (There is too much violence in the media) is a widespread belief among members of the public, researchers, policymakers, and even some producers.

It is not surprising that people in different cultures adhere to different myths. Each culture has a different set of goals and therefore a different perspective on the situation of media violence. For example, producers have the goal of following the most fundamental of all business principles, that is, maximizing the wealth of the owners of their companies. It is understandable that producers would want to defend themselves from criticism from other cultures, so they willingly accept myths such as Myth 6 (The media are only responding to market desires) and Myth 7 (Violence is an essential element in all fiction).

It is useful to challenge our myths periodically—whether those myths be about the economy, America's place in the world, or human relationships—so that we understand what is guiding our thinking. Without such challenges to our thinking, myths control us by focusing our attention on certain things while we ignore others. Perhaps the most dangerous consequence of an unexamined myth is that it makes us feel that we are well informed and do not need to examine our assumptions.

This book is organized to focus attention on 11 myths about media violence. When taken as a set, these 11 myths have formed the walls of a maze that keep us wandering around, trapped in a condition of circular thinking. These myths keep our focus on false information and thereby prevent us from understanding the nature of the problem as well as developing a clear vision for what a meaningful solution would be.

PEELING THE ONION

These 11 myths need to be critically analyzed and challenged. This means that for each claim, we need to get beneath the surface claims, that is, to "peel the onion" so that we can uncover the fallacies in beliefs and in logic.

When we move our awareness to deeper levels, we often find that what we accept as truth on the surface turns out to be a faulty claim when we peel away the layers of opinion and information in order to see things a different way. To illustrate this, let's return to my claim made earlier that the rate of crime is very high in the United States. I presented figures that indicated the

United States has very high rates of violent crime, especially murder, rape, and assault.

Someone who has been following the rates of crime carefully over the past decade could argue that my statement is misleading, because the rates of violent crime have been declining throughout the 1990s in the United States. This argument is valid. From 1990 to 1997, the national crime index dropped 15.4%. The crime index includes violent crimes (murder, nonnegligent manslaughter, forcible rape, robbery, and aggravated assault) as well as property crimes (burglary, larceny-theft, and motor vehicle theft). When looking at violent crime only, there is an even larger drop—16.5%—over that time period (Bureau of Justice Statistics, 1999b). From 1990 to 1997, the rate of rape was down 12.9%, and the rate of assault was down 9.9% (Bureau of Justice Statistics, 1999b).

If we stop the analysis at this point, we are left with the conclusion that crime—especially violent crime—is losing its importance as a significant problem. The rate of violent crime has been consistently dropping for almost a decade, so the factors that once drove up crime rates now seem to be under control. But this conclusion is also misleading. When we expand our analysis, we can see there are several things wrong with such a conclusion. First, the crime rates are still very high despite the recent reductions, and these reductions appear slight when using a larger time frame as context. From 1960 to 1997, the national crime index rose 279.7%, even after accounting for the drop of 15.4% throughout the 1990s. From 1960 to 1997, the overall rate of rape was up 274.7%, and the rate of assault was up 343.9% (Bureau of Justice Statistics, 1999b). Believing that crime is *not* still a big problem is a mistake. It is rather like claiming a person with a temperature of 103.2° is not sick because her temperature is down from 103.4°.

Furthermore, the *declines* seem to have stopped. For example, in 2000, rape and aggravated assault figures indicated an increase of 0.7% and 0.4%, respectively, over the previous year. In the property crime category, motor vehicle theft increased by 2.7%, and larceny-theft increased 0.1% when compared with 1999 data (Federal Bureau of Investigation [FBI], 2001a).

Let's extend the analysis to yet a deeper level by asking: Why did we have reductions in the rates of crime throughout the 1990s, and why might those reductions be a trend that is now over? There are likely to be many factors, but one of the more telling ones is that during the 1990s when the crime rate was going down, the nation's courts were incarcerating more criminals, especially violent felons. From 1990 to the end of 1999, the prison population increased from 292 inmates per 100,000 U.S. residents up to 478 per 100,000—an increase of 64% in one decade. The increases in rates for incarcerating criminals were much faster among violent felons than nonviolent ones. From 1990 to 1999, the percentage of the prison population that was serving time for violent crimes climbed from 46% to 51% (FBI, 2001b).

Removing criminals from society seems to be one successful way of reducing the rate of crime. But how far can we go with this strategy? By the end of the decade the existing prisons reached full capacity or overcapacity, and the incarceration rate had to slow down. At the end of 2000, state prisons were operating between full capacity and 15% above capacity, and federal prisons were operating at 31% above capacity (Bureau of Justice Statistics, 2001).

From a criminology point of view, the problem seems to be not enough prisons. The more prisons you build, the more you remove criminals from society where they commit crimes, and therefore the crime rate will continue to go down. But the influences on rates of crime look different from other points of view. For example, from a sociological point of view, crime is influenced by poverty, child abuse, and the easy availability of guns. And from a media point of view, the problem of crime can be traced in large part to conditioning; that is, perhaps the media are conditioning people to believe that aggression and violence are the means to living an exciting life. Even if we were to lock up all of today's criminals, the media are still helping to train another generation to believe that violence is a successful way to solve problems. Is it a coincidence that the rates of crime, especially violent crime, spiked up shortly after televisions appeared in 99% of American households and that the increases continued until recently, when the rate of incarceration spiked up?

This is a complex problem that requires perspectives from criminology, sociology, media studies, and perhaps more areas. The media do not act alone; they should not be given all the blame for negative effects. But neither should they be ignored; the media are an important factor. This book focuses on what is believed to be their influence and how those beliefs are subtly misleading or plainly wrong.

A CAVEAT

In the following chapters I will be challenging some of the most strongly held beliefs of producers, the public, researchers, and policymakers. My analyses of some of these myths may appear controversial to many readers. But this is the nature of treating certain beliefs as myths, analyzing them, and arguing for alternative perspectives.

Furthermore, some readers may feel offended by a particular analysis. If so, I ask that they take notice that I am likely to offend all types of readers; I am not privileging one group as having superior knowledge and perspectives compared with the others.

I ask readers who are bothered by a challenge to a myth to consider doing two things. First, examine what supports your belief. Are you sure you have enough facts and that those facts are credible? Or do you cling to your belief because it is easier to do so than to change? And second, ask yourself what could be gained by changing your belief. Does your current belief help you see the problem in enough depth that you feel confident that you can protect yourself from the risks of negative effects from media violence? Or does your current belief serve to wall you off from having to assume greater responsibility for your own behaviors?

Also, I need to make a distinction between myths based on a factual claim and those based on a normative claim, because this has implications for how the myth is critically analyzed. Factual claims present a statement of what is, whereas normative claims argue for what ought to be. Normative claims cannot be judged on the same standard as factual claims.

For myths based on a factual claim, the standard is the validity of the argument. An argument is valid if it assembles a sufficient amount of evidence and presents it in a compelling manner. The evidence should come from credible sources and should itself appear reasonable. An example of a myth based on a factual claims is the first myth: Violence in the media does not affect me, but others are at high risk.

In contrast, with myths based on a normative claim, the standard is utility. Utility with this topic means the ability to ameliorate the problem for everyone. Normative claims that would enhance the position of one group over another are less useful in ameliorating the problem than are claims that would on balance help everyone. For example, Myth 2 (The media are not responsible for the negative effects of their violent messages) and Myth 9 (The First Amendment protects the media from restrictions on violence) are based on normative claims. The analyses of myths such as these rely more on examining the varying interpretations of the people in different groups than on determining which interpretations are designed primarily to protect one group's entrenched interests and which are crafted instead to account for the interests of two, three, or all of the groups.

OUTLINE OF THIS BOOK

This book begins with a chapter presenting the context of the problem of media violence. The positions of the people in the four cultures are presented. Then the book presents 11 chapters analyzing each of the 11 myths. The book concludes with a chapter assessing the prognosis for a meaningful solution to the surface problem of media violence as well as the underlying problem of misunderstanding.

The first myth is the widespread belief among individuals that violence in the media does not affect them, but that other people are at high risk. This belief allows people to decouple their fear (that other people are experiencing negative effects and thus behaving in aggressive and criminal ways) from their sense of personal responsibility (that the problem lies within themselves where they are experiencing many of the negative effects and therefore need to change their own behaviors and attitudes).

A second myth is the belief that the media are not responsible for any negative effects in society. Many people believe that the negative effects attributed to the media are caused by nonmedia factors, such as poverty, availability of guns, child abuse, and so forth. Although these factors cannot be ignored, neither can media factors. Instead of blaming one or two factors, it is more useful to recognize that there are many factors in the process of influence and that all the factors work together to increase a person's risk for each of the many negative effects.

Most adults believe that violence in the media primarily affects children. Again, this false belief serves to decouple their fear that the next generation is being poisoned from their responsibility to look within themselves and see that there are many negative effects that are also poisoning them as adults.

"There is too much violence in the media"—this is a common complaint voiced by the public. But the irony is that most people do not regard most of the serious assaults and maimings that are portrayed in the media as being violent. The public has been conditioned to accept a very narrow definition of what is violence—ignoring highly violent acts that are interlaced with humor or that appear in a less-than-real context. People generally underperceive the amount of violence in the media, and if they were not already so desensitized (a major negative effect), they would be far more critical.

Producers of entertainment programming claim that the violence they present just reflects violence in society. However, violence in the media world is both an overrepresentation of violence as well as a distortion compared with patterns of violence in the real world.

Producers of media violence also claim that they are merely responding to market desires. Again, this is a partial truth. Yes, the media are businesses, and as such they must supply what their consumers demand. However, the media also shape markets, and they therefore have created and continue to reinforce the demand for violence.

Many producers claim that violence is an essential element in telling stories. But it is conflict—not violence—that is essential in storytelling. Violence is only one of many tools that can be used to create and heighten conflict.

Many believe that reducing the amount of violence in the media will solve the problem. Again, this is a myth. The problem is less with the frequency of the violence than with the way in which the violence is portrayed. Because violence is portrayed in a negative context, frequency then becomes a problem. However, if violence in the media were portrayed in a positive context, frequency would not be a problem.

Producers of media violence continually claim that the First Amendment is an absolute protection of their freedom of expression. But this is a distortion of the actual wording of the First Amendment, which provides a protection of individuals from the federal government allowing them to speak out and worship as they please. Using a literal interpretation of the First Amendment, there is no protection for businesses who want to market products exclusively for profit, nor is there any protection from product liability.

Is the V-chip a solution to the problem of media violence? No, because the problem with media violence is not a hardware problem, so it cannot be addressed adequately by adding a circuit that can be programmed in all new television sets. Instead, the problem of media violence has more to do with a lack of responsibility to the common good. Congress demonstrated such a lack of responsibility with the way it implemented the V-chip system; that is, Congress allowed the producers of violence to develop their own ratings system, to rate their own programs with no oversight, and to allow producers to ignore the V-chip entirely with no penalty. The producers exhibited a lack of responsibility by first refusing to develop a system, then grudgingly developing one—but one that provides viewers with as little information as possible. As a result few, if any, people use the network rating system.

Finally, perhaps the biggest myth of all is when people believe that there is nothing that individuals can do to make an effect on reducing the problem. People are too dependent on others—such as the federal government—to create regulations to protect them. If people understand the problem better and are willing to change some of their behaviors, they can do a great deal to protect themselves from negative effects.

I conclude the book with a chapter that offers alternatives to the 11 myths. These alternatives are couched in a public health perspective. The problem with media violence ultimately lies in finding a way to reduce the risks of harmful effects to all individuals as well as society while at the same time not restricting artistic expression, legitimate commerce, or people's access to the widest range of messages possible. This is indeed a complex problem. But the immediate problem with media violence is to get the discussion about it "unstuck" from where it is today and has been for the past several decades. Public opinion has been consistently critical for 50 years, and congressional hearings have been largely reruns for 50 years. We need to see the problem from different perspectives so that we can appreciate its many facets and ultimately perceive some fresh approaches to dealing with the problem.

We need to share perspectives and construct some common ground where we can communicate better with one another, rather than continuing to talk past one another until we are all even more frustrated. Therefore, the contribution of the analyses in this book is to "peel the onion" so we can get below the surface and examine the shortcomings of each myth. If this leads to a more informed discussion—replacing a misinformed debate—then this book will have made a contribution to addressing the underlying problem of a lack of understanding about media violence. When we first work to reduce this underlying problem, we will be creating a condition where we can move forward on the surface problem of bringing about change in the behavior of people in all four groups so that the sum of their cooperative effort benefits everyone.

THE 11 MYTHS

1. Violence in the media does not affect me, but others are at high risk.

2. The media are not responsible for the negative effects of their violent messages.

3. Children are especially vulnerable to the risks of negative exposure to media violence.

4. There is too much violence in the media.

5. Violence in the media reflects violence in society.

6. The media are only responding to market desires.

7. Violence is an essential element in all fiction.

8. Reducing the amount of violence in the media will solve the problem.

9. The First Amendment protects the media from restrictions on violence.

10. The rating systems and V-chip will help solve the problem.

11. There is nothing I can do to make an effect on reducing the problem.

ONE

CURRENT CONTEXT

⎯⎯⎯•◦•⎯⎯⎯

The problem of media violence has been with us for as long as we have had mass media. From the earliest days, storytellers have been presenting conflict in the form of violence, and the public has sought out these stories. As each new medium has come on the scene and consumed more of the population's attention, exposure to violence in the media has grown, and along with the exposure, criticism of the violence has also grown. With the arrival of the medium of television into most American households during the 1950s, criticism of media violence became widespread throughout the population. The U.S. Congress picked up on public concern 50 years ago and began holding official hearings on the problem—and those hearings continue up until today. The problem attracted scores of researchers who conducted studies to determine the nature of violence in the media and its potential effects on the population. Despite all this activity and concern, the problem is still with us today; we are no closer to a solution or even an amelioration. Why?

In this book, I will show that the persistence of this problem can be traced to the context in which it has grown. This context is an arena in which four players—the public, producers, policymakers, and researchers—have grappled with this issue in a largely adversarial manner. The primary conflict is between the public and the producers of media violence. The other two groups—policymakers and researchers—have over time been moved into roles to facilitate this conflict.

If all four groups had the same goal and worked together cooperatively, we would likely have seen movement toward a solution. But the groups have had different goals. The public is motivated by a fear that vulnerable elements in society—such as children and unstable people—are being influenced by violent portrayals to learn how to commit crimes and are being stimulated to act on their aggressive drives. The public wants the federal government to exercise some sort of control over producers in order to reduce these risks. Producers are motivated to maximize their profits, which requires them to create programming that they believe will attract the largest audiences.

The other two groups—policymakers and researchers—are facilitators of this central struggle between the public and producers. Policymakers provide a forum for the other three groups to air their concerns. Over the past five decades there have been 28 major hearings by Congress—in addition to less formal sessions—to discuss this problem. Throughout this time, policymakers have been successful at keeping the issue on the public's agenda of problems, but they have not had much success in brokering a compromise that could bring about more of a balance of power and hence a greater sharing of goals.

Researchers have generated a great deal of potentially useful information, but little of that potential has been realized. One finding—that exposure to violence in the media puts people at risk for behaving more aggressively—has worked its way into the public's knowledge base. But there is little evidence that the public, much less producers and policymakers, realizes that there is a broad spectrum of risks or understands the process of influence that can alter those risks. So much of what the public thinks it "knows" about the issue of media violence is based not on factual evidence but on intuitively derived opinions. Researchers have been far more successful at generating valid information about the nature and effects of media violence than they have been at getting the public, policymakers, and producers to understand or accept that information.

Because the goals of the groups differ, each group argues louder in the hopes that its voice will be heard and convince the other groups that its goals are more important than the goals of the other groups. However, as all groups raise their voices, the noise level gets louder, and the ability to understand the other groups gets lost. Frustration builds, and we are locked in a situation where no one really hears or understands the values of the people in the other groups. The players think they know what the other groups are saying, but this is a misperception that leads to misinformation, which then circulates and takes on a life of its own. People accept this misinformation, blend it with their intuitions, and use this dangerous mix to create their opinions.

THE PUBLIC

Over the past several decades, many public opinion leaders have spoken out against media violence (see Table 1.1). Public opinion polls show that the people generally are critical of the media, because they feel there is too much violence in the media and that this violence is causing harmful effects (see Table 1.2).

Although the belief that the media are causing a harmful effect is widespread in the public, knowledge about the nature of the negative effects and how they work seems to be lacking. A good illustration of the misinformed nature of the topic among well-meaning people occurred just after the shootings at Columbine High School in Littleton, Colorado, in the spring of 1999. This horrible event triggered national news coverage that lasted for weeks. This gave columnists a chance to write about violence in our society. One example is John Leo, who writes a weekly column for *U.S. News & World Report*. In his column titled "The Devil With Ms. Jones," Leo (1999a) railed against violence in the media, especially in video games. By arguing for the elimination of violence in the media, his intention was clearly to stir up controversy and elicit strong reactions from readers, which he did. Two weeks after Leo's column appeared, *U.S. News & World Report* published five letters to the editor in response to that column. The ideas expressed in Leo's column and in the five responses provide a good illustration of what is wrong with public opinion on the issue of media violence. Each presents a sliver of insight but misses the bigger picture, so each is faulty not because of what it says but because of what it leaves unsaid. Each is a sound byte that entices the imagination but has little—or misleading—informational value. In one of the reaction letters, the writer chides Leo for blaming the media, saying, "We are a country full of finger pointers. When tragedies occur, we blame the media, the movie industry, the video game industry—the list goes on and on. However, no one bothers to look in the most obvious place, the mirror." Of course, the writer is correct that the adolescent shooters at Littleton had the power to control their actions and should be held responsible. But this should not mean that the media had no role in shaping their values and behaviors. The media should not be regarded as blameless merely because there are also other sources of blame. This is an example of partial understanding. We need to get past the limitation of searching for single causes—life is more complicated than that. There are many factors that shape who we are, and the media are an important—but not the sole—factor in that shaping.

(Text continues on page 7)

Table 1.1   Opinion Leaders Perceive Harm

Public Health Groups

1976	American Medical Association's House of Delegates declares violence an "environmental hazard."
1984	The American Academy of Pediatrics Task Force on Children and Television releases a report cautioning physicians and parents that television may promote aggressive behavior.
1985	The American Psychological Association Commission on Youth Violence releases a report linking television violence and real-world violence.
1992	The American Psychological Association calls for a federal policy to protect the public from the harms of televised violence.
1993	The American Psychological Association says, "There is absolutely no doubt that higher levels of viewing violence on television are correlated with increased acceptance of aggressive attitudes and increased aggressive behavior. In addition to increasing violent behaviors toward others, viewing violence on television changes attitudes and behaviors toward violence in significant ways" (p. 33).
1995	The American Academy of Pediatrics, which represents 48,000 pediatricians, says the evidence is clear: Violence in entertainment makes some children more aggressive, desensitizes them to real-life violence, and makes them feel they live in a mean and dangerous world. "There's no debate. There is clearly a relationship between media violence and violence in the community," says Vic Strasburger, author of the pediatricians' statement and chief of pediatrics at the University of New Mexico School of Medicine. Dr. Strasburger continues, "We are basically saying the controversy is over. There is clearly a relationship between media violence and violence in society" ("Doctor's Push," 1995, p. A16). Similar statements are also released by the American Academy of Child and Adolescent Psychiatry, the American Public Health Association, and the National Association of Attorneys General.
1996	The American Medical Association says, "An extensive body of research amply documents a strong correlation between children's exposure to media violence and a number of behavioral and psychological problems, primarily aggressive behavior. The evidence further shows that these problems are caused by the exposure itself" (American Medical Association, 1996).

Table 1.1 Continued

Government Leaders

1969   The National Commission on the Causes and Prevention of Violence issues a report stating that exposure to television increases physical aggression.

1972   The U.S. Surgeon General issues a report on violence stating a causal link between violent behavior and violence on television and motion pictures.

1982   A National Institute of Mental Health report confirms a link between television violence and aggressive behavior.

1984   The Attorney General's Task Force on Family Violence releases a report claiming that television violence contributes to actual violence.

1991   Deborah Prothrow-Stith, the former Massachusetts commissioner of public health, writes in her book about youth and violence, *Deadly Consequences,* "Children who watch a great deal of violent TV are desensitized to the wrongness of what they are seeing" (Robb, 1991, p. 27).

1993   Attorney General Janet Reno supports the regulation of violence on television, saying that in her opinion, "TV violence legislation will pass constitutional muster" (McAvoy & Coe, 1993, p. 6).

1994   Reed Hundt, Chairman of the Federal Communications Commission (FCC), announces an agenda to support restrictions on violent content on television, saying that the violence children view "affects their behavior negatively to some measurable and meaningful degree" (Eggerton, 1995).

1995   Former Sen. Bob Dole (R-KS), running for President, says that cultural messages affect "the hearts and minds of our young people."
        Sen. Paul Simon (D-IL) says, "We are past questions on the research" (Leland, 1995, p. 16).
        Sen. Ernest Hollings (D-SC) calls the situation a "crisis," because each year hundreds of millions of people witness thousands of deaths. Killing for romance, killing for sex, killing for dinner, and killing for time are just some of the money-making themes coming out of Hollywood (Lutterbeck, 1995).
        Newton Minow, former chairman of the FCC, reflecting on the research studies about media violence, says, "All of them consistently show that television violence contributes to real violence" (Minow & LeMay, 1995, p. 28).

1996   Rep. Joseph P. Kennedy II (D-MA) says, "Study after study has shown that television violence causes aggressive and violent behavior in children who watch it. Despite this growing body of evidence, TV and cable companies continue to broadcast murders, rapes, and gratuitous violence into our living rooms" (Kennedy, 1996).

(Continued)

Table 1.1 Continued

| 1998 | Vice President Al Gore says, "Numerous national experts have demonstrated that children who do view a large amount of TV violence are significantly more likely to exhibit aggressive behavior." He continues, "There's really no serious controversy about that linkage" (Jones, 1998, p. 1). |
| 2001 | In January, U.S. Surgeon General David Satcher says, "Exposure to violent media plays an important causal role in this societal problem of youth violence." He adds that repeated exposure to violent entertainment during early childhood causes more aggressive behavior throughout a child's life (Leeds, 2001, p. A1). |

Consumer Action Groups

1975	The National Parent-Teacher Association (PTA) adopts a resolution demanding that networks and local television stations reduce the amount of violence in programming.
1980	The National Coalition on Television Violence is formed.
1994	Barbara Hattemer, president of the National Family Association, says that television teaches "that violence is an everyday occurrence and an acceptable way of solving problems" (1994, p. 360).
1996	The National Foundation to Improve Television (a reform group in Boston) says, "Three different Surgeons General, the U.S. Attorney General's Task Force on Family Violence, the American Medical Association, the American Academy of Pediatrics, the American Psychological Association, and many others have spoken out about the dangers of television violence" (National Foundation to Improve Television, 1996).
1999	William Bennett, head of Empower America, says, "Almost no one, except for a few blinded by financial stakes, thinks that the popular culture is not having a coarsening effect on our kids." He adds, "The evidence, empirical and anecdotal, is overwhelming." He says that there is an "inescapable logic" that a culture brimming with violence does in fact beget violence (Stern, 1999a). Dr. James E. Savage Jr., director of the Institute for Life Enrichment in Washington, D.C., which focuses on problems of black men, agrees that exposure to violence can lead people to violent behavior. "There's an unconscious part of ourselves that tends to sometimes become uncontrolled," he says. "Society has a lot of loose boundaries as it relates to violence, and it permits this to manifest."

Table 1.1 Continued

Religious Leaders

1985	The National Council of Churches of Christ says that the results of the congressional hearings and research reports indicate a clear causal relationship between television violence and aggressive behavior and that the broadcast industry's demands for absolute proof of such a relationship are "self serving and unprincipled" (Parley, 1985).
1994	Pope John Paul II says that much of the content on television is excessively violent and harmful to the world society.
1995	Rev. Don Wildmon, head of the 1.9 million-member American Family Association, says, "We are beyond a crisis. "We are at the stage of serious business now because [media violence] is affecting everybody" (Lutterbeck, 1995).

Another letter was from a 16-year-old Ohio boy who also complained that Leo was blaming the media. He wrote, "These two [the perpetrators of the Littleton massacre] were obsessed with such things because of latent violent tendencies, not the other way around." He continued, saying that movies and games "are not a whetstone to turn dull male adolescent angst into cold-blooded homicide." This writer sets himself up as the perpetrators' psychologist. How can a person who never met these boys be so sure that things are the other way around? Perhaps things are as the writer guesses, but shouldn't we be more careful to find out first before acting so sure?

Another writer complained that Leo "blurs the lines between reality and fantasy." He says, "It cannot be violence and killing in a video game or in a movie if you are not killing or harming anything that is real. If I take a stick and beat a brick with it, am I killing the brick or committing violence against it? No, of course not. And yet pseudo characters in the video games and the movies are even less real than the brick." This writer exhibits the problem that he himself is complaining about—that is, he blurs the distinction between reality and fantasy. Of course the video game characters themselves are fantasy, but the people who play the games are real people. The playing of a violent video game is not fully contained within a realm of pure fantasy, nor does it take place in the realm of pure reality. The game playing illustrates the interplay between the two. As people learn how to play the game and win, they generalize from those fantasy-generated experiences. We constantly use the lessons learned from the media to guide our actions in real life.

Table 1.2   Public Perceives Harm

1977	A Gallup poll reports that 70% of those polled say there is a relationship between violence on television and the rising U.S. crime rate (Oldenburg & Snider, 1999).
1993	A Gallup poll finds that 88% of respondents say television has either an "important" or "critical" effect on crime.
	A *Los Angeles Times* poll conducted in 1993 finds that 79% of respondents think there is a connection between television entertainment and viciousness in real life ("Most Believe," 1993).
	A *Times Mirror* poll finds that 78% agree that media violence is a factor in the breakdown of law and order (U.S. Department of Justice, 1999, p. 238).
1994	A *U.S. News & World Report* poll finds that 92% of Americans think TV contributes to violence in this country, and 65% think that entertainment programs on television have a negative influence on American life (U.S. News & World Report Online, 1994).
	In a *Parents* magazine poll, 73% agree that "the depiction of violence in the movies, on TV, and so forth is the cause of increased acts of violence in our society" (Diamant, 1994, p. 40).
1995	A Time/CNN survey finds that 76% of those polled say they believe violence numbs people and makes them insensitive to violence; 75% say it inspires young people to commit violence; and 71% say it has the effect of making people believe that violence is fun and acceptable (Lacayo, 1995).
	A Gallup poll reports that 75% believe there is a relationship between television violence and the nation's crime rate (U.S. Department of Justice, 1999, p. 223).
	A *New York Times* poll finds that 56% of those polled believe that media violence contributes to teenage violence.
1997	A *Los Angeles Times* poll finds that 70% say they believe that violence on television causes people to behave violently occasionally; this is an increase from 58% holding such a belief in 1989 (Lowry, 1997).
1999	A week after the April 20, 1999, shooting at Columbine High School, a *USA Today* poll finds that 73% of the public say TV and movies share at least a little of the blame for teen crimes (Oldenburg & Snider, 1999).
	The Annenberg Public Policy Center conducts a survey several weeks after the Littleton shootings and reports that most parents are "deeply fearful" about the Web's influence on their children (Oldenburg & Snider, 1999).
1999	When asked if various media contribute to crime in the United States, 92% say they believed television does; 92% say movies do; 82% say video games do; and 81% say local television news does (Bureau of Justice Statistics, 1999a).

A fourth writer argued that the playing of violent games can have a positive effect. He says, "Violent games (for the majority of people) do not encourage violent behavior. They provide an escape valve for naturally occurring violent tendencies. A good Quake death match is an excellent way to boil off excess stress and frustration." The author, of course, is correct that some people can experience a reduction of aggression by boiling off "excess stress" while playing a violent game. But a catharsis is only one of many effects that could result from playing a highly violent game. For example, in using Quake as a vicarious escape valve for violent tendencies, players might be desensitizing themselves to violence so that over time they lose sympathy for victims.

Finally, a philosophy professor argued that there is much violence in literature and asks, "Would he [Leo] want to restrict teenagers' access to it?" Illustrated here is the problem of regarding all violence as the same and ignoring the context. The context of a Quake game is very different from the context of violence in a fictional narrative in the control of a great author. Playing the Quake game trains people to react quickly with fight-flight reactions and reinforces the mind*less* aggressive response. Encountering violence in a great novel leads readers to think about the nature of violence and to be mind*ful* of its consequences.

Each of these letter writers, as well as Leo himself in his column, make important points about our exposure to violence in the media and its influence on us. But each is limited by his or her narrow perspective. These limitations color what the letter writers say and render their insights naive. Although this set of letters is only one example, it illustrates many of the problems with the general thinking about media violence. It shows a lack of understanding that there are many effects of violence, that the media are an important part (but not the only part) of the process of influencing the effect, that context is more important than the violence itself, that fantasy experiences can have an effect on how we view reality, and perhaps most important, that we need good information in place of intuitive speculation.

In summary, the public is motivated to reduce risks to themselves and especially to their children, but their idea of risk is flawed. The public has a very narrow perspective on the range of negative effects that can—and do—occur from exposure to media violence. The public is concerned primarily about aggressive behavior coming from other people. They do not understand all the negative effects that are possible—and that are probably happening to them. They do not understand how they can protect themselves apart from asking the federal government to do something to reduce the amount of violence in the media.

PRODUCERS

Producers of media violence work for businesses that seek to buy and present programming designed to attract as large an audience as possible. Larger audiences mean higher revenues. When the media businesses can maximize revenues and minimize expenses, they create large profits, and this is their primary purpose for doing business. Violent portrayals are believed to be attractive to large numbers of people and are at the same time relatively inexpensive to produce. Given this entrenched belief, people in the media industries feel threatened when people outside those industries subject them to any kind of criticism and pressure them to reduce the use of violence. When those critics argue that the marketing of violent entertainment and information is harmful to the general population, producers counter that evidence does not exist to support the critics' claim. The industry has always responded with this argument, and this response continues to this day, usually in one of three forms: denial, shifting the blame, and defensive actions.

Denial

In the aftermath of the April 20, 1999, incident in Littleton, Colorado, in which two teenage boys shot and killed 12 of their fellow high school students and a teacher before taking their own lives, criticism flared up again. Many people were blaming the media for presenting so much violence, and many in the media were again avoiding any responsibility for negative effects. For example, the heads of two of the world's largest media corporations, Time Warner CEO Gerald Levin and Seagram CEO Edgar Bronfman Jr., denied any blame for influencing the behavior of teenagers who kill one another and even expressed contempt for the idea and for the critics who make such claims (Stern, 1999b).

Denial comes in many forms. One form of denial is to denounce claims that violence in the media has a negative effect. For example, Wes Craven, director of horror movies such as *Scream* and *Nightmare on Elm Street,* says he does not believe his movies could influence children to recreate such violence in their lives (*"Scream 3* Director," 1999). Also, Fox's executive vice president, George Vradenburg, asserts, "I think most in the television business do not accept the view that what we put on television, what is on over the air, is contributing in any significant measure to violence in society" (Brennan, 1995, p. Y6).

Another form of denial is for people to concede that there are negative effects—but not from the violence on *their* show. Jerry Springer said that although he does agree that the violence in the media contributes to violence in society, he does not believe that his show contributes to violence in society. Springer reasons that his viewers would *not* imitate the violence on his program, because his violence is not glorified like it is in the movies:

> You know, as long as the people that do the fighting and shoot the guns and blow up the buildings are great-looking movie stars and, you know, then we love it. But if it's a show like ours where everyone doesn't look like Arnold Schwarzenegger or Bruce Willis or what have you, and they don't have the big guns that blow people away or the bombs that blow up the big buildings, as long as it's not that, but it's the people who are on our show, all of a sudden we say, Ooh, that's awful, that's disgusting. (*Good Morning America,* 1999)

Springer is certainly right that his guests are not glamorous. But a glamorous role model is not the only factor that can stimulate imitation. If Springer were able to move out of denial, he would realize that viewers are much more likely to imitate the type of violence they see on his show than the violence in an Arnold Schwarzenegger film. It is easier to attack your friends verbally than it is to stab or shoot them.

Another form of denial is for industry people to argue that they are solid citizens and would never produce harmful programming. They claim that they have strong family values just like the people who criticize them. For example, Dick Wolf, producer of *Law & Order,* said that most people in Hollywood have children and nuclear families, which makes them share the concerns of everyday Americans. Also, Sandy Grushow, president of 20th Century Fox Television, which produces shows like the *X-Files* and *The Simpsons,* said that if people throughout the country had contact with Hollywood producers and programmers, they would realize that television executives share the values of "America at large."

A deeper form of denial is to argue that the media do not present violence. For example, Richard Donner, director of the *Lethal Weapon* movies, *Superman, The Omen,* and *The Goonies,* among others, said, "If people see gratuitous violence in any of the *Lethal Weapon* movies, I wonder if they've seen the same movie." He congratulates himself on being socially responsible: "I brought social issues into the *Lethal Weapon* movies, like when Danny Glover's family comes down on him for eating tuna, or the 'Stamp out the NRA' sign up in the LA police station. In the last one the daughter wears a pro-choice T-shirt" (Krasny, 1993). Apparently Donner believes that one scene that has a character wearing a T-shirt with a slogan can affect the audience but that dozens of scenes of violence will have no effect. Also, it is interesting to note that Donner is proud of sending a message to protect the rights of tuna fish, while he ignores what his action scenes are telling the audience about how we should treat humans.

Yet another form of denial is to claim that the amount of violence is decreasing. Jack Valenti said, "I think that what the networks have done in the past 18 months, which is to measurably reduce the amount of violence on TV, is fantastic" (Eggerton, 1995, p. 13). Valenti based his conclusion on the results of a three-year study financed by the National Association of Broadcasters (NAB). This NAB study reported that in its first year of analysis, there were eight television programs that contained violence worthy of concern and that by the second year, the number had dropped to four programs. What Valenti did not acknowledge were the findings of the National Television Violence Study (NTVS), which was conducted at the same time as the NAB study and which examined the same three years of programming across the same channels as the NAB study. Perhaps Valenti ignored the NTVS findings because they were very different from the NAB findings. In the first year of its analyses, the NTVS examined over 2,500 television programs and found violence in 58% of those programs. Furthermore, the NTVS found that the average number of violent acts per hour of television was almost seven. As for changes across years, the NTVS study reported that the percentage of programs with violence went up slightly, to 61% in Years 2 and 3 of the study. Broadcasters, of course, preferred the results of the study they financed, so they had to deny the results of the NTVS. For example, Marty Franks, senior vice president of CBS, strongly disputed the NTVS study, saying, "This study persists in using the same flawed methodology that led several years ago to the twenty-fifth anniversary of *Laugh-In* being named that year's most violent program by simply counting acts of violence without taking dramatic context into account" (Aversa, 1999, p. 3A). It is hard to imagine a more inaccurate statement about NTVS. The entire foundation of the NTVS study was the importance of dramatic context. This study collected information on eight measures of context (such as justification, motives, degree of harm to victim, etc.) for *each* of the 18,000 acts of violence it found. Furthermore, it also recorded information on 11 measures of context (graphicness, explicitness, degree of punishment, etc.) for *each* of the scenes in which violence was found.

Some producers argue that their violence is actually positive or helpful in some way. For example, Disney president Michael Eisner said that violence does have an impact, but a positive one—"a release of tension" (Bayles, 1993). Bob Shaye, CEO of New Line Cinema, distributor of the *Nightmare on Elm Street* horror films, says, "The tales are useful and cautionary. They suggest that evil and harm are everywhere and that we need to be prepared" (Krasny, 1993). Sam Hamm, a writer for *Batman* and *Batman Returns,* argues, "I can remember being scared as a kid at horror films and developing a craving for that sort of thing, but that's what may form imagination in a strong way and that's what creates narrative and inner life. It teaches you to look for stuff that's not safe in the art you enjoy later on." Hamm then moderates his position by adding, "I'm not arguing to expose kids to *Friday the 13th* movies or porno, but I feel there's too much caution about what kids see. Gravitating toward the forbidden is a natural part of growing up" (Krasny, 1993).

Some people deny they have any responsibility for the products they produce. One producer of violent video games told the *Los Angeles Times,* "We make the games we like to play and throw them out into the world. We don't get involved in politics" (Kellner, 1999). Some producers even claim that the games are therapeutic by offering a safe release of anger. "Video games take the place of that [violence and daring] and offer up some of the same images, often in a safer way. They take place inside the house, and people can play them without coming in contact with each other physically" (Kent, 1997, p. C1).

Perhaps the most egregious example of denial of responsibility comes from Wes Craven, director of horror movies such as *Scream* and *Nightmare on Elm Street.* Following the Columbine shootings, Craven and certain other filmmakers were strongly criticized for their ultraviolent plots and graphic images. Craven said that prior to the criticism he had decided to cut down on the amount of blood in his newest film, "but when Congress started citing

Scream as an example of the kind of horrible, reprehensible films out there, we decided not to hold back" ("*Scream 3* Director," 1999). As a backlash against the criticism, he decided to make his film even more graphic.

There is certainly a wide variety of types of denial, but the most convoluted type has to be that expressed by Martin Franks, a senior vice president at CBS, who said he'd read somewhere that television had been blamed for 10,000 murders. Franks said television violence isn't responsible for 10,000 homicides, "but even if we're responsible for one, we have to be careful, and I think we are" (Sullivan, 1998, p. B1).

Shifting Blame

Another popular strategy is to shift the blame onto something else. Three targets are especially popular: guns, parents, and other media. Although each of these deserves its share of blame, notice that none of these industry insiders is talking about *sharing* the blame. Instead, they are arguing for *shifting* the blame away from their industry or shows.

Shifting Blame to Guns. Producer Dick Wolf of the TV show *Law & Order* believes that "we're dealing with the outright hypocrisy of Washington, where many people are calling for steps against television. What about the guns out there? That's the real issue" (Oldenburg & Snider, 1999, p. 1D). Others who shift the blame to guns are Time Warner Chairman Gerald Levin, in a speech before the Hollywood Radio and Television Society (Harrison, 1999); Bob Guccione, now editor and publisher of *Gear* and *Penthouse* magazines (Oldenburg & Snider, 1999); and Fox's George Vradenburg in an interview on *Frontline* (Brennan, 1995).

Some producers argue that although the media in all countries present violence, the murder rate is highest in America because of the easy availability of guns. Producer Henry Winkler said,

> The truth is that wherever you go in Europe, there are American films and TV shows that are just as popular as at home. And you don't have that sense of violence in any other place other than America. . . . They don't have guns. So they don't have kids going through schools on [a] terrible rampage. (Harrison, 1999, p. F1)

Jann Wenner, editor and publisher of *Rolling Stone* magazine, puts his view succinctly: "The reason is easy: It's the guns, stupid." (Harrison, 1999, p. F1). However, the issue of violence in society is not that simple. Guns are a partial reason, but there are others. For years Hollywood has pointed to Japan as an example of a country with a great deal of violence in their media that at the same time maintains a low crime rate because of a strict ban on all guns. However, violence has been escalating in Japan. Recently in a Japanese public school, a man went on a rampage and killed 8 first and second graders and injured 15 other people. His weapon was a kitchen knife, not a gun. Even though Japan still has a strict ban on guns, their crime rate (especially crimes of murder, rape, and arson) has increased 95% in the decade of the 1990s (Reitman, 2001).

Shifting Blame to Parents. Many television writers and programming executives argue that parents should monitor what their children watch. This shifting of blame to parents has been around for a long time. Over 40 years ago, actress Bette Davis argued that parents should be responsible for protecting their children, saying, "Many people are upset by what crime shows do to children. As a professional, I think it's mainly a home responsibility."

This defense flares up when the industry is criticized following a high-profile violent event. Ted Harbert, former ABC Entertainment chief and now an executive at DreamWorks SKG, said, "I don't really agree that you can blame TV or movies in any way for these incidents. I look inward and say, 'Is there anything I'm doing to contribute to this?'" He added, "To me all roads lead back to the parents. Healthy kids can handle violent movies and television. Unhealthy kids can't" (Harrison, 1999, p. F1).

Several weeks after the Littleton shootings in 1999, Jack Valenti shifted blame away from the media by saying that it is up to parents, teachers, and the church to build an "impenetrable moral shield" to protect children. Absent that "moral shield," Valenti said, "no abolition of constitutional rights, no executive order, no congressional law will ever salvage a child's conduct or locate a missing moral core" (Stern, 1999b). This is rather like a factory polluting an area, then blaming the people who get sick for not having an "impenetrable" immune system.

Other Media. Interestingly, many people who defend the content in their own medium are quick to criticize the violence in other media. For example,

Jack Valenti said, "Nobody is looking at the Internet. I don't know of any movies that go into specifics on how to make a pipe bomb. But you can learn that on the Internet" (Wallace & Fiore, 1999, p. B1).

Video games are a popular target of blame. TV producer Robert Singer blames video games, noting that video games put a weapon in the player's hands and give the player points for killing people. Movie producer Sean Daniel (*The Mummy* and *The Jackal*) said he feels the video game industry "is marketing violent materials to youths in America." He argues, "I believe that the video game industry, which has gone completely unregulated, is clearly coming in for its well-deserved attention" (Puig, 1999, p. 1D). Screenwriter Stephen Sommers (*The Mummy*) agreed: "I passed by a video arcade the other day and saw pure violence. They were kicking each other's heads off, and blood was spewing. I would rather my 4-year-old daughter watch most R-rated movies than go to a video arcade" (Puig, 1999, p. 1D).

People in the video game industry shift the blame back onto television. Mike Wilson, CEO of game publisher Gathering of Developers, which distributes *Doom,* says the evening news delivers more violence and more realism than computer games do. "If some network would come out with a show called The Good News, that would be a start. People would watch it. Companies would buy ads, and it would be 'follow the leader'" (Harrison, 1999, p. F1).

Sometimes certain people working within an industry will shift blame from themselves to others working in that same industry. For example, screenwriter Steven De Souza (*Die Hard* and *Die Hard 2*) said, "Every picture I have done has come out more violent than what I wrote." He continued, "I have sat at the screening of one of my movies and been stunned at the level of mayhem that somebody put on the screen" (Puig, 1999, p. 1D). Also, Larry Gelbart, former coproducer of *M*A*S*H,* said, "If there is too much sex and violence on television, the reason that it is so is that the networks want it so. Writers and others are excluded totally from participation in the decision making process. . . . They want it [violence] because they think they can attract viewers. They attract sponsors, and the affiliate stations welcome it" (Cooper, 1996, p. 87).

Defensive Actions

After the shootings in Littleton, Colorado, the media—especially the video game, movie, and television industries—were strongly criticized as contributing to the conditions that led to such a horrible event. People in the industry understandably became very defensive. Their behaviors in that time of stress are revealing. While so much attention was focused on them, they had an opportunity to make some meaningful changes in their content and thus show the public their sincerity in doing their part in making the situation better. What did they do? Their reactions were primarily of one of three types: changing titles of movies, changing release dates, and changing how they promoted their shows. Notice that all of these changes illustrate two things. First, the producers were aware of the public's criticism that their products have too much violence, so they realized they had to do something or risk further criticism. Second, these defensive changes were trivial; none were substantive.

Changing Titles. Following the Columbine High School shootings, some producers examined the names of their ready-to-be-released movies and decided to change their names. For example, Miramax was planning to release a movie named *Killing Mrs. Tingle,* a dark teen comedy about a student's plot to get revenge on her teacher for a bad grade. But after a teacher was killed in Littleton, the studio renamed it *Teaching Mrs. Tingle.* The plot stayed the same—only the name was changed (Stern, 1999a). Wendy Finerman (producer of *Forrest Gump*) changed the title of *Sugar and Spice and Semiautomatics* to simply *Sugar and Spice.* In this film a high school cheerleader becomes pregnant with the star quarterback's child and turns to crime to support herself (Masters, McDowell, & Ressner, 1999).

Changing Release Dates. Another "change" was rescheduling the release of a movie or repositioning a TV program. For example, the release date for *Fight Club,* a bare-knuckle-boxing drama starring Brad Pitt, was pushed back several months from the initially planned release date of August 6 (Masters et al., 1999). Also, Sony moved back the release of *Arlington Road* from May 14 to well into summer. Starring Jeff Bridges and Tim Robbins, this is a paranoia-fueled tale of a man who thinks his next-door neighbors are terrorists (Masters et al., 1999).

As for television, the WB network rescheduled two episodes of its hit *Buffy the Vampire Slayer,* one featuring a kid bringing a gun to school and the season finale showing kids carrying medieval weapons under their graduation gowns. *Buffy* creator Josh Whedon said it was an "ugly coincidence" that the Littleton shootings occurred shortly before the scheduled air dates of the two episodes. Whedon said he did not feel the finale needed to be preempted, but if there had been a single act of violence at a high school graduation, "How horrible would we feel?" Whedon asked (Stern & Petrikin, 1999).

Promoting the Violence Less. Some movie marketing departments toned down their advertising, keeping guns out of the artwork and playing down violence. "We're thinking about it up front at the sketch stage, long before we execute," says Tony Seiniger, whose Beverly Hills ad firm does work for several top studios. He said his clients were thinking about whether actors who are popular with kids should pose with weapons. "Everybody's aware that there's a definite responsibility, the same way we don't have people smoking in ads anymore" (Masters et al., 1999). The Motion Picture Association of America (MPAA), which runs the industry's voluntary rating system, already bans ads in which guns are pointed at heads, and its president, Jack Valenti, says the standards may get tougher (Masters et al., 1999). Of course, these standards apply only to the promos, not to the content of the movies themselves. For example, when Miramax renamed *Killing Mrs. Tingle* to *Teaching Mrs. Tingle,* it also toned back its promotion of the film to depict it as more of a lighthearted kidnapping-and-physical-abuse caper (Stern, 1999a).

Changing titles, rescheduling release dates, and toning down the violence in the advertising for movies all show that producers are sensitive to the issue of social responsibility. But none of these changes deals with the substance of the problem. To the contrary, these so-called changes serve only to mask the existence of media violence while allowing it to continue as a problem. In fact, industry executives see these responses to tragedies as temporary. "If someone passes away in your family, there are certain things you don't say in the week following the death that you might say three months later," UPN CEO Dean Valentine says (Stern & Petrikin, 1999, p. 1).

No matter what happens or how much the industry is criticized, the majority of people in the industry continue with business as usual. There was a strong outcry in the early 1990s about the violence in children's programs, recalls Kathryn Montgomery, president of the Washington-based Center for Media Education. "But in the middle of all that—and the posturing by industry—what you see coming on children's TV is a proliferation of all these action-based programs." Action shows that popped up in 1994, she says, include *Battletech* and *Creepy Crawlers* (both of them by Saban Entertainment); *Gladiators 2000; Ironman; Mutant League; Monster Force; Skeleton Warriors; Super Human Samurai Syber Squad;* and *Tattooed Teenage Alien Fighters From Beverly Hills* (Clayton, 1994, p. 1).

Also, it is business as usual at the *Jerry Springer Show,* although in April 1998, the producers announced they would eliminate all physical violence from the talk show as a positive reaction to well-publicized protests against lewd language and violent outbreaks on the show. But this policy lasted only a few weeks before the show's syndicator pressured the producers to put violence back in, so the brawling resumed (Mifflin, 1998).

POLICYMAKERS

For almost half a century, policymakers have been concerned about the prevalence of violence in the media and its potential effect on the population. The U.S. Congress began holding hearings in the early 1950s, and they have continued holding hearings up to this day (see Table 1.3).

These hearings have been characterized by testimony from a wide variety of people, including social critics, social scientists, movie studio heads, television network programmers, First Amendment lawyers, physicians, parents, and so forth. Although in our democracy it is desirable to ensure that a wide range of voices is heard on important issues, many people expect Congress to do more than simply create forums for debate. Congress must make laws to protect liberty and promote the general welfare of the population, so Congress must sort through all the voices expressed in their forums, decide which are more credible, assess the threats to the population, and then take action in order to reduce the threats. To date, Congress has had little success in this task. For all the effort that has gone into 28 hearings, very little has come out. In the early 1970s, Congress set aside $1 million for new empirical research to increase the knowledge base. In the mid-1970s, the FCC pressured the industry to create Family Viewing Hour, but very quickly other people in the industry took the policy to court and got it rescinded. Then, in the early 1990s, Congress passed the Telecommunications Act, which brought about the V-chip. The V-chip is now part of all television sets sold in the United States, but this is far from moving us closer to a solution to the problem of media violence (see Myth 9).

RESEARCHERS

People in the media research community have been working on this complex problem for most of the 20th century. It wasn't until the 1970s that the

(Text continues on page 26)

Table 1.3   History of Federal Lawmakers
                  Considering the Problem of Media Violence

1952	Congress got involved in the issue in May 1952 when the House Subcommittee on the Federal Communications Commission held hearings to look into television content to determine if programs contained immoral or offensive material. Immoral material was defined as that which places an improper emphasis on crime, violence, and corruption. Chaired by Oren Harris (D-AR), the Subcommittee held hearings for 13 days over a six-month period, taking testimony from broadcast spokespeople and critics.
1954	The Senate Judiciary Committee created a special Subcommittee to Investigate Juvenile Delinquency, which was concerned with the negative influence of television, movies, and comic books. The hearings were held in June and October of 1954 under the chairmanship of Robert C. Hendrickson (R-NJ); these hearings were devoted primarily to industry professionals and executives.
1955	The Senate Judiciary Committee's Subcommittee to Investigate Juvenile Delinquency held a second round of hearings under the leadership of Estes Kefauver (D-TN). These hearings focused on the issue of determining the long-term effects of television on the country's youth. These hearings took testimony from social scientists who had conducted effects studies.
1961-1962	The Senate Judiciary Committee's Subcommittee to Investigate Juvenile Delinquency held a third round of hearings under the leadership of Thomas Dodd (D-CT). The hearings began in June 1961 and went until May 1962, during which time many researchers and industry executives testified.
1964	The Senate Judiciary Committee's Subcommittee to Investigate Juvenile Delinquency held hearings in July and reported that a relationship had been conclusively established between televised crime and violence and antisocial attitudes and behavior among juvenile viewers. However, the subcommittee did not believe that television was either the sole or most significant cause of juvenile delinquency.
1968	Five days after Sen. Robert F. Kennedy was assassinated, President Lyndon Johnson appointed the National Commission on the Causes and Prevention of Violence with Milton Eisenhower as chair. Because the commission was appointed for only about seven months (to the

Table 1.3 Continued

	end of Johnson's term), it relied on existing research and sought testimony from leading experts. The Commission produced a report that did not include any recommendations for legislation, instead saying that there is no single explanation of violences's causes and no single prescription for its control. The report essentially warned the industry to be more careful in its portrayals of violence and warned parents to be more careful in monitoring the viewing habits of their children.
1969	The Senate Subcommittee on Communications, under the leadership of John Pastore (D-RI), held hearings off and on for two years; $1.5 million was allocated to social scientists to fund original research into the effects of television violence on children's and teenagers' attitudes and behaviors.
1969	The Surgeon General's Scientific Advisory Committee on Television and Social Behavior was created. The Committee commissioned social scientists to conduct original research into the effects of television violence on children's and teenagers' attitudes and behaviors.
1971	The Senate Judiciary Committee's Subcommittee to Investigate Juvenile Delinquency commissioned Surgeon General William Stewart and his committee to investigate the effects of televised violence. A budget of $1 million was provided for research and another $500,000 to $800,000 for administrative expenses to produce new research.
1972	The Surgeon General's Scientific Advisory Committee on Television and Social Behavior released a five-volume report, and the Senate held 15 days of hearings on the report. The report concluded that there was a great deal of violence on television and that people were spending more and more time watching this content. Also, they found that viewing violence increases the likelihood that viewers will behave aggressively given certain conditions. However, these conclusions were heavily qualified, and the negative conclusions were largely ignored.
1974	Another hearing was held in the House of Representatives to affirm the credibility of the Surgeon General's Report. House members were willing to broaden the report's implications to realms of obscenity and children's programming and advertising.

(Continued)

Table 1.3 Continued

1975	The death of MacDonald led to the appointment of a new chairperson, Lionel Van Deerlin (CA). The subcommittees had to deal with various Hollywood production communities that had filed lawsuits against the family viewing hour unit.
1975	The chairman of the FCC, Richard Wiley, negotiated an agreement with the broadcast industry in which broadcasters agreed to limit the number of programs that contained violent behavior. The television industry also agreed to restrict its programming during the prime-time hour of 8 to 9 p.m. and also for an additional non-prime-time hour from 7 to 8 p.m. Television broadcasters agreed to add a Family Viewing Hour amendment to the Television Code of the National Association of Broadcasters. It reserved the prime-time hour of 8 to 9 p.m. for programming that would be suitable for a general family audience. It left the considerable interpretation of what would constitute "inappropriate programming" to the individual television networks.
1975	The Writers Guild of America filed a lawsuit against the FCC and the networks arguing that the Family Viewing Hour was an infringement of their First Amendment rights.
1976	Two Congressmen (Van Deerlin and Waxman) held two days of hearings in their districts in Southern California to give people among them in television production a chance to air their grievances. Norman Lear, Grant Tinker, Gene Roddenberry, and Larry Gelbart testified in opposition to the Family Viewing Hour.
1976	In November, a federal judge ruled that the Family Viewing Hour must be rescinded.
1976	The House Subcommittee on Communications, under the chairmanship of Lionel Van Deerlin, held hearings on both sex and violence on television.
1977	In March, the Van Deerlin subcommittee held its last hearing on sex and violence. The subcommittee concluded that the level of violence on television continues to be a cause for serious concern and that responsibility for the level of violence rests largely with the television networks. However, they concluded that: (a) industry self-regulation is a potentially effective way to limit the level of televised violence, and (b) parental supervision is probably the most effective way to curb negative effects of excessive viewing of televised violence by children.

Table 1.3 Continued

1982	The National Institute of Mental Health funded social scientists to synthesize the fast-growing body of research on the effects of television, based on the rationale that 90% of all research focusing on television's influence on behavior appeared in the decade following the Surgeon General's Report in 1972. The 1982 report, titled *Television and Behavior: Ten Years of Scientific Progress and Implications for the Eighties,* is composed of 30 chapters synthesizing the existing research.
1983	In March the House Subcommittee on Telecommunications, Consumer Protection, and Finance held hearings on children and television.
1983	In April, the House Subcommittee on Crime held hearings on crime and violence in the media.
1984	The Senate Subcommittee on Juvenile Crime held hearings on media violence under the chairmanship of Arlen Spector (R-PA).
1986	In June, the Senate Committee on the Judiciary held hearings on TV violence antitrust exemption under the chairmanship of Strom Thurmond (R-SC).
1988-1995	Five congressional hearings (two chaired by Sen. Paul Simon [D-IL]) were held, and 88 expert witnesses testified. During this period, nine new bills were introduced to limit violence on television.
1990	Congress passed the Children's Television Act, which gave the broadcast and cable industry a three-year exemption from the antitrust laws so they could voluntarily cooperate in establishing standards to limit the showing of violence. This Act also asked local stations to file a list of their educational programming for children with the FCC each year.
1993	Both houses of Congress passed resolutions denouncing programming containing violence (H. Res. 202, S. Res. 122). These were part of a tide of bills intended to curb violence on television, cable, and radio ("Summary of bills," 1993).
1993	Companion bills sponsored by Rep. John Bryant (D-TX) and Sen. Dave Durenberger (R-MN) were introduced. These bills required the FCC to establish standards to reduce the amount of violent programming on broadcast television, cable, and radio. A station that violated the standards would be subject to a $5,000 fine. Intentional violations could bring as much as a $25,000 fine, and repeated violations could lead to a revocation of license. Under both bills, the

(Continued)

Table 1.3 Continued

	FCC could exempt "as public interest requires news broadcasts, sporting events, educational programming, and documentaries" (H.R. 2837, S. 943).
1993	In the House, Charles Schumer (D-NY) introduced legislation to establish a presidential commission on television violence that would include the surgeon general, the attorney general, and 26 others appointed by the president. The commission would seek opinions of children, parents, and experts and make recommendations to the president and Congress.
1993	In July, Rep. Joseph Kennedy (D-MA) introduced the "Parents Television Empowerment Act," which required the FCC to set up a toll-free telephone number for complaints about violence on broadcast and cable television. The FCC would publish quarterly reports naming the 50 programs with the highest number of complaints.
1993	Senators Ernest Hollings (D-SC) and Daniel Inouye (D-HI) introduced the Children's Television Violence Protection Act, which prohibited the airing of violent content (as defined by the FCC) during hours when children are reasonably likely to comprise a substantial portion of the audience. It also required stations to provide advisory messages before violent programs.
1993	The Television Violence Report Card Act was introduced in the House by Rep. Richard Durbin (D-IL) and in the Senate by Sen. Byron Dorgan (D-ND). It required the FCC to rate television programs on the amount of violence they contain and to publish the ratings quarterly. The law also required the FCC to identify program sponsors who supported the most violent shows.
1993	In October, Attorney General Janet Reno said that "regulation of [entertainment] violence is constitutionally permissible" (U.S. News & World Report Online, 1994, p. 44).
1993-1994	Bills were introduced in the House by Rep. Edward Markey (D-MA) and in the Senate by Sen. Byron Dorgan (D-ND) that required new television sets to have circuitry, known as the "V-chip," to allow viewers to block programs that have been rated violent by broadcasters and cable networks.
1994	In October, the FCC backed off from its proposed regulation pushing the broadcasting industry to clean up its act on violence. Instead, FCC Chairman Reed Hundt emphasized the importance of self-regulation

Table 1.3 Continued

	by the television broadcasting industry as a means to curb television violence. Hundt said he did not want the FCC to play the role of censor.
1995	FCC Chairman Reed Hundt said that the precedent held by the courts in regulating sexual material provided a foundation for regulating violent material. He said that the government has the constitutional right to enact a curb on violent programming.
1995	Senators Byron Dorgan (D-ND) and Kay Bailey Hutchison (R-TX) introduced legislation to require ratings of television shows on a quarterly basis. The Department of Commerce would award grants to a nonprofit entity such as a university to do the ratings. The ratings would serve as a report card on violence.
1995	In July, President Bill Clinton endorsed congressional proposals to require television makers to install a computer chip that could automatically screen out programs rated as violent.
1995	In August, the House of Representatives approved by a 305 to 117 vote a bill that radically rewrote the nation's communications laws for first time since 1934. The main provisions of the bill deregulated broadcasting, cable, and telephone companies, but the bill also required that the V-chip be installed in television sets.
1996	In January, the landmark Telecommunications Competition and Deregulation Act of 1996 became law. The V-chip provision said that television sets sold in the United States after 1998 had to include the V-chip technology. In the meantime, the television networks were asked to develop their own ratings system that could be used with the V-chip.
1996	In February, the TV industry agreed to create a voluntary television ratings system by the end of the year to warn viewers about programs with sex and violence.
1996	President Clinton summoned entertainment industry executives to the White House and received an industry pledge to produce a voluntary television ratings system by January 1997.
1996	In June, President Clinton announced that television executives had agreed to air three hours of educational programs a week for children.
1999	In August, President Clinton introduced three public service announcements urging parents to talk with their children about television violence.

research base grew large enough for many social scientists to begin taking their expectations seriously that some negative behaviors could be attributed to exposure to violent portrayals in the media. Up until that time, skepticism about the influence of the media was widespread, but it gradually eroded as the research base grew, until now there are only a very few researchers who doubt that exposure to media violence has negative effects.

The formal, systematic study of exposure to the mass media, especially violent content, and its potential effects began in earnest in the late 1920s with the Payne Studies, a set of 13 studies designed to assess the influence of the newest mass medium—movies—on children (Lowry & DeFleur, 1995).

The research built slowly at first until the late 1960s, after a decade of assassinations (John F. Kennedy, Robert Kennedy, Martin Luther King), dramatic rises in crime, and general civil unrest (protests against American involvement in the Vietnam War). At this time, the U.S. Surgeon General assembled a task force to generate more research and thus create a sound basis to inform governmental policy on this issue.

As the research base grew, skepticism about media influence waned, especially among those scholars most directly involved with conducting research on this topic. Several of the more prominent of these effects researchers were appointed to the first major research commission on this topic—the 1970 Surgeon General's Task Force on Media Violence. The Task Force was controlled primarily by people from the media industries, so the warning voices of the researchers were smothered in the 1972 report issued by the Task Force. People in the media industries felt that the researchers on the Task Force were premature with their pronouncements, because they felt the research base was too small and contained studies with flaws in their designs. However, as these media scholars continued with their research and as that research influenced other scholars to study the topic of media violence, the set of findings grew more extensive. The size of this research base is now some-where around 300 carefully designed and executed empirical studies that have undergone rigorous peer review and have been published in the most respected scholarly journals. In addition to this core of highest-quality research studies, there is another set of publications—numbering up to 3,000—in which other scholars have reviewed those findings, synthesized new insights, or promulgated the central conclusion: Exposure to violence in the media increases risks of harmful effects.

Over the past two decades, virtually everyone who carefully reads the body of research on this topic has become convinced that exposure to media violence increases the probability of negative effects such as fear, desensitization, and even the behavioral effect of disinhibition. A "disinhibition effect" is the lowering of a person's natural inhibitions against performing in an aggressive manner. The body of research clearly shows that when people are exposed to violent portrayals in the media, they are more likely to behave in an aggressive manner when given an opportunity immediately following the exposure (Andison, 1977; Carlson, Marcus-Newhall, & Miller, 1990; Comstock, 1985; Comstock & Strasburger, 1990; Friedrich-Cofer & Huston, 1986; Geen, 1994; Hearold, 1986; Heath, Bresolin, & Rinaldi, 1989; National Institute of Mental Health, 1982; Paik & Comstock, 1994; Roberts & Maccoby, 1985; Rule & Ferguson, 1986; Wood, Wong, & Chachere, 1991). Also, people in the medical community have joined together to issue strong statements (see Table 1.1). For example, the American Medical Association, the American Academy of Pediatrics, the American Psychological Association, and the American Academy of Child & Adolescent Psychiatry issued a statement that said, "The effects of violent media are measurable and long lasting. Moreover, prolonged viewing of media violence can lead to emotional desensitization toward violence in real life" (Albiniak, 2000, p. 14). The belief in a connection between exposure to media violence and negative effects now seems intuitively obvious, akin to other beliefs that seem intuitively obvious to us, such that criticism of the belief seems unreasonable.

Resistance From Some Researchers

Several decades ago, when there was not much of a research base for making claims about the effects of media violence, it was reasonable to doubt the claim that portrayals of media violence led to harmful effects to individuals and to society. Many media effects researchers were skeptical about the claim that exposure to violence could be harmful (Howitt & Cumberbatch, 1975; Jones, 1971; Kaplan & Singer, 1976; Kniveton, 1976; Lesser, 1977; Singer, 1971). At the time, the field of media research was going through a transitional phase because scholars were disappointed about not finding the powerful effects they had expected to find. As a backlash, many scholars took the position that the influence of the media was weak at best. Then in the 1960s, researchers began looking for more modest effects rather than the one "big powerful effect" of the media. Researchers designed studies to examine the influence of various kinds of content on different kinds of people, especially on children, people living in high-crime neighborhoods, and people with high trait aggressiveness. This line of research was generally successful in showing that different people were affected in different ways by exposure to media violence.

Although acceptance of the research evidence is not unanimous, the number of people who continue to believe there is no link between exposure to media violence and negative effects has dwindled to a very few. For example, during the 1980s, Jonathan Freedman continued to publish several critiques of the existing social science research (Freedman, 1984, 1986). Today, the lone dissenting voice in the research community is Jib Fowles, who recently published a book titled *The Case for Television Violence* (1999).

Criticism and debate are usually signs of a healthy research community. People who challenge the conventional interpretations of research findings are essential to the growth of knowledge. But in order for criticism and challenges to be useful, they need to be based on an informed analysis that challenges researchers with criticism that gives researchers deeper insights into their shortcomings so that they can be overcome. Fowles's (1999) criticism is based on the same point that was used more than 40 years ago, that the individual research studies exhibit flaws. To be fair to Fowles, he is right that there are flaws in the body of research. However, there are no research studies that are completely free of flaws. No one has ever designed and executed the perfect research study. Furthermore, perfection, although a worthy goal, can never be fully achieved. This is why science is progressive—new studies improve on past studies and thereby knowledge grows. Researchers are constantly trying to improve past studies by using better samples, better measures, better stimulus materials, better procedures, and better analyses. It has always been this way, and it always will be. There is no end point to knowledge; we can always construct better ways to explain our world.

Given this progressive process in the generation of knowledge, the question becomes: Are we far enough down this research path to see patterns in the research findings that consistently show up in study after study? The answer is yes. The question then shifts to: Can we have confidence that the findings of these research studies reflect the reality of media influence, or are the findings anomalies that have been generated by flaws in the research studies? Fowles (1999) believes that the findings are anomalies and dismisses all the research. However, other scholars think through this body of research more carefully. They notice that although flaws vary across studies, the findings of negative influence still consistently emerge. Because the findings are consistent across studies, each of which has a different set of flaws, the findings appear so robust that they are stronger than the flaws and therefore cannot be ignored. In fact, the flaws in the individual research studies serve less to support the argument that the findings are faulty and more to support the argument for the robustness of the findings. Fowles misses this point. To use an analogy, it is as if Fowles is arguing that because no automobile is without flaws (poor gas mileage, bad safety record, overpriced, etc.), automobiles are therefore not a useful form of transportation. In this analogy, the flaws do not wipe out the usefulness of automobiles as a form of transportation; automobiles can still be improved in many ways, and there are many cars in junkyards, but none of this prevents us from regarding automobiles as a viable form of transportation. With media violence, each study has its flaws, but the body of research is very useful in helping us understand how media violence influences us in different ways. Of course people are not automobiles. But even though people are far more complicated than automobiles, the point illustrated by the analogy still holds—that is, each research study contributes to knowledge is some way, however minutely, and there comes a time when the accumulation of research reaches a point where we can no longer say we know nothing about a topic. We have long since passed that point with media violence.

Misinformation

There is misinformation in the research community. The most visible bit of misinformation is the claim that the research base is 3,000 publications. Actually, there are 300 empirical studies; the remaining publications are articles that promulgate the empirical findings. However, a research base of 300 studies is still quite large. The studies within that research base are also quite consistent. The 3,000 number is an exaggeration, and this is unfortunate because it gives critics some ammunition. But the conclusion that exposure to media violence leads to negative effects is not invalidated by the exaggeration. There is still a relatively large and strong research basis.

A more serious problem with the research base is that it is not more broad. That is, it is essentially limited to three negative effects—disinhibition, fear, and desensitization. If you look at the entire research base, about 70% of the studies confirm a disinhibition effect, 10% a fear effect, 10% a desensitization effect, and the remaining 10% suggest a variety of other negative effects.

Another problem with the research is that although it is strong in pointing out that there is a problem, it is less strong in helping craft a solution. Researchers have identified risk factors that increase the probability that a person will have a negative effect from the exposure, but they haven't produced much insight into how the risk factors work together. Therefore, research can only suggest a partial solution, and other groups are not willing to act on such a weak foundation.

CONCLUSION

Misinformation characterizes the current context underlying the problem of media violence. This misinformation is crystallized into a set of 11 beliefs— what I refer to as myths. Belief in these myths impoverishes the context by channeling our thinking into unproductive areas. The myths continue to wall us off from alternative perspectives that together would allow us to see the problem of media violence in a broader context. The current narrow context contains no useful solutions to the problem of media violence. We need a broader perspective in order to see ways to gain control over reducing the risk of negative effects and thus ameliorating the problem.

The purpose of this book is to analyze each of the 11 myths and reveal their faulty nature. I am not arguing that exposing the faulty nature of these myths will automatically lead to a solution to the problem. However, I do believe that unless we can move beyond the myths and thus broaden our perspective on the problem, we are locked in a context that guarantees that we will fail to do anything of substance to address this serious and persistent problem.

TWO

MYTH 1

Violence in the media does not affect me, but others are at high risk.

———•◦•———

M ost people do not believe that media violence has had any negative effect on them. In public opinion polls, typically 88% of people say that the media have not affected them personally (Whitman, 1996).

This belief is faulty. The media continually and profoundly affect everyone, and when the messages are violent, people are at risk for a variety of negative effects. However, people do not perceive these negative effects happening to them in their everyday lives—not because those effects don't exist, but because people do not know what to look for as evidence of the effects.

This myth persists primarily because people have a very narrow view of negative effects. They think in terms of high-profile criminal acts of violence, so if you ask the typical person, "Does violence on television and the movies have any effect?" most people will say yes—recalling a horrible instance where someone copied a violent criminal act that was in a movie or in the news. However, if you were to ask those same people if violence on television and movies has had an effect on them, most would say no. Thus, most people believe that other people are at risk whereas they are free from risk. This difference in perception between one's self and others has been labeled the "third-person effect."

The reason for this third-person effect with media violence is that few people believe they behave aggressively after watching violence, but they have ample evidence from news reports that others are influenced to behave aggressively. There are frequent examples of copycat crimes and of kids going on shooting sprees at school in imitation of movie and video game violence. Also, many adults notice their children imitating violent television characters they see on action adventure shows or on the *World Wrestling Federation*. We all remember children (or even ourselves as children) racing around the house chasing siblings and pets while imitating many of the movements and even the sounds from violent portrayals. But we know we do not behave that way now, so we believe there is no effect on us. However, there are effects—we just need to take a broader view to see what they are.

TAKING A BROADER VIEW ON EFFECTS

What are the effects of exposure to media violence? This is an extremely important question. The media research that has examined the influence of media violence on individuals and society contains indications of several dozen such effects (see Table 2.1). Of course, not all of these effects have the same degree of research support. One of these effects—disinhibition—has a great deal of research to support its existence, and several other effects—fear and desensitization—have substantial empirical support also. It is bad enough that people typically overlook the presence of these three effects in their everyday lives, but there are many more than three negative effects. The other effects have attracted the attention of some researchers, but none of these other effects has generated more than a few studies. This is not to say that these other effects are not important. Many of these other effects may be found to be more powerful and more widespread than the three that are well documented. To be sure, we will have to wait for researchers to provide a series of careful tests on each. But in the meantime, it is worth considering a broader spectrum of risk.

Before I describe each of these effects across a broader spectrum, it is first important to illuminate two characteristics underlying this set of effects. These two issues are timing of effect and type of effect.

Timing of Effects

When the public looks for evidence of effects from exposure to media violence, they notice examples that happen immediately after the exposure. If

Table 2.1   Broad Perspective on Effects of Media Violence

Type	Immediate	Long-Term
Behavioral	Imitation and copying	Generalizing novel behaviors
	Triggering	Long-term triggering
	Disinhibition	Malformed superego
	Attraction	Training behavior
Physiological	Fight-flight reaction	Physiological habituation
	Excitation transfer	Narcotizing
Emotional	Temporary fear	Emotional habituation
	Desensitization	
	Catharsis	
Attitudinal	Opinion creation or change	Reinforcement
		Cultivation of fear
Cognitive	Learning facts	Generalizing factual patterns
	Learning behaviors	Acquiring social norms
		Programming thinking
Societal		Moving mean
		Changing institutions

two boys are watching a violent car chase on television and then begin chasing each other around the house while tackling and hitting each other, most people will conclude that the television viewing triggered the subsequent mayhem. Such examples make it easy to see a link between the viewing and the effect. Immediate effects—like this example—are those that happen during exposure or within a very short period of time afterward. These effects can either dissipate within minutes—such as an increase in heart rate and blood pressure—or can last for a long time—such as a vivid memory of a horrible act. The key characteristic about immediate effects is that they are fairly observable by researchers. For this reason, it is relatively easy to attribute the effect to the stimulus preceding it.

However, when looking for outcomes of exposure to media violence, we should not limit ourselves to immediate effects. There are also some negative effects that take a much longer time to show up. If we ignore these, we will greatly underestimate the influence media violence has on us.

Long-term effects do not occur after a single exposure to media violence; they manifest themselves only after an accumulation of exposures, so if you do observe one of the long-term effects immediately after a particular exposure, it is shortsighted to blame that one exposure. Rather, that exposure should be regarded as "the straw that broke the camel's back." When trying to understand a long-term effect, it is important to understand that the cause of an effect is an accumulation of exposures as well as other factors and not only the most recent exposure. In addition, it is important to understand that even if a particular exposure is not followed immediately by an example of a negative effect, the exposure could still have had a partial influence, because it contributes to the accumulation of exposure. This is a major reason why we have more research evidence on immediate effects than on long-term effects. With a long-term effect, the researcher has to document the contributions in the accumulation and then be around when the effect eventually manifests itself. This is prohibitively time consuming to do with individuals, but some researchers have been successful at approaching the research challenge from a more macro perspective, in which they look for patterns in the aggregate. Two examples will illustrate this. In 1973, Tannis MacBeth Williams studied the children in a Canadian town before and after the town got television service. She found that the behavior of the children in general did not dramatically change immediately, but that two years after the introduction of television, the rates of hitting, shoving, and biting among first and second graders had increased by 160% (Williams, 1986).

Also, Brian Centerwall (1993b) conducted a macro study in which he examined murder rates in the United States, Canada, and South Africa after the introduction of television. In each country, 10 to 15 years after television began providing programming, murder rates doubled. Centerwall explained the lag by reasoning that it took that long for the first young children exposed to television to come of age. Even looking at other factors—the baby boom, urbanization, the rise of firearms—he claims that none of those factors was as viable an explanation as TV (Leland, 1995).

The general public has been slow to understand and accept lagged effects of media influence. However, these same people have no trouble accepting the belief that eating high-calorie, high-fat foods for years can lead to clogging of a person's arteries, that inhaling cigarette tar or asbestos over the years can lead to lung cancer, or that daily practice on the tennis court can lead to a high degree of tennis skills.

Type of Effect

Effects can show up as a change in our behavior, but they can also manifest themselves in nonbehavioral ways. They can influence automatic bodily functions, emotions, attitudes, and knowledge.

Behavioral effects are those where people are activated to perform some action. Most of the experimental effects research has been focused on behavioral outcomes. Researchers expose participants to violent portrayals and then watch what the participants do in response.

Physiological effects are those that influence a person's automatic bodily processes, which are usually beyond our conscious control. For example, watching violence can increase our heart rate and blood pressure. A horror film triggers rapid breathing and sweaty palms.

The media can make us feel things. They can trigger strong emotions such as fear, rage, and lust. They can also evoke weaker emotions such as sadness, peevishness, and wariness.

The media can create, alter, and reinforce attitudes. When we are exposed to many violent occurrences in the media, we might form the opinion that the world is a mean and dangerous place. Also, over the long term, the media can reinforce and give greater weight to an existing opinion, making it more and more resistant to change.

Cognitive effects are intellectual ones in which the mind acquires new information. We can learn how to commit a complicated crime by watching it portrayed on television. Or the cognitive effect could be more subtle, such as producing a generalization, such as when we "learn" that crime is a serious problem after we see criminal acts portrayed each and every night on the local news.

The five types of effects I have explained here are keyed to the individual person. But there are also broader effects that change society and our institutions. When society is changed, we eventually are influenced to change. This is an indirect effect of the media violence. Thus it is possible for us to avoid all exposure to media violence but still be influenced by it indirectly through the way society changes.

The effects that I present in this chapter should not be regarded as the definitive list of all the effects that could result from exposure to media violence. These 26 effects are those about which we have some evidence. As we continue to conduct more effects research, we may find that we need to add more to this list.

THE IMMEDIATE EFFECTS

The following list contains 12 immediate effects and descriptions of each.

1. Imitation and Copying Behavior

This is the effect that the public focuses on most when thinking about protecting people from the influence of media violence. This is understandable, because copying behavior is very easy to spot, and it is very easy to see the link back to the media content.

The imitation effect is much more prevalent in children than adults (Bandura, 1978, 1979, 1982, 1985; Centerwall, 1993a, 1993b; Comstock, Chaffee, Katzman, McCombs, & Roberts, 1978; Liebert & Schwartzberg, 1977; Tan, 1981; Walters & Willows, 1968). For example, Centerwall (1993b) says that children as young as 14 months "demonstrably observe and incorporate behavior seen on television" (p. 56). Children are aware of their copying violent acts. In a survey of young children, 60% said they frequently copied behaviors they had seen on television (Liebert, Neale, & Davidson, 1973).

2. Triggering Novel Behavior

Triggering is not the same thing as imitation, where someone mimics behavior witnessed in the media. Triggering refers to the media's stimulating a person to act in a violent manner that is not copied from a specific media portrayal. The person acts violently in a novel way to fit the situation at hand. An example of this is "wilding," the term for when teenagers commit violent crimes for fun or out of curiosity (Baker & Gore, 1989). Teens get pumped up by watching violent movies and television programs, listening to violent CDs, and playing violent video games. They want to act out their aggression, so they behave violently in new ways. This happens at rock concerts where bands sing about how bad the government and police are and urge listeners to strike back. The crowds get pumped up, but they strike out at each other and their physical surroundings rather than the government. For example, on the last night of Woodstock 99 some concert goers pushed over a lighting and sound tower. In 1998 alone, 5,711 people were injured while attending rock concerts. One security company executive said, "Bands are more prone to incite the audiences than they used to be." Thus attendees get swept away with hard-driving appeals to violence and later question what they did (Kleiner, 1999).

3. Disinhibition

Exposure to media violence can reduce viewers' normal inhibitions that prevent them from behaving in a violent manner. Although the disinhibition effect can occur immediately after viewing, it can also last over time, especially when viewers are continually exposed to violent messages (Baker & Ball, 1969; Chaffee, 1972; Comstock et al., 1978; Goranson, 1969; Hapkiewicz, 1979; Liebert, 1972; Liebert et al., 1973; Liebert & Poulos, 1975; Liebert & Schwartzberg, 1977; Maccoby, 1964; Roberts & Schramm, 1971; Shirley, 1973; Stein & Friedrich, 1975; Tan, 1981; Tannenbaum & Zillmann, 1975). This is the most researched and well-documented effect of exposure to media violence.

David Grossman, a former Army Ranger, a psychologist, and the author of *On Killing: The Psychological Cost of Learning to Kill in War and Society* (1996), points out that the military takes in recruits who have "a powerful, God-given resistance to killing your own kind." To turn recruits into soldiers, the military must reduce the recruits' inhibitions and they do this with psychological conditioning. The military has been very successful with this conditioning. Army officials had discovered that only 15 to 20% of U.S. soldiers in World War II actually fired their weapons in combat, but by the time of the war in Vietnam, the "fire rate" had been increased to 95%. The Army psychologists were able to do this by reprogramming the values of the soldiers.

4. Attraction

Many people are attracted to violence, maybe not all the time, but there come times when people want to see a violent show. If it were not for this effect, violent CDs would not sell, and horror movies would have no audiences. When you add up all the time and money spent by millions of people each year in seeking out this kind of content, this must be regarded as a major effect. (See Myth 6 for more on this effect.)

5. Fight-Flight

Exposure to violence can temporarily arouse people physiologically. During exposure, a person's heart rate and blood pressure increase. These physiological changes are the body's way of getting ready to respond to the violence as if it were a real threat to the viewer. This type of arousal usually dissipates within an hour after exposure (Doob & Climie, 1972; Tannenbaum & Zillmann, 1975).

6. Excitation Transfer

Violence presented in the media tends to arouse viewers and hence is an energizer. People do not necessarily need to use that energy in an aggressive manner—they can transfer that energy to other outlets. For example, people who are exposed to a strongly violent portrayal can become highly aroused (heightened heart rate) and are ready for action. If there are sexual reminders in their environment, they will be likely to stay highly aroused but shift into a sexual mode. The arousal needs direction, because arousal by itself is not guided. If the viewer guides the energy into positive directions, then the exposure to violence can have a prosocial value. Whatever the direction, the energy from the arousal is short lived and usually dissipates within several minutes after exposure (Zillmann, 1971, 1982, 1991).

7. Temporary Fear

Violence in films and on television can produce intense fright reactions (Blumer, 1933; Cantor, 1994; Cantor & Hoffner, 1990; Cantor & Reilly, 1982; Cantor & Sparks, 1984; Cantor, Wilson, & Hoffner, 1986; Cantril, 1940; Dysinger & Ruckmick, 1933; Himmelweit, Oppenheim, & Vince, 1958; Osborn & Endsley, 1971; Sapolsky & Zillmann, 1978; Schramm, Lyle, & Parker, 1961; Sparks, 1986; Sparks & Cantor, 1986; von Feilitzen, 1975; Wertham, 1954; Wilson & Cantor, 1985). Fright as an immediate emotional response typically lasts only a short time, but it may endure on occasion for several hours or days, or even longer. It is composed of the components of anxiety, distress, and increased physiological arousal that are frequently engendered in viewers as a result of exposure to specific types of media productions (Cantor, 1994).

8. Desensitization

The media can reduce our emotional reactions. For example, Grossman (1996) argues that television and movie violence is desensitizing the young. When children watch graphic violence in movies and TV shows and also play realistic violent video games, it breaks down their natural resistance to killing.

Children are being exposed to such media violence at earlier ages. "The average preschooler in America spends approximately 23 hours a week watching television before they [*sic*] even go to school, and that's not good," says Grossman (Sullivan, 1998, p. B1). "The net effect on children up to 4 or 5 years old is they can't tell the difference between television and reality," he said. "As far as they're concerned, when they see someone on TV being shot, stabbed, raped, kicked, brutalized, degraded, murdered, punched—it's as though it were actually happening." And, he said, "What we sow when the child is 2, 3, 4, 5 years old is what we reap 15 years later." Exposing children to media violence "is a form of child abuse," argues Grossman. "It is identical to what the military does in basic training. But instead of doing it with a drill sergeant on an 18-year-old volunteer, we're doing it to 3-year-olds over the public airwaves, in order for the networks to increase their ratings" (Sullivan, 1998, p. B1).

9. Catharsis

Catharsis is an effect that gives viewers release from their own aggressive drives when they vicariously participate in the violence that they see in drama. The idea of catharsis as an effect of exposure to entertaining messages goes back to the writings of Aristotle; the idea resurfaced with Freud and more recently with media effects researchers (Feshbach, 1972). Media portrayals of violence have been found to help people with weak imaginations experience catharsis, because these people have difficulty fantasizing (Feshbach, 1972). Also, people with well-developed imaginations are more able to become absorbed in violent portrayals and thereby discharge their anger (Gunter, 1980).

Catharsis is categorized here as an emotional effect, because it is usually experienced by people as a purging of negative emotions, such as fear or anger. But catharsis also has a physiological component, because catharsis can only work if a person is in a relatively high state of arousal. Without high arousal, there is no energy or drive to dissipate.

This is one effect that is regarded as very controversial by media effects researchers, with a few researchers claiming to have found support for this effect (Feshbach, 1955, 1961, 1972; Feshbach & Singer, 1971), whereas many other researchers have challenged this research (Berkowitz, 1962; Comstock et al., 1978; Liebert, Sobol, & Davidson, 1972; Wells, 1973). As of now, the research community is skeptical of such an effect, but this effect continues to have a great deal of intuitive appeal.

10. Immediate Creation or Change of Attitudes

A person's attitude can be created or changed with as little as a single exposure. For example, researchers have shown that when people are exposed to a violent television program, they will show an immediate drop in sympathetic attitude (Drabman & Thomas, 1974; Molitor & Hirsch, 1994; Thomas & Drabman, 1975). Among children and adults, even watching a single violent film can make people temporarily less aware of and less concerned about aggressive acts in others (Drabman & Thomas, 1974).

11. Learning Specific Acts and Lessons

If learning is defined as the acquisition of facts so that they can be recalled later, then exposure to media messages can certainly lead to an immediate learning effect. For example, when we watch the evening news we learn about which crimes were committed today.

Learning need not be planned—it can be incidental to the motive we have for media exposure. Incidental learning takes place when we do not intend to learn (maybe our motive is for entertainment) and when the sender of the messages is not intending for us to learn anything. For example, as we watch a movie we might learn how to defend ourselves with our fists or how to give someone we dislike a severely witty tongue lashing.

12. Learning Behaviors

People can learn behavior patterns by watching characters perform in the media. For example, children might watch a cartoon in which characters beat each other over the head with rubber hammers and show no harm. The children do not imitate the behavior patterns they see, because there are no rubber hammers available to them. But this does not mean they have not learned how to perform a particular aggressive behavioral sequence. Now let's say that the next day those children are in a toy store where they see some rubber hammers. Those hammers are likely to cue the memory of the cartoon. At that time, the children may pick up some hammers and begin hitting each other over the head; if they do, their behavior has been activated by their previous learning. But even if they do not hit each other over the head, they have still learned the behavioral sequence and its lack of consequences (Caprara et al., 1984).

LONG-TERM EFFECTS

Long-term effects are those that do not show up during the exposure but build up slowly and subtly over time, which makes them harder to perceive. When we do see evidence of something that may be a long-term effect, it is relatively difficult to make a strong case to attribute the influence to the media, because it is difficult to envision all the links in the chain of events that connect the observed effect back to the accumulation of media exposures over years of viewing.

1. Generalizing to Novel Behaviors

The media can influence behaviors—not just in specific actions, but in a general, long-term manner (Comstock et al., 1978; McHan, 1985). The resulting effect can show up as behavior that is very different from any of the particular portrayals viewed by that person, because viewers can generalize from particular violent behaviors to a broader class of behaviors. For example, after watching multiple acts of physical violence in which the powerful physically subdue the weak, some people gradually alter their behavioral patterns to become more verbally aggressive.

2. Long-Term Triggering

Some researchers have hypothesized that television teaches people to commit criminal behavior—such as larceny—indirectly. For example, Hennigan and colleagues (1982) argue that exposure to affluent lifestyles on television along with high levels of advertising for consumer goods teaches viewers over time that in order to be happy in America (or even to be part of the mainstream), you need to attain a high level of materialism. Poor people who cannot buy many goods are being tempted to commit crimes in order to acquire more possessions. During the course of decades of watching portrayals of violence linked with materialism, people's levels of frustration and anger increase. Then one day, a person might be in a shopping center and begin shoplifting.

3. Malformed Superego

Freud (1933) conceptualized a superego that governs our primal drives. This superego is something that is acquired through experience as people learn what is acceptable behavior in their society. One of the lessons imposed by the superego is the avoidance of aggression and violence.

Centerwall (1993a) argues that television, with its flood of violent messages, stunts a person's growth of superego:

> Television is not merely a poor source for the child seeking to shape an ego ideal: it actively disrupts the process of superego formation, increasing the likelihood that the child will enter adulthood with a superego that is weak and poorly organized. Violence follows. (p. 192)

He points out several reasons why this is so. First, the messages of television are chaotic, so that a person is exposed "to as many different value systems as there are channels" (Centerwall, 1993a, p. 192). Centerwall (1993a) also says that television leaves to children the difficult task of synthesizing the values in all the messages they see. Also, television gives children no discipline or even any feedback on their behavior. Thus children are left to develop their superego in a moral vacuum.

4. Training Behavior

The media can shape our behavior by training us. For example, Grossman (1996) points out that one of the jobs of the military is to train soldiers to kill. He expresses alarm over seeing video games on the open market that are similar to the military's training simulations. Grossman argues that these first-person-shooter video games are training players how to kill other people by teaching hand-eye coordination so that players can be more skilled at shooting. The best killers receive the highest rewards. The worst of these games—Doom, 007 Golden Eye, Duke Nukem, Postal, Quake, and Redneck Rampage—are also the most popular (Grossman & DeGaetano, 1999). These games are fun and also give players a sense of power and provides immediate reinforcement (Healy, 1990). Over time, this reinforcement conditions players to seek out this type of action.

5. Physiological Habituation

This is the building up or increasing of physiological tolerance over the long term. With repeated fight-flight responses, the human body gradually builds up a resistance to the exposure to media violence. For example, the first time a person sees a horror film, the body responds with a fight-or-flight reaction by substantially increasing the heart rate and blood pressure. As the person continues to view horror films over the years, the body's reaction to this stimulus is not as substantial: The heart rate and blood pressure still increase, but not as much. With repeated exposures, people build up a higher physiological tolerance to this type of message. In the extreme case, with massive exposure to this type of message, people might even extinguish all physiological reactions to horror. Researchers have found that children who are heavy users of TV (25 or more hours of viewing per week) are much less responsive to television violence in terms of physiological measures of arousal than are very light viewers, such as those who watch less than 4 hours per week (Cline, Croft, & Courier, 1973).

6. Narcotizing

Not only does habitual viewing of violence over time dull our reactions, some people continue to crave the strong "arousal jag" they used to get from violent exposures. Thus violence acts like a drug in the sense that people become more dependent on it over time. In its extreme case, this narcotic of violence can lead to addiction. Like with other narcotics, television violence loses its strength on users over time, so users need stronger doses to get the same pleasant feelings. In order to experience the same degree of arousal, they search out more graphic and stronger forms of violence (Zillmann, 1982).

This belief that media violence could act as a narcotic has been around for many decades. Blumer (1933) warned of media possession, in which viewers lose control over their feelings and perceptions. Preston (1941) asserted that people could become addicted to media horrors. Himmelweit, Swift, and Jaeger (1980) claimed that people can become as habituated to beatings and car chases as they can to barbiturates. They speculated that producers of empty excitement action series "might be tempted to increase the dosage and opt for even more violent happenings . . . but this could be self-defeating since habituation to the new level might soon set in" (p. 95).

New York Times columnist Frank Rich (1998) likens the public's taste for media violence to an addiction and says that the media are just giving the public what it wants. According to Rich, video games are especially addictive— providing a drug-like response—so playing is exciting.

Murray Straus, who has studied patterns of violence in American families for decades as director of the Family Research Laboratory of the University of New Hampshire, provides support for this characterization of media violence as an addictive drug. He explains that "people get inducted into violence in infancy. Since probably half of all children have been hit by their parents as infants, before speech, it just becomes built into the personality" (Robb, 1991, p. 27). People then look to the media to continue with violence, but media violence loses its shock value fairly rapidly, researchers have found, so more and more violence is needed to maintain the thrill.

7. Emotional Habituation

Some portrayals are presented so often we can no longer treat them with wonder or awe. Our tolerance has been increased so that those things that used to horrify or even upset us no longer do. This is especially important with the issue of violence. Viewing TV violence leads to lowered sensitivity to aggression and violence, and when people are exposed to violence continuously for a long period of time, this lowering of sensitivity is reinforced.

Exposure to a great deal of violence can lead to a lack of remorse. In 1993 in Houston, Texas, two teenage girls (14 and 16) were walking home one summer evening when they were attacked by six teenage boys (aged 14 to 18) who raped and murdered them. The youths offered no explanation for their crimes, nor did they show any remorse. One of the suspects had been featured in a television news report on gangs in Houston the night before the crime. In that news report, the suspect lifted a beer can and made a toast, saying, "Human life means nothing" ("Houston Knows Murder," 1993). In this case, the youth was emotionally dead; extreme violence, even murder, could no longer evoke an emotional response in him. Another example is from an interview on National Public Radio with a teenage gang member who, without a shred of remorse, said he would kill without a second thought. He and his friends had seen *The Terminator* and for months afterward were pumped up, wanting to be just like that movie's futuristic murder machine.

Some have made the argument that watching a great deal of television stunts a child's emotional development. Children experience high levels of exposure to television—by the time a child reaches the age of 5, he or she has been exposed to about 6,000 hours of television. Couple this with the average image being on the screen only about 3.5 seconds before being replaced with another, then another. This leaves no time for reflection. This frenetic pacing short-circuits the natural emotional development that people need to become healthy human beings; it strangles the development of children's own voices and denies them their imaginative powers:

Some neuro-anatomists argue that excessive TV viewing—more than four or five hours per day, seven days a week—ultimately takes a serious cognitive toll. They believe the limbic system of the brain—the mysterious, sub-cortical part of the brain that researchers designate as the image-making center—develops more slowly when a young person spends half of his or her waking life in front of the TV set. (Sanders, 1994, p. 39)

Also, TV presents so many images to viewers that viewers do not have to generate their own images; they do not practice "what-if" situations and thinking things through. They can't even fully process much of what they do experience on TV—there is too much. Viewing weakens their will. TV takes over and gives them all their excitement; people don't have to generate their own entertainment any longer (Sanders, 1994, p. 42).

One of the explanations for emotional habituation is that when people spend more and more time with pseudo-emotional connections with fictional characters in the media, they build up less experience with emotions in the real world. Television viewing makes people think they are experiencing emotions, but these are not real because they are not two-way emotions—that is, there is no interaction. Viewers cannot influence the behavior of TV characters, so there is no emotional exchange. Emotions require physicality, that is, people to touch each other; TV does not provide this. Without adequate emotional development, people do not develop a sense of guilt or conscience (Sanders, 1994, p. 125).

On the positive side, people can also become desensitized to the things they fear through repeated exposure to these violent characters and actions in the media. For example, experimenters have shown that gradual, repeated showing of frightening material in a nonthreatening environment can gradually reduce children's fear of particular characters, such as the Incredible Hulk (Cantor & Sparks, 1984; Sparks & Cantor, 1986) or the Wizard of Oz (Cantor & Wilson, 1984; Wilson, Hoffner, & Cantor, 1987).

8. Long-Term Reinforcement of Attitudes and Beliefs

Because the media provide so many messages of violence and because those messages are usually presented with the same cluster of contextual factors, viewers' existing attitudes about violence are reinforced over time. This is a consistent conclusion of many research studies (Cline et al., 1973; Drabman & Thomas, 1974; Greenberg, 1975; Kaplan & Singer, 1976; Thomas & Drabman, 1975; Thomas, Horton, Lippincott, & Drabman, 1977).

9. Cultivation of Fear

There is a good deal of research support for the hypothesis that heavy exposure to the world of television, which is saturated with violent portrayals, leads people to construct unrealistically high estimates of risk of victimization and a corresponding belief that the world is a mean and violent place (Bryant, Carveth, & Brown, 1981; Carveth & Alexander, 1985; Gerbner et al., 1977; Hawkins & Pingree, 1980, 1981a, 1981b; Morgan, 1983, 1986; Ogles & Hoffner, 1987; Potter, 1991; Rouner, 1984; Signorielli, 1990; Weaver & Wakshlag, 1986; Wober, 1978; Zillmann & Wakshlag, 1985).

The person who first established the existence of this effect, George Gerbner, argues that television presents a mean-world syndrome that culti- vates "feelings of insecurity, vulnerability and mistrust, and—despite its sup- posedly 'entertaining' nature—alienation and gloom." He contends that violence is used to define social relations between characters. "Some kids see themselves as more likely to be victims than other kids, and they develop a greater sense of vulnerability." In his research, he found that heavy viewers were more likely to call for severe punishments for criminals and to have bought new locks, watchdogs, and guns for protection (Leland, 1995).

Gerbner's original conceptualization of cultivation in the late 1960s was based on the assumption that all messages were the same across the television landscape. Therefore, it did not matter what people watched, only how much they watched. As the television landscape has changed over time, with many more channels and specialized niche programming, subsequent research has demon- strated that it matters what a person watches. People who watch programming with more violence will be more cultivated to believe the world is a mean and violent place (Hawkins & Pingree, 1981a; Potter, 1991), as are people whose viewing is dominated by violent programming (Potter & Chang, 1990).

The argument has been made convincingly that the media have created a moral panic with all their coverage of crime and violence. For example, Chiricos (1996) points out that in the early 1990s there was a particular fixa- tion on high-profile crimes in the national news media and that during that time the percentage of Americans ranking crime and violence as the nation's foremost problem jumped from 9% to 49%.

Alton (1994) writes that there is a serious problem of fear in Britain, "where women are frightened to travel alone on public transport in the evening or leave their children alone in a public park." He contrasts this with 20 years ago, when people felt safe to walk the streets and the parks. "We call this a free and permissive age—but what has happened to true freedom and the things we were once permitted to do without fear?"

Fear of victimization is widespread in the United States. There are 192 million guns in private hands in this country; 46% of those owners say the reason they have a gun is for self-defense—perhaps that is why 65 million of those guns are not rifles or shotguns but handguns (Simon, 2001, p. A5).

10. Generalizing Patterns

A person watches a local news program and hears a story about a house that was vandalized in an area near his apartment. Then he hears a story on radio about a local bank that was robbed. Next he reads the newspaper and sees that there was an assault in his town last night. He has learned three facts—one from each message. But later that night he might generalize from these three facts and draw a conclusion that the crime rate is very high in his town. This specific conclusion was not given to him by the media, but the media provided him with some facts that set up his jump to this conclusion.

The mass media have been found to provide consistent messages that lead viewers to construct generalizations about how much crime and violence there is in society (Gerbner, Gross, Jackson-Beeck, Jeffries-Fox, & Signorielli, 1978; Hawkins & Pingree, 1982; Potter, 1994). Sometimes this generalization process results in a conclusion that is very much unlike the real world. When this happens, one of three conditions exists: (a) the person has acquired false information from the media, (b) the person has been exposed to an imbalance of information (extreme depth in one narrow area and no breadth) and this gives a distorted picture, or (c) the person has accumulated a great number of facts and has not properly sorted or organized them.

11. Learning Social Norms

The learning of social norms is a special case of generalizing patterns. People can generalize a pattern from individual media exposures without that pattern being a social norm. For example, through repeated exposure to media violence, a person overestimates the rate of crime and the percentage of crimes that are cleared by an arrest. Although these are generalizations, they are not social norms. Social norms are generalized patterns from social information, rather than factual information. Social norms deal more with the rules of behavior in social situations rather than with society's factual parameters, such as the numbers of lawyers, crimes, trials, and executions—all of which have real factual indicators. But social norms have no factual foundation in the sense that they are either accurate or not.

As people gradually construct their generalizations about social norms from viewing individual media portrayals of violence, they look at how that violence is portrayed. For example, viewers have been found to generalize to a social norm that violence is OK to use in certain situations when they frequently see it justified in those situations (Collins, 1973; Hoffner & Cantor, 1985; Kaplan & Singer, 1976; Leifer & Roberts, 1972; Linne, 1971; Siegel, 1958; Thomas & Drabman, 1978).

Also, the sheer repetition of violent portrayals is enough to lead people to generalize that violence is a typical way of dealing with problems in society. This is why there is a relationship between the amount of exposure to TV violence and a willingness to use violence, to suggest violence as a solution to conflict, and to perceive violence as being effective (Liebert et al., 1973; Tan, 1981).

12. Programming Us How to Think

Young brains are being programmed differently because of the stimulation of television. In their book *Stop Teaching Our Kids to Kill,* David Grossman and Gloria DeGaetano (1999) argue that media violence weakens our ability to react properly to violent messages, rather like AIDs weakens a person's physical immune system. Grossman and DeGaetano say that "AVIDS" ("Acquired Violence Immune Deficiency Syndrome") "weakens appropriate cognitive, emotional, and social development, causing more children to become increasingly vulnerable to other violence-enabling factors in our society such as poverty, discrimination, drugs, and the availability of guns" (p. 64).

The brain development that occurs between the ages of 0 and 6 is phenomenal. And an overemphasis on any particular activity robs children of the opportunity to do a range of activities, which is so important to building neural networks. Many things that adults see as play are very important for children. When they bounce a ball, they are learning hand-eye coordination, muscle coordination, and the elementary rules of physics. If they are doing it with a friend, they are learning to read cues of socialization. A well-loved video can seem like a friend. But a parent must ask: Is this a good friend, and are the visits in moderation? (Churnin, 1998).

13. Moving the Mean of Society
Toward More of a Fight-Flight Mentality

Envision the aggregate of society arrayed as a normal distribution, with most people clustered in the center in terms of their socialized beliefs and behaviors regarding violence. On one side of the distribution (the prosocial tail) are the people who have a very high degree of inhibition preventing them from behaving aggressively; also, these people have a high degree of sensitivity to violence and sympathy for all its victims. On the opposite side of the distribution (the antisocial tail) are the people who have very low inhibitions toward behaving aggressively; also, these people have very low levels of sympathy for victims of violence.

When violence permeates the media year after year in all kinds of programming and when the message of that violence is antisocial (violence is usually justified, successful, and harmless to victims), the mean of society is likely to move gradually in the antisocial direction. That is, the norms of society (as evidenced by the beliefs and behaviors clustered close to the mean) will show a gradual movement in the direction toward a fight-flight mentality. The fight component is exhibited by an erosion of inhibitions to behaving in a violent manner. The flight component is exhibited by a gradual increase in generalized fear along with an erosion of sympathy for victims of violence.

When television is introduced into a country, there is an increase in the violence and crime rate in that country, especially crimes of theft (Campbell & Keogh, 1962; Centerwall, 1989; Furu, 1962, 1971; Halloran, Brown, & Chaney, 1970; Hennigan et al., 1982; Schramm et al., 1961; Williams, 1986). Within a country, there is also a relationship between the amount of exposure to violence that a demographic group typically experiences in the media and the crime rate in neighborhoods where those demographic groups are concentrated (Messner, 1986). Finally, there is some evidence that when a high-profile violent act is depicted in the news or in fictional programming, incidents of criminal aggression increase subsequent to that coverage (Phillips & Hensley, 1984). These studies have been criticized for demonstrating only covariation, not causation. That is, merely because two things occur at the same time does not mean that one has caused the other. That is one of the biggest challenges of conducting this type of broad-scale research. It is very difficult to make convincing claims for causation, because there are usually many alternative influences that could be responsible for the effect.

Societies have drawn a line out on the antisocial tail that divides socially tolerated antisocial behavior (such as rudeness, selfish aggression, etc.) from antisocial behavior that the society cannot tolerate (usually labeled as criminal behavior, for which society has prescribed clear penalties). All societies have a few people with extreme deviant behavior—that is, those people who have crossed the line set by society.

As the entire distribution shifts more toward a fight-flight mentality (antisocial direction), not only are there observable differences in the mean, but there are also observable differences at the tails of the distribution. As the antisocial tail also moves to more of a fight-flight mentality, there are more people on that tail who have crossed the line. Also, it takes even more outrageous behavior to label someone truly deviant.

One example of moving the mean is that a very violent movie such as *Home Alone 2* is categorized as a "family" film. Violence in movies and on television has desensitized children so much that they laugh at human suffering, while their point-and-shoot video games have conditioned them to act out aggression. We have all gotten to the point where it takes much more to shock us. The boundary that defines civil behavior has moved.

14. Changing Institutions

When violence permeates the media year after year in all kinds of programming and when the message of that violence is antisocial, institutions feel the influence and gradually change. For example, the criminal justice system experiences stronger conflicting forces. On the one side is greater fear in society, which leads to asking this institution to be more aggressive in removing deviants from society and thus to reduce the fear. On the other side is a greater tolerance for many forms of deviant behavior that have become relatively less threatening to society (thefts and assaults) compared with other more deviant acts (such as bombing public buildings, sending letter bombs to individuals' homes, and teenage snipers killing classmates in public schools).

In a larger sense, the entire institution of government seems to be changing as a result of these conflicting forces. On the one hand, the public is asking government for more personal freedom, perhaps as a way of getting back some of their lives, which they perceive as being taken away by their increasing fear of others. But on the other hand, the public asks for a more authoritarian response (more laws, more law enforcement personnel, and stronger punishments) to the shifts in society.

The educational system has also changed to deal with the stronger fight-flight mentality among students. Instead of being able to operate at higher levels, where students can concentrate on more abstract ideas, teachers must respond to more basic concerns of students concerned about survival.

Religion may be changing as people turn to that institution more out of a generalized fear or out of a rejection of the changing norms of society. Also, religions may be more aggressive at drawing the line of acceptable behaviors in order to stop the shift of society in an antisocial direction. Thus religion becomes more concerned with moral issues than spiritual ones. The focus may be shifting more toward prescribing everyday behaviors and away from focusing on the awe and mystery of creation and humans' place in the universe and eternity.

The institution of family may also be changing as a result of these forces brought about by media violence. Perhaps the generalized fear has made parents less trusting of their children. Perhaps couples are less willing to deal with their arguments by looking for peaceful solutions and being willing to compromise. Instead, couples may be looking for more fights to act on their aggressive impulses, may feel more justified in those confrontations, and thus may want to dominant the other in their resolutions. Such adversarial behaviors are likely to lead to more breakups and more people choosing to live alone.

CONCLUSIONS

The myth that violence in the media affects others but not me will continue as long as people have a narrow perspective on what is a negative effect. A narrow perspective includes only those things that show up in other people and those things that usually occur immediately after the exposure. Until people understand that there is a wide variety of effects—many of them subtle and many that take a long time to manifest themselves—people will continue with their limited range of awareness. People need to be made aware of the variety of negative effects on their behavior, physiology, emotions, attitudes, and knowledge—especially those that manifest themselves only after repeated exposures over a long time. As long as people use a very small radar screen to scan for the occurrence of negative effects in their lives, they will continue to miss most of them.

THREE

MYTH 2

The media are not responsible for the negative effects of their violent messages.

———•◦•———

A 12-year-old boy in Ft. Lauderdale, Florida, killed a 6-year-old playmate by smashing her skull while imitating a pro wrestler he had seen on television. Lionel Tate was arrested for first-degree murder. The 166-pound boy with a below-average IQ flung the 48-pound Tiffany Eunick into a metal staircase after asking her if she wanted to play wrestling. His defense focused on his being influenced to behave aggressively by his exposure to television violence, specifically shows about professional wrestling (Clary, 2001a). This defense failed, and he was convicted of first-degree murder (Clary, 2001b).

In the Tate case, as with several other cases in which the defendant tried using the "media made me murder" defense, the jury convicted the defendant, reasoning that people have free will and should be held accountable when they decide to commit a serious crime. Do people have free will? Of course. Should people, even adolescents, be held accountable for their actions? Yes. But concluding that people should be held accountable for their actions is not the same thing as saying that the media exert no influence on people. Accountability and influence are two distinct issues.

People who defend the industry frequently use the myth that the media are not responsible for negative effects. The effectiveness of this myth as an argument relies on confusing the two issues of accountability and influence.

When we separate the two issues, we can clearly see that the media are in fact responsible for negative effects—that is, the media exert a negative influence on people who are exposed to violence in the media. This is not to say that the media are the *only* factor or even the most important factor leading to a negative effect. But the media *are* an important factor, and their influence should not be ignored.

To understand the extent of the media's role in bringing about negative effects, we should think in terms of a "process of influence." This broader perspective on effects gives us the means to consider not only manifest effects but also process effects. Manifest effects are observable changes in behavior, physiology, emotion, attitude, or cognition. We should not think of these manifest effects as blossoming forth suddenly after a single exposure to media violence. Rather, it is more useful to think of them as a result of a process of influence. People are constantly experiencing this process of influence. As various factors (about the content, about the situation, and about the people themselves) wax and wane throughout this process, levels of risk increase and decrease. Every once in a while the risk level becomes so high that a particular person begins exhibiting a particular effect, such that we can observe a manifest effect. Because process effects are not observable, it is tempting to think that they do not exist or that they are not important. However, it is even more important for us to understand the process effects than the manifest effects, because when we comprehend the process of influence we can control the process effects and thereby determine which manifest effects we will eventually experience. Once we observe a manifest effect, we have lost control over its occurrence. In contrast, if we can control the factors in the process of influence, we can decrease our risk of negative manifest effects.

The process of influence is complex. This is why it is possible for 12 people who watch the same violent movie to have a dozen different reactions. Illuminating the process of influence is difficult and remains one of the biggest mysteries in media research. Critics of the research would say that the process is so complex and there are so many things we do not know about this process that there is nothing we can do. That is a pessimistic reaction. I prefer to be more optimistic. Although we do not have the entire process mapped out at this time, we do have a good idea of the major factors influencing that process. We have moved far from our initial state of ignorance on this effects process. Researchers need to share what we now know, and people who acquire even a partial understanding of how this process works will be much more able to increase their control over their risks. We also have some useful general ideas about how the process works. In the following sections, I will first illuminate what we know about the nature of the process of effects, and then I will list the major factors that we know influence risk.

THE NATURE OF THE PROCESS OF INFLUENCE

To comprehend the complexity of the process of influence, it is helpful to focus on four ideas. First, there are multiple factors interacting simultaneously. Second, the causal process is probabilistic. Third, not all factors have the same degree of influence. And fourth, some of the influences are direct, whereas others are indirect.

Multiple Influences

When an act of violence dominates press coverage, the public searches for something to blame. For example, during the week after the horrible shootings at Littleton, Colorado, radio call-in shows and letters-to-the-editor pages were deluged, and the following emerged as the targets of blame for the tragedies: parents, copycats, the media, the Internet, guns, the free-love generation, gun control, the bombing of Serbia, large schools, the movie *The Matrix,* permissiveness, conformity, the movie *The Basketball Diaries,* the loss of family values, education cutbacks, the rocker Marilyn Manson, violence on television, bullying in school, the rock group KMFDM, the improper storage of firearms, the 40,000 killings children will see on television and in the movies by the time they are 18, cults, loners, the lack of counselors in schools, and the movie *Natural Born Killers* (Gordon, 1999).

It seems like every person has his or her favorite target of blame. All of these positions are right, and they are all wrong. They are all right in the sense that these factors are likely to have contributed to the shootings—at least we cannot rule any out completely. However, they are all wrong in asserting that one factor is to blame and the others are not. The process of influence that leads up to the manifestation of a negative effect is constructed from many factors. Attributing blame to any one factor is foolhardy, unless that factor's influence is explained in the constellation of all other contributing factors. We must shift the question from "Which factor shall we blame?" to "What are all the factors active in the process of influence, and how do they work together to produce the manifest effect?"

Probabilistic Causation

If you slam your finger in a car door, you experience an immediate painful effect. You know without doubt that the car door slamming was the cause of the effect of the pain in your finger. This is a simple illustration of cause and effect.

In everyday life, we look for simple, direct connections to make sense of our world. The press and policymakers want a simple explanation for the crime, fear, and callousness in our society. Is media violence to blame or not? They want researchers to tell them that X and Y cause negative effects in a direct, causal manner—no exceptions. When researchers explain that they are unable to make such a statement, all sorts of destructive reactions are triggered. Producers of violent stories claim that they are off the hook. Policymakers argue that without a "smoking gun" directly linking media violence with serious, widespread negative effects in society, they cannot expend all the political capital they would need to take on a powerful industry. And the public remains confused.

Acknowledging that there is no simple, direct causal relationship does not leave us with the conclusion that there is no effect from exposure to media violence. There are many process effects, as the various factors increase and decrease our risk levels. In order to appreciate these process effects, we must think in terms of probabilistic causation, not deterministic causation. In the earlier example, the slamming car door led directly to the pain in the finger. This is regarded by social scientists as deterministic causation, because the cause *determined* the outcome. However, when dealing with the issue of media influence, it is foolhardy to look for manifest effects that are determined by the media alone. Instead, it is more realistic to look for many factors that work in concert with the media to increase or decrease probabilities of manifest effects occurring.

One of the implications of shifting thinking away from determinism is to recognize that there are no "sufficient conditions" for an effect—that is, no single factor is sufficient to guarantee an effect. Instead, effects result from the interaction of many factors acting together. Among those factors, some may be necessary, that is, the effect could not occur if one of these were missing. However, many of the factors are not even necessary; factors can be substitutable. To illustrate this point, think of the example of making a fire, which requires three things: heat, oxygen, and fuel. Each of these is a necessary condition, but none is sufficient. Also, there are many different types of fuel that can be substituted for each other. In media violence effects research, there are no sufficient conditions; most, if not all, are substitutable. If one day the heat in your attic reached a point high enough to lead to combustion, it would not be accurate to say that the heat determined the fire; instead, the heat acted in concert with the fuel and oxygen in the attic—the *set* of three factors is responsible for the fire. But we cannot hold the heat blameless simply because if the heat had existed without any fuel, there would have been no fire.

Thus it is more useful to think less in terms of deterministic causation and more in terms of probabilistic causation. Trying to use a very simple idea of causation as a tool to explain a very complicated phenomenon is a prescription for failure.

Differential Influence

Not all factors have the same degree of influence on changing risk levels. Some are strong influences, and others are weak. Also, not all of these probabilities are positive—that is, not all of the factors *increase* the probability of an effect. Some can *decrease* the probability of an effect. Also, it follows that it is possible that the influence of two factors could cancel each other out if one were positive and the other negative. For example, think of a situation in which you are watching an action movie. You like the hero and find him funny, strong, and attractive. That might increase the probability moderately of your wanting to imitate the character. The hero is provoked and responds with violence. The justification for the violence might strongly increase the probability of an effect. The hero is successful with the violent act. This also strongly increases the probability. But then the movie shows the victim of the violence suffering. The victim's innocent family is also suffering. This decreases the probability (perhaps even canceling out all the positive probabilities already built up) that you would want to imitate the hero's violent actions. In this example, different factors in a portrayal can have different (or even opposite) influences.

It is also important to factor characteristics about viewers into the "probability equation." Viewers are often different from one another, so when two people are exposed to the same media violence, they can react very differently.

To illustrate, let's say that Greg watches a violent fight on television and sees that the perpetrator was attractive and rewarded. Greg then begins behaving aggressively. Here, the violent message leads to aggressiveness. If Cindy has poor attention skills as she watches the same violence, she might not understand the meaning of the violence and may become confused, not aggressive. The violence in this case leads to confusion. And Marcia watches the same violent message but laughs at it, because she thinks it is farcical and unrealistic. In this case the violence leads to laughter. From these three examples, can we say that violent messages lead to aggressive behavior? Yes, but only with Greg. There is no general pattern of effect, but this does not mean that all three were not affected. In this example, all three people manifested an effect, but those effects were different because of the factors (cognitive developmental stage, degree of identification with characters, sense of humor, etc.) attributable to the three people. Can we then conclude that the media had no effect on these three people? Of course not. The media violence was a factor in the process of influence for all three, even though all three processes of influence moved in different directions to different manifest effects. It is too simple to conclude that the media violence had no effect on these people simply because they all manifested a different effect subsequent to exposure. It is a mistake to think of media exposure as a discrete factor that works by itself in determining an effect. Instead, media exposure must be conceptualized as something that bonds with other factors in differential ways to move risk levels incrementally toward various manifest effects.

Direct and Indirect Influences

The media effect process *can* be direct. For example, we might read about a violent crime and encode the details, thus experiencing a cognitive effect. Or we might be watching television and see an attractive character commit a justified act of violence, which triggers us to behave rudely when our viewing is interrupted by a telephone call to the wrong number.

The effect can also be indirect, such as through institutions, which try to socialize us by instilling values about violence, among other things. Reimer and Rosengren (1990) remind us that the important agents of socialization in modern societies are the family, the peer group, the work group, church, law, school, and large organizations representing popular movements and interest groups. The mass media can influence these institutions, which in turn influence us. For example, it has been argued that the media have changed the way families are structured, so the children of today are raised in a different manner than were the children of several generations ago. In certain families, the media violence resonates with existing family values about aggressiveness and serves to reinforce those values (see McLeod & Chaffee, 1973). But in other families, the media violence goes against the grain of values, so a child's intense exposure to both family and media serve to put a child in a state of confusion. This, too, is an effect of exposure to media violence.

FACTORS IN THE PROCESS OF INFLUENCE

There are many factors active in the process of influence. The media are an important influence, but there are others. How else can we explain that although many people are exposed to the same media content, there is still a range of reactions? People of different ages and in different parts of the United States are exposed to the same media but display drastically different violence levels. TV violence does not account for the fact that the murder rate among black teens in Washington, D.C., is 25 times higher than that of white teens living a few blocks away. It doesn't explain why, nationally, murder rates doubled among nonwhite and Latino youth over the last decade but declined among white teens. Furthermore, white 16-year-olds have lower violent crime rates than black 60-year-olds, Latino 40-year-olds, and white 30-year-olds. Also, America's biggest explosion in felony violent crime is not street crime among minorities or teens of any color, but domestic violence among aging, mostly white baby boomers (Males, 1996).

In this section, I will show that we need to consider nonmedia as well as media factors. It is also shortsighted to argue that the media have no influence, even when there appears to be no direct, immediate connection between a particular effect and a particular media message.

Media Factors

Researchers know a great deal about what factors are likely to lead to negative effects (see Table 3.1). Notice that prevalence of violence is only one of the categories of influence. The context of the portrayals is also important. In addition, media effects research has made good progress in delineating a list of contextual factors that are associated with negative effects.

Table 3.1   Media Factors in the Process of Influence

Frequency of Violence

Risk increases when:

- There are higher rates of violence in the exposures

Television World Profile on Frequency:

- Since the early 1950s, between 60 and 80% of all television programs have contained at least one act of violence.
- The average rate for violent acts in fictional television programming over the past 40 years has been between six and eight acts of physical violence per every hour of programming.
- Violence is prevalent in the news: If it bleeds, it leads.

Context of Violence

Risk increases when:

- The perpetrator is rewarded or at least not punished
- The perpetrator is attractive or a hero
- There are no serious consequences (such as pain or harm) to the victim
- When the action is portrayed as being justified
- Violence is portrayed in a realistic setting with realistic characters
- Violence appears in a humorous context
- Violent portrayals are arousing

Television World Profile on Context:

- Less than 30% of the violence is portrayed as being punished.
- About 40% of perpetrators are portrayed as attractive.
- Only 15% of violent incidents portray serious consequences (such as pain or harm) to the victim.
- More than one quarter of violent action is portrayed as being justified.
- Over half of the violence is portrayed in a realistic setting.
- More than 40% of violent action appears in a humorous context.

SOURCE: Abstracted from Potter (1999).

Frequency of exposure is related to effects. Some effects can occur after only one exposure, such as cognitive encoding, generalizing to novel behaviors, disinhibition, triggering, immediate emotional reaction, immediate change of attitudes, temporary physiological arousal, and catharsis. Other effects require a gradual accumulation of exposures over a long period of time, such as learning social norms about violence, cultivation of fear, reinforcement of attitudes, habituation, narcotizing, attraction to the fringe, and changing institutions. Also, some of these immediately occurring effects can be reinforced or altered over time with additional exposure to media violence.

Although the frequency of violence in the media is usually the focus of criticism, the process of influence is shaped much more by the context of the violence. People use the web of contextual factors to interpret the meaning of violent portrayals. The interpretive process is complex. Among those influencers are contextual factors that are part of how the violence is portrayed, and some of these factors can reduce the risk of a negative effect. Thus, not all violence is bad; some portrayals of violence can teach us to behave in a prosocial manner.

Given the factors of risk, the television world clearly puts viewers at high risk (see Table 3.1). On television, violence is typically portrayed as glamorous, successful, and sanitized (NTVS, 1999). This formula for violence teaches us all that violence is acceptable and even desirable. Thus, what matters most is the type or treatment of violence. Screen mayhem that is rewarded will encourage aggression, but violence that is punished will inhibit aggression. By this logic, a heroic John Wayne movie might do more to increase risk than a senseless slasher movie, especially if the villain is punished. Of course, viewers are more likely to be offended by the slasher movie. But they are more likely to consider John Wayne a role model, and the risk for many negative effects—such as imitation and disinhibition—are increased much more by a positive role model than by a portrayal that gives offense.

Interpretations of reality are likely to be cued to the setting, the genre, and the matching of characteristics in the portrayals to real life. Humor also plays a complex role in the perceptions of viewers, and there are several major reasons for this. One reason is that there are many different types of humor. Another reason is that humor can be used in many ways, either to heighten dramatic effect, as a catharsis from serious scenes, or as a trivializer of otherwise serious situations. But perhaps the most important reason is that humor appears to be very personal, that is, each person is likely to read the cues differently and find a different reaction to the humor in a violent act. The complexity of understanding the factors of fantasy and humor is magnified in the genre of cartoons, where these two highly interpretive factors work in interaction and lead to the public's opinion that cartoons do not contain violence.

The effect of exposure to media violence is influenced by nonmedia factors such as society and the viewer (see Table 3.2). Viewer susceptibility is based on factors in the viewers' environment as well as their traits and states.

Societal Factors

People in the media industries often defend themselves from criticism by pointing out that the blame belongs to factors in society—such as lack of socialization, child abuse, poverty, and lack of gun control. These are factors that are important in the process of influence, and there are many who make the argument that societal factors are far more powerful than media factors are (Bok, 1998; Males, 1996).

We should not regard the factors as being independent from one another; they are all related. Many of the societal factors interact with media factors. What I mean by an interaction is that the influence of societal factors—although important by themselves—is even stronger when they work in conjunction with media factors. For example, let's consider the interaction of poverty and the media. People living in poor neighborhoods are likely to experience crime at a higher rate than people living in middle-class or rich neighborhoods. In poor neighborhoods, it is likely that there are more criminals living close by and that these criminals will have an influence on socializing the children growing up in those neighborhoods. Adults—especially the elderly—in these neighborhoods are more likely to lock themselves in their homes, and they are more likely to watch television, where they will see a great deal of crime and violence. This double dose of exposure to crime will make them even more fearful of their neighborhoods (Gerbner, Gross, Morgan, & Signorielli, 1980). Also, as people in poor neighborhoods watch television, they are reminded that they do not have the resources to afford the large houses, fancy cars, and luxurious lifestyles they see on television. This can lead to anger and frustration. Television shows them that violence is a successful means of getting what you want, especially if the violence is justified, as it is with the heroes. Thus over time, poor people can feel that something is wrong with a rich country's allowing poor people to be continually deprived. It is not the American way to be poor. It *is* the American way to take matters into one's own hands and create a different world.

If there is child abuse in the household, the probability that the child will become violent is high. Children are socialized by their parents. One example

Table 3.2   Nonmedia Factors in the Process of Influence

Society and Environment

- Poverty: People with little money who live in high-crime neighborhoods are at greater risk.
- Availability of weapons: The more weapons, especially guns, that are in a society, and the easier it is to obtain one, the greater the risk.
- Family life is an important contributing factor. Children who are abused by parents, who watch more violence, and who identify with violent heroes more are at higher risk. Also, children who get less support and who are members of families with higher-stress environments are more vulnerable.
- Viewers who perceive cues in a real-world situation that remind them of violent media portrayals are at higher levels of risk.

Viewer Traits

- Socialization against aggression is also important. Children in households with strong norms against violence are at lower levels of risk, but those in households where parents exhibit sociopathic belief systems are at higher risk.
- Psychological traits: People at lower levels of cognitive and moral development are at higher risk. People with higher levels of exposure (which is related to low socioeconomic status [SES], lower IQ, ethnic minorities, and immigrant groups) are at higher risk. Children who have lower IQs, who have learning disabilities, who are emotionally disturbed, and who are generally more aggressive are at higher risk.
- Demographics: Younger children, boys, people of lower SES, and minorities are at higher risk.

Viewer States

- Viewers who are upset by the media exposure (anger or frustration) are at greater risk.
- The more a person, especially a child, identifies with a character, the more likely the person will pay attention to, encode information about, and be influenced by that character's behavior. People are more likely to identify with characters who are attractive, who are portrayed as good, and who are heroes.

Exposure Situation

- Viewers who are more analytical and critical during exposures to media violence are at lower risk. If instead the exposure environment presents

Table 3.2 Continued

many distractions, such as extraneous noise, people talking, and other
demands on one's attention, the exposure is likely to be experienced in the
automatic processing perceptual channel, and the viewer will lose control
over the effects process.

- Greater control does not directly lead to avoidance of negative effects. In
  order for the self-reflexive processing to be more powerful, viewers need to
  be at higher levels of cognitive, moral, and emotional development and to
  have more elaborated scripts from which to work.

SOURCE: Abstracted from Potter (1999).

of this is with smoking. Children of smoking parents are three times more
likely to smoke by age 15 than children of nonsmokers (Males, 1993).

Children socialized by violence learn that violent behavior is the norm. But
television is also socializing viewers that violence is a typical means of solving
problems and that there are many people who deserve violent treatment. Thus,
children raised by child abusers who see lots of violence on television get a
double dose of violent socialization.

Another important societal factor is the availability of guns. There are
192 million guns in private hands in this country, and right now more than
30 million of those guns are loaded and unlocked (Simon, 2001). When guns
are easily available and people see repeated portrayals of the use of guns on
television, there is a high risk of interaction. On television, more than one
quarter of all violent acts involve the use of a handheld firearm. Viewers are
being socialized to associate violence with guns. When guns are seen by
people in real-life settings, there is a triggering of memories about specific
portrayals of violence from media portrayals (Berkowitz & LaPage, 1967).
People recall those portrayals, and they also frequently experience the emotions they felt during those media portrayals. Therefore, guns appearing in real
life are strongly linked in people's minds to the television portrayals. How
often is this link triggered? It depends on the person. But with the average
television viewer seeing more than 40 acts of gun-related violence per week,
it is likely that the association occurs frequently.

The National Rifle Association used the slogan "Guns don't kill people;
people kill people." It is true that a gun needs a person to pull the trigger, so

guns by themselves do not result in violence. But it is also true that if a person squeezes his or her trigger finger and there is no gun, the person cannot shoot someone. Guns are a contributing, but not the sole, factor in violence. When guns are easily available, the risk of violence increases, and in this country, guns are easily available, even to children. The American Medical Association reports that 5.8 million households with children have guns; that in 58% of those households, those guns are accessible to children; and that in 11% of those households, not only are they accessible to children, but they are also loaded (Simon, 2001).

Factors About the Viewer

The traits of a viewer are also part of the process of influence. Traits are the internal psychological characteristics that shape our behavior. Concerning vulnerability to violent messages, a person's cognitive, emotional, and moral development are especially important. As children age, their minds mature to allow them to operate at higher cognitive channels. Because young children differ in their ability to attend to, process, and make meaning of media messages compared with older children and adults, they experience different effects from exposure to violence in the media. People see images on TV and in the media before they see the real thing in life. With violence, often they never see a truly violent occurrence, so they are left with the media images as their reality. But when they do see a murder or a serious accident, it becomes just another image.

Lt. Col. Dave Grossman, an expert in the psychology of killing, observed that in the attacks in schools at Pearl, Mississippi; West Paducah, Kentucky; Jonesboro, Arkansas; and Springfield, Oregon, the teenage killers "suffered an inferiority complex and were enthralled by violent images from television and film." Grossman, who is also a former West Point psychology professor and Army Ranger, continued, "What all of the killers have in common to a certain degree was this tremendous fascination with media violence" (McCain, 1998).

Viewer states are also important. States are temporary conditions, such as feelings of frustration or anger. For example, Harvard psychiatrist James Gilligan, who spent years interviewing murderers in Massachusetts, has concluded, "Nothing stimulates violence as powerfully as the experience of being shamed and humiliated" (Dority, 1999, p. 7). Also, experimental research is quite clear on the following point: People who are angry or frustrated are much more likely to act in an aggressive manner. Once their anger or frustration dissipates, within an hour or so, they will return to their normal behavior patterns, which are typically nonaggressive.

Motivation for watching violence is a state that changes depending on our mood and what is happening in our lives. There appear to be four types of motives: gore watching, thrill watching, independent watching, and problem watching (Johnston, 1995). These motivations are related to dispositional characteristics (fearfulness, empathy, and sensation seeking) as well as cognitive and affective responses. For example, some viewers seek out graphic horror for excitement and for the opportunity to demonstrate mastery over fear. These viewers report a positive affect both before and after viewing. But viewers who watch because of anger, loneliness, or personal problems report negative feelings after viewing and attribute these feelings to the exposure; however, these people usually have negative feelings before the exposure. The type of person who is most at risk for subsequent violent behavior is the gore watcher, who is an adventure seeker and is low on both empathy and fearfulness.

AN IRONY

There is a very troubling irony with this myth. The irony is attributable to two different ways of defining *responsibility*. In one sense, responsibility means having an influence in changing or causing something. Given this definition, the media are responsible in part for any manifest effect, and they are certainly responsible for changing risk levels in the process of influence. Using this definition of *having influence*, belief in this myth is clearly faulty.

But there is also another way to define *responsibility*, which is the characteristic of being trustworthy, having the ability to choose between right and wrong, and accepting one's fair share of accountability. Given this definition, belief in this myth *is accurate*—that is, the media are indeed *not* responsible.

When people in the media industries claim that the media are not responsible, they usually mean that they are not the cause of negative effects. The irony is that when they defend themselves with this myth, the utterance of those words in itself confirms that they are not responsible, but only in the other sense of the word—that is, they are not recognizing their accountability.

CONCLUSION

Media messages are constantly exerting an influence on all of us. Much of that influence is neither direct nor immediate. Instead, the majority of that influence is through a complex process that involves many contributing factors, each of which ratchets up (or down) the probability that we will experience a variety of effects. Each of us is an individual with a different psychological makeup, history of socialization, and pattern of media use. Thus we all have different interpretations of the messages we see, and we find ourselves at different points along the process of effects. This is why a given violent movie does not have exactly the same effect on everyone. The argument that everyone is not directly and immediately influenced by a portrayal of violence in the same way cannot be taken as evidence that the portrayal is not having some influence on all who see it.

This dual perspective on media effects (manifest and process) raises some important questions. If there are so many different factors and so many differences among people, how can we ever hope to find a pattern of effect? If everything is so fragmented across individual viewers, how can we ever address this problem as a society? These questions are important and present a significant challenge to researchers. Although social scientists will never be able to predict the behavior of any particular individual with certainty, they can develop more insightful explanations about how risk levels change in the population as a whole. That is a significant contribution. With over 100 million households in this country with televisions, with those televisions turned on an average of 42 hours per week, and with about 60% of the programming presenting some violent content, there is a great deal of exposure to television violence in the population. If we are to move toward constructive solutions to the problem of media violence, we need to make good assessments about what the risk levels are in society and what factors are responsible for increasing those risks of negative effects.

We must get beyond the limited thinking that unless an effect clearly manifests itself, no influence has taken place. Even if we cannot observe any outward manifestations of behavioral change, our exposures are continually altering our levels of risk. Although difficult to observe—or even to understand—the process of influence never stops.

Furthermore, although individual portrayals of violence may exert some influence by themselves, we need to understand that the contribution of the media in the process of influence is better understood in combination with many other factors. Research that examines the influence of media violence by itself—without taking into consideration how those portrayals interact with many other factors—greatly underestimates the influence of the media.

FOUR

MYTH 3

Children are especially vulnerable to the risks of negative exposure to media violence.

————•◦•————

There is a widespread belief that children are especially vulnerable to negative effects from media violence in general compared with adolescents and adults. It is easy to understand why we would focus on protecting children. We commonly believe that children are highly vulnerable to harm in the world. Children have less experience than adolescents and adults do. They also have not yet developed a high degree of thinking ability (Piaget & Inhelder, 1969), emotional control (Goleman, 1995), or moral reasoning (Kohlberg, 1981). When children are very young and their minds are relatively undeveloped, they have difficulty distinguishing fantasy from reality. They often do not understand the "make-believe" nature of the monsters in movies (Cantor, 1994). Given these inabilities, certain kinds of violence would generate a great deal more fear in children than in adults. Therefore, we believe that children are less capable of protecting themselves from harm. It is our job as parents to protect our children and to teach them how to avoid harm, so the idea of their vulnerability is constantly on our minds.

When thinking about the media and the potential for harmful effects from exposure—particularly to violence—there is ample evidence that children as a group are given a special status. First, when we look at the list of consumer advocacy groups that have been created to help educate the public about the risks of all kinds of media exposure and to put pressure on Congress as well as the media themselves to change—or at least to label their content—we can see that many of those groups focus on children (see Myth 11). Children Now, Coalition for Quality Children's Media, and Maryland Campaign for Kids' TV all reference children in the names of their organizations. Furthermore, Parents' Choice and the TV Parental Guidelines Monitoring Board also indicate a focus on children. Even among the groups that do not explicitly reference children in their names, a perusal of their materials makes it clear that children are treated as a special group. There are no counterpart groups that focus especially on protecting adults or adolescents. Why are there no groups with names such as "Coalition for Quality Television for the Elderly" or "National Campaign to Protect Adults Against Media Violence"?

A second body of evidence illustrating that children are regarded as an especially vulnerable group is in the behavior of public officials. Throughout the past three decades of congressional concern on the issue of media violence, all of the proposed legislation has focused on protecting children. These bills fall generally into one of three categories: safe harbor, report cards, and blocking devices (see Potter & Warren, 1996). Members of Congress periodically have proposed the identification of a safe harbor, with restrictions on programming during the time period when children are watching television in large numbers. Safe harbor bills tend to restrict violence during the early evening hours, but they say nothing about the other hours of the day when adolescents and adults are viewing. A second type of congressional bill deals with the creation of report cards, in which television programs are rated for violence, among other things, so that parents can make informed choices about what they will allow their children to view. The third type of proposal is the blocking device—such as the V-chip—which allows parents to program their television sets so that shows with certain ratings can be prevented from appearing on their screens. The latter two types of proposals have the potential for helping adults as well as children, but this potential was lost in the implementation, when the television networks decided to use an age-based system for rating their programs. The V-chip currently relies on a modification of the MPAA rating system, which is keyed to age, with one level of restriction up until age 13 (PG-13) and another up until age 17 (R) (see Myth 10). The assumption clearly is that once a person has reached age 17, he or she is somehow beyond the risk for the negative effects that people under the age of 17 are.

It is easy to accept the belief that children are especially vulnerable to negative effects from exposure to media violence when we think of examples that we have observed in our everyday lives. When a family watches a horror film, it is the children who exhibit the most extreme reactions and who have the nightmares. Also, when we see copycat behaviors, it is usually children playing cops and robbers in the backyard or wrestling in the den. These effects are easy to observe, because they happen almost immediately after the exposure. With these types of effects, it is likely that children are more vulnerable than adults. But recall from Myth 1 that there is a wide range of effects, and many of them are not observable immediately after an exposure to violence. Because children appear more vulnerable than adults on a few of the more observable negative effects (such as imitation, temporary fear, and learning behaviors), it does not automatically follow that children are also more vulnerable to all effects, or even to the majority of negative effects.

What makes this a myth is not that the public believes children are vulnerable when in fact children are not—this is not where the faulty thinking lies. Instead, this is a myth because of the limited thinking that children are *especially* vulnerable. This limited thinking is what makes it easy for adults to compartmentalize the vulnerability to others and thereby feel that they themselves are not vulnerable, thus releasing them from the responsibility to be vigilant with their own exposures.

I need to make it clear that I am not arguing that children are invulnerable to negative effects from exposure to media violence. They *are* vulnerable (see the following for good summaries of that research evidence: Cantor, 2000; Comstock et al., 1978; Hearold, 1986; Paik & Comstock, 1994; Potter, 1999). I do not dispute the conclusions of that body of research. However, if you look at the research evidence carefully, you will see that adolescents and adults are also affected in negative ways. But the public and policymakers overlook the risks to adolescents and adults in their rush to protect children. Although this concern for children is good, it is a serious mistake to fail to show at least as much concern for other age groups.

What are the pillars undergirding the belief that children are especially vulnerable to media effects? In this chapter I will analyze five of the arguments that are typically advanced. These five are as follows: (a) children's exposure to the media is high, (b) children have difficulty distinguishing between reality and fantasy, (c) children's abilities to deal with the media are limited by developmental stages, (d) children have a lack of experience, and

(e) research clearly shows that children are vulnerable. Let's examine each of these five to determine if children warrant special protection.

As you will see from the following analyses, children are not special if we define *special* as "unique." All age groups are susceptible to negative effects from exposure to media violence. Even if we define *special* as "unusually vulnerable," children appear to be much less special than older groups. The following analyses are designed to expand your thinking and to consider potential reasons why adolescents and adults should also be considered to be as vulnerable as children, and perhaps—with certain effects—more vulnerable.

ARGUMENT #1: CHILDREN HAVE HIGH EXPOSURE TO THE MEDIA

One argument is that children are especially vulnerable because they typically watch so much television. Compared with other age groups, is children's annual exposure to television—and hence violence—higher? The answer is no. There are other age groups that have even higher exposures to media and violence. For example, Comstock and Scharrer (1999), in the most current review of the literature on television exposure patterns, say that the average person views about 22 hours and 40 minutes of television per week. The amount of viewing among older children (6 to 11 years) and adults (18 to 64 years) is about equal—that is, adults are exposed to as much television as are children. When we look at a larger span of age, we see that younger children (2 to 6 years) watch less than the average, and older adults (54 to 65 years) watch much more than the average—22.5% more. Therefore, if we use the annual amount of television exposure as a criterion for selecting the most vulnerable age group, we would select people 54 years and older.

The issue of differences in vulnerability becomes even clearer when we think beyond annual exposure to cumulative exposure. For example, by the time children finish high school, they will have spent at least 16,000 and possibly as high as 20,000 hours in front of the television. Much of television content is violent, so children's high exposure to television translates into high exposure to violence—as many as 100,000 acts of violence by age 18. That is indeed a very large number, but that number grows even larger with each passing year, and by the time viewers reach their mid-50s, the number is three times as high as when they graduated from high school. Because many of the negative effects of exposure to media violence are long-term ones (see Myth 1), it stands to reason that people who have seen more than 250,000 acts of violence on television over five decades would be more at risk for negative effects—especially the long-term effects—than children who have seen 50,000 such acts over one decade.

This exposure argument is therefore faulty. Instead of supporting the contention that children are *especially* vulnerable to negative effects from exposure to media violence, it provides much stronger support for older people being more vulnerable than children are.

ARGUMENT #2: DIFFICULTY DISTINGUISHING BETWEEN REALITY AND FANTASY

For a long time, media researchers have been concerned with the issue of how children perceive reality in the media and how that influences their vulner-ability. For example, Van der Voort (1986) argued that young children have more difficulty than adults do in distinguishing between reality and fantasy and concluded that children are therefore more susceptible to negative effects. At first this sounds like good reasoning. But when we examine the findings of scientific research, it becomes clear that this claim is faulty for two reasons.

One reason this claim is faulty is that people *underestimate* the ability of many children to know the difference between reality and fantasy. Children can be fairly sophisticated in judgments about reality, because they take into consideration multiple factors, as do adults.

The argument that children have difficulty distinguishing between reality and fantasy treats children as bewildered beings who do not have the mental capacity to make accurate judgments. However, researchers who carefully interview children have found that even young children are concerned about making these distinctions accurately and exhibit a degree of sophistication in making their interpretations. For example, Sherry Turkle (2000) has inter-viewed children about their interactions with computers and other forms of new technology. She argues that children do not make simple categorical deci-sions about whether computers and video games are alive or not. Typically children will puzzle over the nature of a computer and explain that in some ways the computer has lifelike qualities (it can ask questions and provide answers) even though it is not really alive (it does not eat or sleep). Children have several middle categories between alive and not alive. Likewise, children have several categories of reality. Children's judgments about the reality of media portrayals are based on the consideration of many factors, and this results in perceptions that there are degrees of reality across those portrayals. It is not a simple categorical decision; a portrayal is not simply reality or fantasy.

The judgment of reality is multidimensional. For example, researchers have found that children—like adults—often make judgments about the reality of a program along three dimensions: magic window, social utility, and identity (Dorr, 1986; Hawkins, 1977; Potter, 1986, 1988). The magic window judgment is the concern about the actualities of the portrayals on television, that is, whether something portrayed on television actually happened (e.g., news stories). The social utility judgment is based on whether viewers believe they can use the information in the portrayal in their own lives. The more fantastic the characters and actions, the less viewers believe they can translate that information into something they can use in their day-to-day interactions with people. The identity judgment is based on a feeling of parasocial involvement with particular characters. The closer a viewer feels to a character, the more real that character is to that viewer.

Viewers make judgments on these three dimensions in an independent manner; that is, if a program is perceived as highly realistic on one dimension, the person may or may not perceive the show as being realistic on the other two dimensions. For example, *Star Trek* is likely to be regarded as fantasy when considered along the magic window dimension, but it can be regarded as highly realistic by many on the identity and social utility dimensions.

Another important point to consider is that differences in judgments of reality in media portrayals are likely to be larger among people of the same age compared with the differences in judgments across different age groups. Not every child of the same age is making the same judgments about reality. For example, Van der Voort (1986) reported that perceptions of reality and degree of identification with characters vary substantially at any given age. In his research he found that some children became absorbed in watching the violent videos and judged the violence to be realistic, which led them to a stronger emotional reaction, which led to a belief that the violence was terrible, which did *not* lead to aggressive behavior in real life. In contrast, other children, who were also absorbed in viewing violence and believed it to be realistic, were found to have an uncritical attitude toward program violence, which led to their being more jaded and less emotionally involved, which led to more aggressive behavior in real life.

A second reason why this argument is faulty is that most people overestimate the ability of adults to distinguish between reality and fantasy. Many adults exhibit the same problems that are attributed to children. An example to illustrate this point came about with the farcical comedy called *Gilligan's Island,* which premiered in the fall of 1964. This 30-minute weekly television series featured seven characters who were marooned on an island somewhere in the Pacific Ocean. After about six episodes had aired, the show's producer, Sherwood Schwartz, was contacted by the Coast Guard and told that they had received several dozen telegrams from people who were complaining that the military should send a ship to rescue these seven people. Those telegrams were serious. Schwartz was dumbfounded and called it the "most extreme case of suspension of belief I ever heard of." He wondered, "Who did these viewers think was filming the castaways on that island? There was even a laugh track on the show. Who was laughing at the survivors of the wreck of the S. S. Minnow? It boggled the mind" (Schwartz, 1984, p. 2).

Although true, this example might appear silly, because there would be only a very small number of adults who would mistake the happenings on *Gilligan's Island* for events in the real world. But this is not to say that adults have a clear grasp on where reality leaves off and fantasy begins. For example, how many adults believe the matches in the World Wrestling Federation television programs are real? How many adults who watch "docudramas" have difficulty perceiving the line between what actually happened and what was fictionalized? How many adults have trouble distinguishing between the reality and fantasy in facts presented by political candidates in mediated debates? How many adults realize that news programs, with their selection filtering processes and story construction formulas, substantially change the picture of what actually happens and instead present a sensationalized version of what the world is like?

In 2001, one of the most popular shows on television was *Survivor,* which bills itself as "reality television." This show purportedly takes 16 real people and puts them in a wilderness setting where the individuals depend on each other for survival (food, shelter, fire). At the same time, they compete against one another for $1 million. In what sense is this show real? The players were selected from thousands of applicants not because they were ordinary people but on the basis of their potential attractiveness to audiences and their ability to generate conflict. The situation is artificial in the sense that none of these people lives his or her typical life in the wilderness, and none has played this game before—or any game for $1 million. Although the setting looks like a wilderness, there are camera crews, sound engineers, producers, and all their support people of medics, cooks, and helicopter pilots. The 16 players are not really alone in the wilderness. The show is not scripted in the sense that the dialogue has been written by a member of the Writers Guild of America. But each contestant carefully writes his or her own lines, in the sense that their interactions are highly calculated to put themselves in the best position to win the game. Also, the show is carefully edited to present to the viewing public the most dramatic version of what takes place. The 960 hours over the course of the 40 days of the game are edited down to about 10 hours that are shown to the public. That is only 1% of what happened. This example makes us confront the issue of where we draw the line between reality and fantasy when something appears in the media. Also, do most adults make this distinction better than most children do?

As we age, we do not automatically acquire the ability to make accurate differentiations between reality and fantasy. Believing that we do may be the strongest evidence that our belief in what we think is the reality of the situation is actually a fantasy. Misperceptions of reality are not limited to children.

In summary, the argument that children are especially vulnerable because they have much more difficulty than adults do at differentiating reality from fantasy is faulty. The belief underestimates children's abilities by assuming that they are limited to making simple and inaccurate judgments about the reality of portrayals. It is also faulty in its assumption that adults have a superior ability and a higher degree of willingness to think through their judgments about the degree of reality in media programs. Because the degree of belief in reality is associated with higher negative effects, adults are as vulnerable as children are (Potter, 1986; Rubin, Perse, & Taylor, 1988).

ARGUMENT #3: CHILDREN'S COGNITIVE DEVELOPMENT IS LIMITED

Another argument for why children should be regarded as being a special group is that their cognitive abilities are limited during childhood, and therefore they are more susceptible to negative effects from the media. In order for this reason to provide strong support for the contention that children should be treated as a special group, we must accept two arguments. First, we must accept that the limitations of children contribute to the risk of negative effects.

Second, we must accept that adults do not have similar limitations. Let's examine the validity of these two arguments.

Children Are Limited Cognitively

Many people believe that children have cognitive limitations that contribute to their risk of negative effects. The primary support for this contention comes from the developmental theory of Jean Piaget. According to his theory, a child's mind matures from birth to about 12 years of age, during which time it goes through several identifiable stages (Smith & Cowie, 1988). Until age 2, children are in the sensorimotor stage; then they advance to the preoperational stage from 2 to 7 years of age. Children then progress to the concrete operational stage, and by 12 they move into the formal operational stage, at which time they are regarded as having matured cognitively into adulthood. Children lack the full capacity for cognitive functioning until about age 12—the onset of adolescence. Therefore, children are different from adolescents and adults because of their lower level of cognitive development. Thus we can draw a clear distinction between childhood and adolescence at age 12 in terms of cognitive development (Piaget & Inhelder, 1969).

Is developmental stage linked to media effects? The answer is yes. But a child's cognitive limitations do not translate consistently into higher vulnerability. There are times when children's cognitive limitations actually protect them from negative effects. For example, Collins (1973, 1983) found that young children are less able to understand relationships between motives and aggression, and therefore they may be less prone to imitate inappropriate behaviors. When certain motives or cues occur in a child's real-life environment, the child will not be able to make the association between those cues and the image of violence he or she saw in the media. Thus very young children seem to be protected from an imitation effect because they do not understand the significance of violence as a tool for solving problems and do not see the utility in imitating it.

Over time, stage theories such as Piaget's explanation of childhood cognitive development have been seen as less useful predictors. Stage theories of childhood cognitive development have come under criticism for being too discrete (e.g., see Gardner, 1983). Critics say that even Piaget cannot consistently demonstrate that all children of a given age are operating at the same developmental stage. There are differential rates of cognitive development.

Information-processing theories, which look at the second-by-second processing of messages, demonstrate that children of exactly the same age can process the same messages in very different ways. Also, it has been found that children attach different meanings to the symbols in a message, because children differ in their real-life experiences as well as in their contact with the media. Also, researchers have been finding that Piaget underreported the abilities of young children (Bryant & Kopytynska, 1976; Donaldson, 1978; McGarrigle & Donaldson, 1975; Moore & Fry, 1986) and even infants (Bower, 1965; Bremner & Bryant, 1977; Butterworth, 1981).

The research on media violence clearly indicates that factors in children's environments influence their rates of development and hence their understanding of these messages. For example, children of low SES enjoy the violence in programs more, approve of violent behavior more, and identify with television characters more than do children of higher SES (Van der Voort, 1986).

Family life is also an important contributing factor (Josephson, 1987). For example, children who are abused by parents watch more violence and identify with violent heroes more (Heath et al., 1989). Children being raised in high-stress environments get less familial support and are more vulnerable to the effects of media violence (Tangney, 1988; Tangney & Feshbach, 1988). In contrast, children in households with strong norms against violence do not have their behavior affected as much (Heath et al., 1989).

Because of all the different factors that influence children, they develop at very different rates. Some young children are able to process meaning from the media as well as some adults are.

Adults Are Fully Developed Cognitively

The second argument we must accept in order to believe that children's development is more limited than adults is that adults really are significantly more developed than children are. The strongest support cited for this argument is from Piaget's theory, which posits that people reach the final stage of cognitive development (formal operations) at age 12. At this point, Piaget's theory says, children are fully developed cognitively and therefore are capable of adult thinking. Many researchers have tested this claim, and it appears to be faulty, according to King (1986), who conducted a review of the published literature that tested the formal reasoning abilities of adults. She concluded that "a rather large proportion of adults do not evidence formal thinking, even among those who have been enrolled in college" (King, 1986, p. 6). This conclusion holds up over the 25 studies she analyzed, including a variety of tests of formal reasoning ability and a variety of samples of adults 18 to 79 years old. In one third of the samples, less than 30% of the respondents exhibited reasoning at the fully formal level, and in almost all samples no more than 70% of the adults were found to be fully functioning at the formal level.

Many adults never reach the cognitive developmental level of formal reasoning, which is the passage into adulthood according to Piaget. Also, there is considerable evidence that as people age throughout adulthood, there continues to be development on many kinds of cognitive abilities, and this development varies significantly across adults. For example, Mines and Kitchenor (1986) build on the work of Piaget but argue that the stage of formal operations is not the ultimate step of cognitive development in humans but rather is one step in a longer sequence of intellectual development that continues throughout adulthood. Also, other researchers (Kitchenor, 1983; Neimark, 1979) have argued that the tests of Piaget's stages of formal thinking are really assessments of a person's ability in hypothetico-deductive reasoning and logical-algebraic thinking. They then raise concerns that adult thinking is more complex than this one type of thinking and that adults develop their thinking abilities in many different areas.

There is a growing literature that documents how adults continue to experience cognitive changes throughout their lives. For example, Sternberg and Berg (1987) show that throughout adulthood, people's intelligence changes, not so much in the level of IQ but in terms of a shift in type from fluid to crystalline. Fluid intelligence is the ability to be creative and see patterns in complex sets of facts. Crystalline intelligence is the ability to memorize facts. Sternberg and Berg say that

> crystallized ability is best measured by tests requiring knowledge of the cultural milieu in which one lives, for example, vocabulary and general information, whereas fluid ability is best measured by tests requiring mental manipulation of abstract symbols, for example, figural analogies and number series completions. (p. 4)

Sternberg and Berg (1987) point out that research has shown that "whereas crystallized ability seems to increase throughout the life span, although at a decreasing rate in later years, fluid ability seems first to increase and later to decrease" (p. 4).

There is also evidence that a person's mind can continue to mature throughout adolescence and adulthood in terms of cognitive style, which is a person's approach to organizing and processing information (Hashway & Duke, 1992). Although many people continue to mature in their cognitive style well beyond childhood, others don't. Cognitive style is a continuum of abilities, and there are many adults who are not far away from childhood on this continuum. A person's cognitive style is reflected in his or her abilities in several areas, including field dependency, tolerance for ambiguity, conceptual differentiation, and reflection-impulsivity.

Although Piaget's stage theory of cognitive development has been very influential in helping us understand how children's minds mature in their abilities to solve problems, we must move beyond the limitations of this theory as we see greater complexities in the development of the human mind. This development does not reach an ultimate stage at age 12. Instead, the human mind develops along many cognitive dimensions throughout life. Furthermore, this development is not uniform. Some people develop very quickly and exhibit adultlike problem-solving abilities while still in elementary school, whereas some adults of retirement age still have not reached a level of reasoning that Piaget claimed was characteristic of 12-year-olds.

To this point, I have been talking about cognitive development only, but there is evidence that humans also develop emotionally and morally. Children and adults develop emotionally throughout life. Awareness and control of emotions includes components of being able to read emotions (empathy), having emotional self-awareness, harnessing emotions productively, managing emotions, and handling relationships (Salovey & Mayer, 1990). It is not difficult to see how each of these would be related to media effects. People who have higher development along these lines would have stronger and more appropriate emotional reactions to violence in the media while exercising greater control over their personal behaviors in real life.

Emotional development is closely linked to cognitive development (Goleman, 1995). For example, very young children cannot follow the interconnected elements in a continuing plot; instead, they focus on individual elements. Therefore, they cannot understand suspense, and without such an understanding, they cannot become emotionally aroused as the suspense builds. So a child's ability to have an emotional reaction to the media messages is sometimes low not because of a lack of ability to feel emotions, but because of a lack of ability to understand what is going on in certain narratives.

Emotions and cognitions are also closely linked throughout adulthood. Goleman (1995) explains,

> We have two brains, two minds—and two different kinds of intelligence: rational and emotional. How we do in life is determined by both—it is not just IQ, but emotional intelligence that matters. Indeed, intellect cannot work at its best without emotional intelligence. (p. 28)

In addition to cognitive development and emotional development, people also develop morally throughout childhood and continue through adulthood. Like Piaget, Lawrence Kohlberg has studied the development of children. Whereas Piaget was concerned with cognitive development, Kohlberg focuses on moral development. He envisions three levels of moral development: preconventional, conventional, and postconventional (Kohlberg, 1966, 1981).

Kohlberg argues that the preconventional stage begins at about age 2 and runs to about 7 or 8. This is when the child is dependent on authority. Young children depend on their parents and other adults to tell them what is right and to interpret the world for them. The child's conscience is external; that is, the child must be told by others what is right. Inner controls are weak.

During the conventional stage, children develop a conscience for themselves as they internalize what is right and wrong. They distinguish between truth and lies. Their behavior is still motivated by the threat of punishment.

The postconventional stage begins in middle adolescence, when some people are able to transcend conventional notions of right and wrong as they focus on fundamental principles. This requires the ability to think abstractly and therefore to recognize the ideals behind society's laws. This level is characterized by a sense that being socially conscious is more important than adhering to legalistic principles.

Advances in moral development do not necessarily come with age. For example, Van der Voort (1986) found no evidence that children judge violent behavior more critically in a moral sense as they age. He found no reduction in the approval of the good guys' behavior. And as children aged, they were even more likely to approve of the violent actions of the bad guys. So although children acquired additional cognitive abilities with age, they did not necessarily acquire additional moral insights. There is a range of moral development among people of any given age. Also, older children do not automatically have higher moral development than younger children do.

In summary, there is ample evidence that people develop cognitively, emotionally, and morally over the course of childhood and that this development does not stop at adolescence but continues throughout one's entire life. Furthermore, it is important to note that not everyone at a given age is at the same level of development; there are significant differences across people at any particular age in terms of their cognitive, emotional, and moral abilities. It is likely that there are many adults who are not as highly developed cognitively, emotionally, or morally as many children.

The way people use their abilities to think, feel, and judge is what determines their levels of risk of negative media effects. Age has been used as a surrogate variable for these more accurate predictors. But age is a poor surrogate, because research has shown that there are many more differences within people of the same age than there are differences across ages.

ARGUMENT #4: LACK OF EXPERIENCE RATIONALE

Children are regarded as having less worldly experience than older people have. For example, Dorr (1986) uses this reasoning as the basis for her argument that "children may accept program content as accurate 'information' when other more knowledgeable viewers know it to be otherwise" (p. 13). This statement seems valid on its face, but let's examine it more closely in the context of media violence. When we think of "experience" with violence in the real world and in the media world, there may be two fallacies underlying the belief that older people automatically have more experience.

Experience Fallacy

Let's analyze the claim that children are more vulnerable to the effects of media violence compared with adults because they have less experience. The key question becomes: Experience with what? Adults generally have more experience than children with lots of things—balancing checkbooks, raising a family, following sports teams, driving, and so forth—but most of these experiences would have no influence on vulnerability to media violence. The key kind of experience that would make a big difference when assessing vulnerability to media violence is experience with real-world violence. The incidence of being involved in a violent crime in real life is so low that adult experience is not much more than children's experience on average. Of course, an adult living in a high-crime neighborhood is likely to have been involved in a violent crime multiple times, but then so are children living in the same neighborhood. So neighborhood, not age, is the key factor. Also, violence is prevalent in some families with child abuse, but in such families, the violence is experienced by children and adults alike. The key factor here is type of family, not age.

Although most adults have never witnessed a crime or an act of serious violence in their real lives, they have witnessed many such acts in the media. Therefore, adults clearly have much more experience with crime and violence compared with children—but this experience is limited to the media world. If we then argue that greater exposure to media violence leads to greater vulnerability to negative effects, it must follow that adults are more vulnerable than children *because of* their greater experience.

Adults, of course, have more experience compared with children in general. But do adults have more of the type of experience that would reduce their vulnerability to media violence? The answer appears to be no. Adults' greater experience with violence is purely from the media world, and this type of experience is what increases vulnerability. When it comes to real-world experience with violence, the key factors that predict vulnerability are neighborhood and type of family rather than age. So real-world experience with violence does not necessarily separate adults from children in terms of vulnerability.

Logical Fallacy

If we accept the premise that children are at greater risk for harm because they have less experience with the world and with the media, then does it logically follow that we should work to keep that experience limited? If the assumption is that one's ability to protect oneself from risk increases when one's experience increases, then how can it follow that limiting a person's experience is a good thing to do? The desire to protect children seems motivated more by an implied preference that negative effects should show up later, when one is an adult, rather than earlier, when one is a child. If we act on this preference, we are protecting the child in a cynical sense by not showing concern for the person who will eventually become an adult. If adults really want to help children build a strong experiential base to use to protect themselves, then adults should follow through on this concern and expose children to violence in the media but do so in a consciously therapeutic manner. If adults really want children to learn prosocial attitudes and behaviors from their exposure to violence, then adults need to watch with children and help those children process the narratives carefully so that they do not fall prey to the misleading meaning in those messages.

Some people argue that children need more real-world experience *before* they are able to handle media world portrayals. That is a reasonable argument, but does it apply with the content of media violence? What do we gain by waiting for a child to experience real-world violence before we are assured that the child's experience has increased enough that the child is ready for media-world portrayals of violence? Again, we can see the argument breaks down, and we are left in a position of absurdity.

The key to building useful experience is that it is more than summing up exposures. For experience to be useful as a protector from negative effects, it must be a quality exposure in which the "innocent" (a child or someone with little experience with violent content) is guided by another person to show the innocent how to handle the exposure. This quality exposure can happen at any time during childhood. An innocent who has quality exposures at age 5 will have a very different childhood in terms of risk of negative effects from exposure to media violence than another child who has no quality exposures.

It is faulty to believe that higher age translates into more experience, which is then valuable as a protector from the risks of exposure to media violence. Mindless years of exposure to media violence do not mean that a person has grown in understanding of risks. Only the experience of active and critical viewing can increase a person's ability to reduce risks. Age and experience are not the same thing.

ARGUMENT #5: RESEARCH CLEARLY SHOWS THAT CHILDREN ARE VULNERABLE

When research on the effects of violence in the media was begun, first with film (Charters, 1933) and then with television (Schramm et al., 1961), the focus was on children's exposure and how children were affected. Since that time, children have remained on center stage through the report of the Surgeon General's Scientific Advisory Committee on Television and Social Behavior

(1972) and its follow-up a decade later (Pearl, Bouthilet, & Lazar, 1982). In between those classic milestone studies (Lowry & DeFleur, 1995), hundreds of individual research efforts examined the influence of the media on children. Scholars who have carefully reviewed all those research studies conclude that children are vulnerable to harmful effects from their exposures to violence in the media (Baker & Ball, 1969; Comstock et al., 1978; Hearold, 1986; Liebert & Schwartzberg, 1977; Paik & Comstock, 1994; Potter, 1999).

Reviews of the research also conclude that nonchildren are also vulnerable to negative effects, especially when we look beyond imitation and examine a broader range of effects. If we are concerned only with copycat behaviors or immediate fear responses, then most of the research (but not all) has been conducted on children, so it is understandable that children have been shown to be highly vulnerable to negative effects. But with other effects, there are relatively large research literatures that have relied predominantly on adult samples. For example, we can draw confident conclusions of a disinhibition effect, and most of the studies in this literature have been conducted on college-age participants. The same can be said for the growing literature on the desensitization effect. In fact, the major theoreticians and researchers (Berkowitz, Donnerstein, Geen, Linz, and Zillmann) of these two effects have dealt almost exclusively with adult participants.

CONCLUSION

There is a strong intuitive appeal to each of these five arguments that children are especially vulnerable to negative effects from the media. But all of these arguments are faulty. They are not faulty in the sense that they are wrong about children being vulnerable to negative effects from exposure to media violence. Children *are* vulnerable and should be protected. But children represent only one group that is vulnerable. People in all age groups are vulnerable, and there is good reason to believe that on many negative effects, older people are even more vulnerable than are children.

Being an adult does not necessarily mean that one is more highly developed cognitively and can therefore protect oneself better from the influence of media violence. Adults also have problems distinguishing fantasy from reality. Having more years of experience with life is not necessarily a shield against negative effects if that experience is dominated by mindless exposure to the media and few real-world encounters that could moderate the media influence.

We should protect children from risks of negative effects from exposure to media violence. But the risks do not stop at puberty. It is a serious lapse of responsibility to ignore the importance of protecting adolescents, adults, and the elderly.

FIVE

MYTH 4

There is too much violence in the media.

————•◦•————

Public opinion polls consistently reveal that people think there is too much violence in the media (see Table 5.1). The misperception underlying this belief is found in the difference between the way researchers identify violence and what the general public regards as violence. Because these two groups exhibit a very different idea of what violence is, the results of researchers' analyses of media content do not seem relevant to the public, and at times, these results can even seem silly. For example, when researchers report that among the most violent shows are *Tom and Jerry, Road Runner, Three Stooges,* and *America's Funniest Home Videos,* the public cannot relate to such findings. Most viewers would not regard any of these programs as violent. Some critics look at this situation and conclude that social scientists must be using poor definitions of violence (Morrison, 1993). The public feels it has reason to regard researchers as "fuzzy thinking academics" who have lost touch with reality.

MAJOR DIFFERENCES IN DEFINING VIOLENCE

Researchers and the public do agree that there is a great deal of violence in the media—too much. But this agreement is specious, because they are not think-ing about the same thing when they say they agree.

Table 5.1   Public Opinion About Amount of Violence in Media

- A 1975 Gallup poll found that two thirds of Americans found the present level of violent programming unacceptable (Cooper, 1996).
- A 1992 Associated Press poll found that 82% of Americans feel that movies are too violent (O'Donnell, 1992).
- Based on a 1993 poll, 70% of Americans feel that entertainment TV has too much violence, and 57% think that TV news gives too much attention to stories about violent crime (Galloway, 1993).
- A 1994 *Parents* magazine poll found that an overwhelming majority of Americans—87% of those questioned—say that the media "contains too much violence" (Diamant, 1994).
- In a 1995 Time/CNN survey, 52% of adult Americans said they are very concerned about the amount of violence depicted in movies, television shows, and popular music; another 25% said they were fairly concerned; only 9% said they were not concerned at all (Lacayo, 1995).
- A 1997 nationwide poll by the *Los Angeles Times* found that two thirds of people think that television programming has gotten worse over the last decade, with 90% believing that television now has more violence and sex than it did 10 years ago (Lowry, 1997).
- A 1997 *USA Weekend* write-in poll generated 21,600 responses, with 92% of those respondents saying they regarded television content as more offensive than ever, especially in terms of violence, sexual content, and vulgarity (Salvoza, 1997).

Scientific Definitions

Social scientists have been studying the amount of violence in the media for decades using a methodology called content analysis. In order to use this methodology, researchers must begin with a clear articulation of what they intend to measure, in this case the occurrence of violent acts. Over the years, many different scientific analyses have been conducted using a range of definitions (see Table 5.2). Despite some differences, the overlap in definitions is substantial. Also, when researchers add unique elements to their own definitions of violence, this allows them to determine how the widening (or narrowing) of the definition affects the subsequent counts of how much violence appears in the media.

Let's examine some of the definitions used by researchers so we can identify what concerns them most about media violence. The prevalent definition

Table 5.2   Scientific Definitions of Violence

Gerbner:	"The overt expression of physical force, with or without weapon, against self or other, compelling action against one's will on pain of being hurt or killed, or actually hurting or killing" (Gerbner et al., 1978, p. 179). Furthermore, Gerbner's definition requires that the violence be plausible and credible, which rules out idle threats, verbal abuse, or comic gestures with no credible violent consequences. The violence may be intentional or accidental. Also, violent accidents, catastrophes, and acts of nature are included. Any act that fits the definition, regardless of conventional notions about types of violence that may have "serious" effects, is coded. This includes violence that occurs in realistic, serious, fantasy, or humorous contexts. "Accidental" violence and "acts of nature" are recorded because they are always purposeful in fiction, claim victims, and demonstrate power. (Signorielli, 1990, p. 89)
NTVS:	"An overt depiction of a credible threat of physical force or the actual use of such force intended to physically harm an animate being or group of beings. Violence also includes certain depictions of physically harmful consequences against an animate being or group that occur as a result of unseen violent means" (NTVS, 1996, p. 1-48).
Williams, Zabrack, and Joy:	"Physically aggressive behaviors that do, or potentially could, cause injury or death" (1982, p. 366).
Mustonen and Pulkkinen:	"Any action causing or attempting to cause physical or psychological harm to oneself, another person, animal, or inanimate object, intentionally or accidentally. Psychological harm was understood as assaulting another's self verbally or non-verbally, e.g., by threatening, forcing, submitting, or mocking. Verbal reports of aggression and

(Continued)

Table 5.2 Continued

	aggression without clear visual cues were not coded" (1993, pp. 177-178).
Potter et al.:	"Any action that serves to diminish in some physical, social, or emotional manner" (1995, p. 497).
Potter and Ware:	"Any attempt by one character to harm another character" (1987, p. 672).
Greenberg, Edison, Korzenny, Fernandez-Collado, and Atkin:	"That which is psychologically or physically injurious to another person or persons whether intended or not, and whether successful or not" (1980, p. 102).

used by researchers was developed over three decades ago by George Gerbner and his colleagues at the University of Pennsylvania. Gerbner's research team used this definition consistently for over 25 years in annual analyses of television content, and they influenced other researchers to also use their definition, either in whole or as a basis for their own definitions. Using this definition, Gerbner and others typically find that about 80% of all network prime-time and Saturday morning television programs have contained at least one act of violence over the past several decades. They also found cycles of violence ranging from 7 acts on average per hour during some years to as high as 10 acts per hour during other years (Cumberbatch, Lee, Hardy, & Jones, 1987; Halloran & Croll, 1972; Iwao, de Sola Pool, & Hagiwara, 1981; Kapoor, Kang, Kim, & Kim, 1994; McCann & Sheehan, 1985; Mikami, 1993; Sherman & Dominick, 1986; Slaby, Quarfoth, & McConnachie, 1976).

The central idea in Gerbner's definition is that violence is physical force that has the potential to harm. This is also the central idea of all the other scientific definitions. Those other definitions differ in terms of how they treat some issues surrounding this core idea.

There is one important characteristic that is shared by all the definitions of researchers: All the definitions treat violence as realism. By this I mean that the definitions specify conditions about an act that would allow it to be coded as violent, and once it is identified as an act of violence it does not disappear when it appears in certain contexts. For example, if one character takes a hammer and smashes the hand of another character, that is violence. It still is considered violence if it is done in a humorous context (e.g., *The Three Stooges*) or a fantasy context (e.g., *Bugs Bunny*). The act of hurting another person with a hammer is violence regardless of context. Researchers typically code the contexts so they can present figures about how much violence is presented as humorous and how much is presented in a fantasy context. But the context does not camouflage or excuse the violence; the context is treated as additional variables that also need to be analyzed.

Public's Definition

The public treats violence as a primitive term; that is, people all know what it is and believe they all share the same definition. They use the word with confidence that others will know what they mean; there is no need to define it explicitly in conversations. However, when members of the public are asked to write a definition of violence, they have a great deal of difficulty. They know it when they see it, and that is enough. In my experience, I have found that people become surprised when I show them the decisions that scientists typically consider when formulating their decisions. For example, look at the questions in Table 5.3.

Before you read any further, try the following exercise. Get a pencil and a piece of paper. Attempt to write your definition of violence in one sentence. When you finish, think about the violent portrayals you have seen in movies and on TV. Does your definition work well? Does it identify what would be violent in news shows? In an episode of *The Three Stooges*? In Saturday morning cartoons? With video or computer games?

The task of defining violence appears to be an easy one at first, but it turns out to be very difficult to write a definition that would provide adequate guidance to judge whether something is violent or not across all the nuances of portrayals across all media. Most people become frustrated with this task as they realize how complex it is to articulate precisely what they had previously believed they understood clearly. The reason for this is that *violence* is a primitive concept; that is, we all know it when we see it, but it is nearly impossible to write down a good definition. Another example of a primitive term is *red*. You cannot write a definitional rule for what is red and what is not, but you have high confidence that you know what it is and can spot it when it occurs.

We deal with many primitive concepts in our everyday life—love, chair, freedom, sex. We all "know" what these mean even though we cannot specify

Table 5.3   Key Elements in Definitions of Violence

1. Does the act have to be directed toward a person? Gang members swing baseball bats at a car and totally destroy it. Is this violence?
2. Does the act have to be committed by a person? A mudslide levels a town and kills 20 people. Do acts of nature count? Remember that nature does not write the scripts or produce the programming.
3. Does the act have to be intentional? A bank robber drives a fast car in a getaway chase. As he speeds around a corner he hits a pedestrian (or destroys a mailbox). Do accidents count?
4. Does the act have to result in harm? Tom shoots a gun at Jerry, but the bullet misses. Is this violence? Or what if Tom and Jerry are cartoon characters and Tom drops an anvil on Jerry who is momentarily flattened like a pancake. A second later Jerry pops back to his original shape and appears fine.
5. What about violence we don't see? If a bad guy fires a gun at a character offscreen and we hear a scream and a body fall, is this violence even though we do not see it?
6. Does the act have to be physical (such as assaults), or can it be verbal (such as insults)? What if Tom viciously insults Jerry, who is shown through the rest of the program experiencing deep psychological and emotional pain as a result? What if Tom embarrasses Jerry, who then runs from the room, trips, and breaks his arm?
7. What about fantasy? If 100 fighting men "morph" into a giant creature the size of a 10-story building that then stomps out their enemies, does this count as violence?
8. What about humorous portrayals? When the Three Stooges hit each other with hammers, is this violence?

an adequate definition for any of them. We learn the meanings of primitive words through experience as other people point out examples and label them for us. After we have experienced many examples, we become confident that we will know something when we see it, but we can never express a clearer definition of it.

If people have a lot of difficulty expressing their definitions of violence, how can I know that people have a very different definition than do researchers? I found this out quite by accident when running an experiment to test how people use the information in the plot of television shows to interpret the meaning of the violence. Some of my colleagues and I showed some people an episode of *Walker, Texas Ranger* and asked them to rate the amount of violence in that program (Potter, Pekurny, Pashupati, Hoffman, & Davis, 2000). We divided our television viewers into three groups. One group watched the version of the episode as it had been broadcast. We labeled the broadcast version of the show "high violence," because it contained 62 violent acts—punches, kicks, shootings, and so forth. The second group saw the same episode but with some of the violent acts edited out. It contained 47 violent acts and was labeled "moderate violence." The third group saw the "low-violence" version, which contained 13 acts. This low-violence version was the same episode with as many acts of violence as possible edited out without destroying the meaning of the plot. After viewing their version, each of our participants was asked to fill out a survey instrument that contained a question asking them to rate the amount of violence on a 10-point scale, with a 1 being *no violence* and 10 being *extremely high amount.* The ratings of the people in the low-violence group averaged a 5 on this 10-point scale. This is about what we expected—a middle rating of violence. However, we were very surprised when we found that the average rating of the high-violence group was only 6. Although the difference in the number of acts of violence (13 acts vs. 62 acts) was substantial, the difference in participants' ratings of the degree of violence in those shows was trivial (5 vs. 6).

How was it possible that the perceptions of violence differed so little across groups? To answer this question, we examined responses to other questions and found no good explanation until we looked at our viewers' estimates of the number of violent acts. (The postviewing survey instrument also had a question asking viewers to estimate the number of violent acts that were in the show they had just seen.) The patterns of these estimates were startling. Among the low-violence group, some of our viewers said they saw no violent acts. Recall that this episode contained 13 clear acts of violence. The average estimate across all viewers in this group was only two acts, and no one said they saw more than six acts of violence. All our viewers were underestimating the number of violent acts. This tendency to underestimate was even more substantial among the viewers in the high-violence group who saw the version with 62 violent acts. Among those viewers, the highest estimate was 14, and the average estimate across all participants in this condition was only 4 acts.

We began searching through the research literature to see if other researchers had found similar patterns. Despite the literature on media effects' being very large, we found only one study on this point. In Holland, Van der Voort (1986) conducted a similar study on children as well as adults and found that they rated the frequency of violence in particular programs lower than the frequency found in scientific content analysis. He explained, "Programs that are extremely violent according to 'objective' content analysis can be seen by children as hardly containing any violence. This, for example is the case with violent cartoons of the *Tom and Jerry* type" (Van der Voort, 1986, p. 329).

Clearly, television viewers are perceiving things very differently than are scientists who make systematic counts of violent acts in programs. It is apparent that the public is missing many acts that scientists regard as violent. Why are there such big differences in perceptions of violence? In order to answer this question, let's first take a look at the public's definition of violence, then we'll take a look at how media researchers define violence.

Because the public treats media violence as a primitive concept, it is impossible to specify the public definition of violence directly. The only way to understand how the public defines violence is to observe what people point out as violence and then work backward, if possible, to make a list of characteristics and conditions that reflect the meaning of the term in everyday usage. When we do this, we can spot three such factors that capture much of the essence in the way the public conceptualizes the idea of violence in the media.

The first of these factors is graphicness. The more a portrayal shows blood and gore, especially in close-ups, the more viewers will consider it violent. Several studies have been conducted in which people are asked to rate the violence in a story and then to rate those stories on other characteristics (Potter & Berry, 1998). This relationship between graphicness and a viewer's perception of violence is strong for all kinds of people: males as well as females; religious and nonreligious people; people who have been a victim of violence in their real life as well as those who have not; people who are politically liberal or conservative; and people who watch little television as well as those who watch a great deal.

Closely related to graphicness is the characteristic of offensiveness. If portrayals are not offensive—that is, evoking a negative feeling—then viewers do not pay much attention to violence compared with other program features (British Broadcasting Corporation, 1972), or when they do pay attention, it is not an important element that takes away from their enjoyment of programs (Diener & De Four, 1978; Diener & Woody, 1981). But when a violent portrayal is unusually graphic, it interrupts viewers' flow of enjoyment, and viewers experience strong negative emotions.

The second of these factors is that the public seems to define violence more in terms of the way the act is portrayed than the degree of harm to the victims. For example, if a character fires a gun and kills another character offscreen, the public will not regard this as violence. However, if a character slaps a child without justification, and we see the imprint of the slap grow dark red on the child's face as her lip trembles and she breaks into silent tears, viewers would criticize this incident for being highly violent. Thus a slap to the face can be considered more violent than a murder.

A third factor of the public's definition of violence is that humor is a camouflage. It appears that when humor blankets violence, the public does not see the violence. This is taken for granted by all kinds of people. An anecdote will illustrate this. In the winter of 1996 I was meeting with the staff of the Viacom Standards and Practices Department in New York City. These seven women are charged with previewing the content to be aired on Viacom's cable channels of MTV, VH1, and Nickelodeon. I was watching a music video while the seven women in the room explained how they screened music videos to determine if those videos met their standards or if, in their judgment, there were things in the portrayals that would offend viewers. For an hour the women showed parts of music videos and explained how they asked the various music groups to remove or tone down certain images that they felt were demeaning to women. Finally, when I was given a chance to ask a question, I said, "What about violence in the videos?" Several women were eager to answer that they were sensitive to that issue and that the videos did not have any direct scenes of violence, although violence was implied in certain lyrics. Then I asked about violence on Nickelodeon. There was a rather long pause as the women looked at me as if I were a third grader who had just claimed that two plus two equals seven. One of the women looked very puzzled and said, "But there is no violence on Nickelodeon." I returned the puzzled look and replied, "What about your Saturday morning shows such as *Bugs Bunny* and *Ninja Turtles*?" Her puzzled looked turned into a big smile as she said, "But those are not violent. Those are cartoons!" Were these women naive? No, they had a highly sophisticated understanding of violence—as defined by the general viewing public. These women knew that the public was not concerned by the actions—even the most brutal—portrayed in cartoons.

What is the reason for humor's ability to camouflage the violence? It appears that humor tends to remove the threat of violence. In order for viewers to consider something violent, they need to feel a degree of personal threat. This insight can be found in the work of Barrie Gunter in Great Britain. He reported that viewers' ratings of the seriousness of violent acts were higher as the fictional settings were closer to everyday reality in terms of time and location. In contrast, "Violence depicted in clearly fantastic settings such as cartoons or science-fiction were perceived as essentially non-violent, non-frightening and non-disturbing" (Gunter, 1985, p. 245). Other researchers also report that people were much more concerned with acts that had a higher probability of occurrence, meaning the likelihood of the act's happening to them in everyday life (Forgas, Brown, & Menyhart, 1980).

In summary, the public uses a conception of violence that is keyed to three factors. First, there is graphicness. The more blood and gore shown in a portrayal, the more the portrayal risks offending viewers, and the more viewers will object to the act as being violent. Second, the seriousness of the action itself and the way the act is portrayed is more influential in the decision of what is violence than is the portrayed harm to the victim. Third, people allow humor to camouflage violence. Humor reduces the feeling of personal threat to viewers and thereby eliminates the sense of violence.

Implications of the Differences

Does it matter how we define violence? Of course it does. The way you define violence in large part determines how much violence you will perceive in the media. Let's return once again to your definition. Analyze your definition by answering the eight questions in Table 5.3. If you answered no to all eight questions, you would have a very narrow definition of violence. If you were to use that narrow definition to examine systematically the content of television, you would find about one act of violence per hour on average. In contrast, if you answered yes to all eight questions, you would have a very broad definition of violence. Using a broad definition, you would find about 40 acts per hour on television. Of course, there are shows that contain no violence—such as most game shows, cooking shows, home shopping shows, and so forth. There are other shows—such as action-adventure shows—that display very high levels of violence.

If you are like most people, you excluded acts that result in no harm to the victim (Question #4), acts that take place offscreen (#5), verbal acts (#6), fantasy context (#7), and humorous context (#8). Many people would also rule out property harm (#1), acts of God (#2), and accidents (#3). That leaves a very narrow definition—much narrower than the definitions typically used by researchers.

When we use the typical definition used by media researchers, such as the one developed by Gerbner and his colleagues, the rate is about eight acts per hour on average. Because the typical American household has the television set on for about 42 hours per week, this computes to about 17,500 acts of violence coming into a household each year through the television set. In contrast, if we use the public's definition, this number would be reduced substantially, because only about 2% of these 17,500 acts are highly graphic. Thus, whereas researchers look at the television landscape over a year and perceive 17,500 acts of violence, the public looks at the same landscape and perceives about 300 acts per year. Thus the public's criticism that the media present too much violence is based on a level of tolerance below 300 acts per year. Using this same level of tolerance, imagine the degree of criticism if the public were able to perceive the full extent of the problem.

Clearly, the public and researchers perceive very different amounts of violence in the media. These differences in perceptions of amount are directly traceable to differences in definition. Whose definition is better? The answer to this question lies in our perspective on harm.

WHY THE DIFFERENT DEFINITIONS?

So far in this chapter, we have seen that there is a big difference in perception between the public and researchers in terms of how much violence there is in the media. In analyzing this difference, we see that the more fundamental difference is a definitional one. The question now becomes: Why are the definitions of the public and researchers so different? To answer this question, we need to extend the analysis one step further and consider the most fundamental difference between the public and researchers, and this is the issue of harm. There are three ways to consider harm: potential harm to characters, "as-if" harm, and potential harm to viewers.

Potential Harm to Characters

This type of harm is a key factor in the definitions of researchers. If Harry fires a gun at Tom, researchers would typically regard this as a violent act even if the bullet misses Tom, because Tom is put at risk for serious harm when Harry aims and fires the gun at him. If the gun goes off by accident and Tom is hit by the bullet, most researchers would consider this an act of violence.

Also, if Harry and Tom are cartoon characters and Harry shoots Tom's head off as a joke and Tom grows his head back in the next scene, this would still be regarded as an act of violence by most researchers.

The public does not view media violence from this perspective. The public typically screens out threats that do not result in physical harm. When there is physical harm, the public discounts the act if it is an accident or if it occurs in a fantasy context, such as an animated cartoon. Also, the public screens out acts that are not portrayed in a relatively graphic manner. Because of the screening and discounting, the public is not viewing violence from the same perspective as researchers do.

The portrayals of violence in the media play into the public's definition. Most violence on television has been sanitized, that is, there is very little blood and gore, even when a character is shot or hit 20 times. When people watch sanitized violence—even at high rates—they are not shocked and therefore are not bothered by the violence. Also, when the violence is trivialized—such as when it is shown in fantasy and humorous contexts—people are not shocked and thus do not criticize the portrayals. This explains why most people do not think of cartoons as violent (Howitt & Cumberbatch, 1975), despite the fact that carefully conducted objective analyses of media content continually find cartoons to have the highest rates of violence of any type of television program (Gerbner, Gross, Jackson-Beeck, Jeffries-Fox, & Signorielli, 1976; Greenberg et al., 1980; NTVS, 1996).

"As-If" Harm

Some depictions of violence make the viewer think about what it would be like to be the victim in the portrayal. When a viewer is drawn into the action through identification with some characters and those characters experience violence in the plot, viewers tend to feel threatened and harmed as if they too were in the action. Up to a point, this can be an enjoyable feeling for viewers. When the action follows a simple, recognizable formula, viewers can delight in the danger and suspense knowing eventually that they (through their characters) will prevail. However, if they feel that their characters are being roughed up too much or if they lose faith that their characters will prevail, viewers become very uncomfortable in their as-if experience. They feel harmed, not entertained. This leads to negative feelings and criticism.

There are certain factors that can increase the pleasure of the as-if experience. Enjoyment increases when viewers' identification with particular attractive characters increases and when the actions that happen to these characters are sanitized. Pleasure is heightened even more when these particular characters then feel justified when they begin retaliating in a glamorized and successful manner. In contrast, viewers who identify with the victim of an act of violence that is depicted as highly graphic will feel a high degree of personal threat and experience a strong sense of fear, vulnerability, or disgust. These are negative emotions, so viewers would find the exposure highly unpleasant, and this would then trigger criticism. For example, if an entertainment program depicts disgusting characters performing graphic physical harm to innocent characters, the public will be offended and regard these depictions as highly violent. But if the perpetrators are the attractive characters and they are portrayed as being justified in committing violent acts against the ugly victims, viewers will identify with the perpetrators and not be offended. Or if a news program shows bodies being removed from a house in a local neighborhood while the reporter says the crime is apparently unmotivated and police have no leads, a viewer will feel a high degree of personal vulnerability as a potential next victim. But when viewers see bodies removed from a battlefield in a remote foreign country, they do not feel vulnerable.

Viewers are constantly looking for pleasant as-if experiences. Violence helps increase the pleasure when it is portrayed as creating a pleasant sense of danger for viewers; when viewers feel at risk but only from minor (sanitized) harm; and when the heroes with whom they identify retaliate with appropriate and justified (even if graphic) harm against the villains.

Potential Harm to Viewers

The most important key to appreciating the problem with this myth—as well as the entire problem of media violence—is to understand the potential risks for negative harm to viewers. Although at first glance this type of harm might appear to be very similar to as-if harm, the two are very different. The harm in as-if harm is a perception by viewers that they are in danger as they suspend belief and become part of the story. This perception of danger is gone as soon as the story is over or whenever the viewer turns away from the story. In contrast, harm to viewers refers to the range of harmful consequences to the viewers in their real lives as a result of the exposure to media violence. The harm usually occurs after viewing and increases with additional exposures over the course of a person's real life. This type of harm is the most dangerous, because it is largely unperceived by the viewers.

Recall from Myth 2 that there are several dozen potentially negative effects from exposure to media violence. These include immediate effects (such as learning behaviors, disinhibition, excitation transfer, etc.) and especially long-term effects (such as desensitization, false generalizations about violence, emotional habituation, increasing physiological tolerance for violence, changing social norms, and many other negative effects). The public is aware of few of these effects. Also, recall from Myth 3 that viewers are constantly altering their level of risk for each of these effects. Again, the public is largely unaware of the process of influence or any of the changes that take place within them. Media researchers are aware of these risks and of the factors in the context of the media portrayals that significantly alter those risks. Therefore, when researchers analyze media content for violence, they build their definition of violence and their analysis of context on this awareness.

Risk of harm to viewers is influenced in large part by the type of content. So for example, if you are exposed to many violent acts of nature (Question #2 in Table 5.3), even though there is no intention to harm, you are increasing your risk for a fear effect. In contrast, if you are exposed to many violent acts that are verbal rather than physical (#6), you are increasing your risk for an imitation effect, because it is easier to imitate a vicious insult than a physical assault. And if you are exposed to many violent acts that are in children's cartoons (#7 and #8), you are increasing your risk for a desensitization effect, because the violence is trivialized in such portrayals.

Risk of harm is also influenced by the context of the portrayal. Media researchers know that there are many factors that contribute to risk, and this is why their definitions of violence are much broader than the definition used by the public. Researchers are more concerned with how the context of violent portrayals affects viewers' interpretations about the meaning of that violence. After all, the primary reason why media researchers bother to count how much violence there is in the media is to assess potential harm to viewers and to identify the types of programs that present the greatest risk to the viewers in their real lives.

IMPLICATIONS OF THE DIFFERENCES

There are some important implications stemming from the differences between how social scientists conceptualize violence and how the public defines it.

The context of the violence is important to researchers, as it is to the public, but with scientists, context does not cancel out the existence of a violent act. For example, let's say in a *Bugs Bunny* cartoon one character intentionally shoots another character through the heart. The public would say that this is *not* an act of violence *because it takes place among cartoon characters*. Scientists would say that this *is* an act of violence *and that this act of violence takes place in the context of fantasy and humor*. Scientists decouple the judgment of whether an action is violent from the judgments about the context and record all the information. This results in a more complete database that can be used to account for all the violent acts as well as partitioning certain kinds of violence by content. The violence can be profiled in terms of how much of it takes place in a serious versus humorous context, how much takes place in a realistic versus fantasy context, how much is depicted with harm to the victim versus no harm, how much is justified versus nonjustified, and so forth. Thus scientists have many categories for violence, each of which has been shown to contain significant numbers of occurrences in media portrayals. By discounting violence through context, the public ignores many of these categories and therefore fails to notice many of the types of violence in the media.

From the public's point of view, sanitized violence is not a problem, because viewers do not feel offended by such depictions. If this mindless entertainment draws them into an as-if experience, they do not feel personally threatened. The public wants formulaic action, that is, safe, sanitized violence (no graphicness, low harm) that does not threaten them (not shocking, low reality), where the good guys are strong and prevail (high revenge, high justification), and with heavy doses of fantasy and humor. When the public sees this formula in action, they perceive no violence and there is no need to complain.

However, remember that the public misperceives violence in the media. The public's definition of violence is so narrow that people are not consciously seeing most of the violence to which they are being exposed continually in the media. Furthermore, their definition is so idiosyncratic that even if all the violence—as defined by the public—were removed from the media, the public would be at *more* risk of negative effects, not less risk. This observation is reflected in two ironies. If it were not for these ironies, belief in this myth would be less harmful. But as you will see, this misunderstanding of what media violence is creates a huge barrier between the public's apparent concern and a constructive solution.

Graphicness Trap

One irony is that people are complaining about the amount of violence in the media while at the same time missing more than 90% of it! Imagine the complaints if the public were not already so desensitized to the point that it takes a highly graphic act to offend them. People can watch one movie with a great deal of violence and see none of it. But if they watch a second movie with one graphic act of violence, they will believe that the second movie was far more violent than the first. Explicit blood and gore count as violence, while all other forms of violence—especially humorous and fantasy—do not count.

To further deepen this irony, the shows with the greatest saturation of graphic violence are children's cartoons—and this is a genre that few people think is violent at all. In cartoons there is a great deal of hitting, punching, shooting, dropping anvils onto heads, stuffing dynamite down rabbit holes, and hanging on to projectiles that rocket into the sides of cliffs or accelerate toward earth. But these are meant to be funny, and so—for many viewers— they do not count as violence.

Complaints Misplaced

The second irony is that the kind of violence that upsets people the most is precisely the type of violence that they need to be exposed to more. In contrast, it is the violence that most people do not complain about—or even perceive— that is doing them the most harm.

If a show presents a highly graphic act of violence, people will complain. *But this is a good thing.* It shows that people are sensitive and that these portrayals can outrage them. When these portrayals fail to outrage them, this is clear evidence that they have succumbed to the negative effect of desensitization. The fact that people do not complain about the moderately or low-level graphic acts is an indication that they have become desensitized to much of the violence.

Desensitization is only one of many possible negative effects. Let's examine another negative effect—disinhibition. We have natural inhibitions toward behaving physically aggressively to the point of harming others. When we are exposed to a portrayal of a relatively minor physical act of aggression where the characters are attractive, are justified in their actions, and get away with the action without punishment, our inhibitions erode a bit. When we are exposed to a half dozen of these portrayals every hour for years, our inhibitions substantially erode. And if we are totally unaware of this happening, we cannot stop or control its effect on us.

Another effect is imitation. People complain most about the highly graphic acts of physical violence, but these depictions are not likely to lead to much imitation. Much more easy to imitate are the relatively minor forms of physical violence and especially verbal violence. We are much more likely to imitate a character who delivers a wicked tongue lashing that humiliates another character than we are to imitate a character who stabs another character to death. The public does not regard verbal aggression as violence, yet insults and harsh criticism can cause more harm to a person than cuts and bruises. The emotional and psychological damage can last a lifetime. Yet verbal aggression comes to us "flying under our radar," that is, we do not notice it. The television networks, which are continually being criticized for the amount of physical violence, have not increased those rates over the past 30 years. However, the number of acts of verbal violence has increased dramatically since the 1970s. Seldom does the public complain about verbal violence, because it is not noticed.

CONCLUSIONS

Yes, there is too much violence in the media. The public holds this belief today as it has for the last several decades. Members of the public support this belief based on their bad experiences with the as-if type of violence. But there is very little unpleasant as-if type of violence compared with other types, so the public is greatly underperceiving the amount of violence in the media. The irony is that when the public is asking for a reduction in violence, they are really asking for a reduction in what is a very small base. Furthermore, a reduction in this type of violence would not solve the problem of reducing their risk of harm—only their risk of being offended.

Our beliefs can get us into trouble if they are not informed. When we are guided by misinformation and misperceptions, we often ask for the wrong things. Even when we are sincerely motivated to solve a problem, we need to build our strategies from a good understanding of the nature of the problem. If we do not make understanding a first step toward a solution, we are likely to set off on a path that will make things far worse. For example, in 1993, there were at least 10 bills pending in Congress proposing various legal attacks on televised violence, but not one of the measures tried to define "violence" or specify the kind of violence the legislators were targeting (Denniston, 1993). The lawmakers were acting out of a positive motivation to respond to a problem identified by the public. However, their efforts were so misinformed that they had no chance of moving toward a solution to the problem. Their proposals had only the negative effects of angering media producers and further frustrating the public.

Replacing this myth is one of the first things that must be done before we can start moving toward a solution to the problem of media violence. We need to share a definition of media violence that is both broad and based on potential harm to viewers. As long as the public is stuck in its present perspective, it will continue to ask for the wrong things. When we are navigating through the waters of entertainment, we should not complain about the tip of the iceberg and be offended that it is in our way. Instead, we should be thankful for the warning—a warning that alerts us to a much bigger mass lying below the surface. That which we cannot see presents a far greater risk to us.

SIX

MYTH 5

Violence in the media reflects violence in society.

———◦•◦———

In the film *Money Train,* a criminal attempts to rob a subway token seller. The criminal sprays lighter fluid into the token seller's glass-enclosed booth, then throws in a lit match. The makers of the film claimed they were depicting a real crime method. When someone copied the action depicted on film, the movie makers deflected criticism by arguing that the copying of the fictional crime validated their claim that the movie was only reflecting real life (Leland, 1995).

It is common for producers to argue that violence is a part of everyday life and that the media are only reflecting the violence. This has been an argument used by people in the industry for a long time. For example, three decades ago, Baldwin and Lewis (1972) interviewed the producers of the top 18 series on prime-time network television at the time and found producers who held the opinion that it would be fantasy to act as if violence did not exist.

There is a kernel of truth in the argument that violence in the media reflects society. Violence has existed for much longer than any of the media, so the media cannot be blamed for creating the concept of violence. However, the key word in the myth is *reflects.* Are the media merely holding a mirror up to something in the real world? Or are the media distorting and amplifying the violence from the real world? In this chapter, I will show that if the media are holding a mirror up to the real world, it is a fun-house mirror that reflects back a greatly distorted picture. For this reason, the claim that the media are merely reflecting violence in society is a myth. There are four arguments that show the faulty nature of this belief. These arguments concern distortions in frequency, type of violence, characters involved in violence, and context.

FREQUENCY IS AMPLIFIED

The key to understanding the frequency argument is to find out how much violence there is in the media and then compare that to some real-world figure. This is not as easy to do as it might seem. It is very difficult, if not impossible, to get a good frequency figure for either the media or the real world. However, let's use what we do know to construct some good estimates.

The best information we have for the frequency of violence in the media is limited to television programming, where many careful content analyses have been conducted. We don't have good frequency figures about violence in films, books, magazines, newspapers, video games, or the lyrics of popular music. So let's use only the figures from television, realizing that our numbers will be a severe underestimation of the total number of violent depictions in all media. The NTVS found about 18,000 acts of violence in each of its three composite weeks of programming. That is about 936,000 acts per year. The analyses conducted by NTVS were limited to only 23 channels and only 17 hours per day. If we extrapolated out to 24 hours per day and 50 channels (the number received by most television households), we arrive at about 2.6 million violent acts. Extrapolating beyond the limits of the NTVS sample (which excluded news, documentaries, and sports), it is reasonable to estimate that the average household has access to about 3 million acts of violence per year from the single medium of television.

How do we find the real-world figure for violence? There is no way to count all acts, but perhaps we can derive a good estimate from national crime figures. In 1999, there were about 11.6 million criminal offenses (Federal Bureau of Investigation [FBI], 2001b), but about 88% of these were property crimes where the victim was not present; only 12%, or about 1.4 million, were violent crimes, which include murders, forcible rape, robbery, and aggravated assault (U.S. Department of Justice, 1999).

Thus if people were able to watch all television programs provided by their cable TV company in a given year, they would view 3 million acts of violence. If at the same time, they were able to witness all violent crime during that year, they would see 1.4 million acts. Granted, this is not a perfect comparison, but the media number is so much greater than the real-world number that it is clear that the media present far more violence per year than occurs in real life. If the comparison is inaccurate, it is likely to err on the side of placing the numbers too close together. Recall that the NTVS used a fairly narrow definition of violence that focused on physical force intended to hurt other people. This definition did not include idle threats of violence, nor did it include verbal violence. So most of the acts recorded by NTVS are likely to be criminal. Also, if the violence in video games, films, books, magazines, and newspapers were included, the 3 million figure would be much larger.

Let's take our comparison one step further. To this point, the comparison has been between total occurrences of violence. No person could ever witness all the occurrences. With television, the average person views about 23 hours of television per week (Nielsen, 1998). That would mean that the typical viewer will see about 6,700 acts of violence on television per year. How likely is a person to witness an act of violence in real life? Again this is impossible to determine with accuracy, but it is safe to conclude that the number is much smaller than 6,700. There are about 1.4 million violent crimes each year. Let's assume that each violent crime has one perpetrator, one victim, and two bystanders. That would mean about 5.6 million people were involved in some way in a violent crime in their real lives last year—assuming no one witnessed more than one crime. That would put the probability of seeing a real-world crime at 1 chance in 49. Another way to say this is: On average, a person is likely to witness one violent crime in his or her real life every 49 years. During that same 49-year period, the average person is likely to witness about 328,000 acts of violence on television.

To make matters worse, these calculations are likely to be an *under*estimation of the degree of distortion for two reasons. First, the calculations are limited to exposure to violence in only one medium—television. Add to this all the violent messages a person is exposed to in films, newspapers, magazines, video games, radio, CDs, and the Internet. Second, the amount of violence in the media is growing, especially in nonentertainment programming such as news programs. A recent report released by the Maynard Institute for Journalism Education in Oakland, California, stated that while homicide rates dropped 33% in this country from 1990 to 1998, homicide news coverage on network television increased 473% (Texeira, 2001, p. B3). So news shows, which are purportedly reality programming, are not only portraying a very unrealistic pattern concerning crime, but they are moving more and more in the direction of distortion. Dori Maynard, author of the research report, said she does not believe the press sets out to distort reality, but they do so anyway. "I don't say they are ill meaning; they just don't see it" (Texeira, 2001, p. B3). Clearly the media are not simply reflecting the violence in the real world— they are *greatly* amplifying it.

PROFILE OF THE TYPE OF VIOLENCE IS UNREALISTIC

We can move beyond the comparison of frequencies and look at the type of violence. Again, the available figures on media violence are limited to television.

If the television world in its fictional narratives and news programs replicates the real world, then we should expect to find that most of the crime is not violent, but again this is not the case. The smallest percentage of aggression should be at the most serious end of the spectrum—that is, physical acts that result in great harm should account for a small percentage of all aggressive acts. For example, the FBI Uniform Crime Report statistics typically indicate that of all crimes, murder was 0.1%; rape, 0.8%; robbery, 3.5% (and only 1.1% were robberies with injuries); and aggravated assault, 7.9%. Most of the crime is property crime, which includes burglary (18.0%) and larceny-theft (59.8%) (FBI, 2001b).

Clearly, in the real world only a small percentage (about 12.3%, or about one act out of eight) of crime is violent. But this is not what the nonfiction shows on television tell us. A few years ago, I conducted an analysis of the content in a composite week of nonfiction (primarily newscasts) television along with some of my students at Indiana University (Potter et al., 1997). The findings of that study were startling. When we limited our focus to criminal aggression only, we found much higher rates of serious violence on news and "reality" programming than in the real world. In this study, we began with a base of 832 criminal acts (those in the assault, attack on property, and theft categories). Of these, 541 (65.0%) depicted serious violence (assaults resulting in death or great harm, bombings, and arson). In the real world, only 18.5% of all crimes were violent in 1995. Also, in the real world at that time, assaults accounted for only about 15% of all crimes, whereas thefts of all kinds accounted for about 77% of all criminal behaviors. However, in our analyses of television, we found that thefts accounted for only 3% of all criminal behavior. Similar findings also appear in the work of other analyses of television content. For example, Oliver (1994) examined the content of "reality programs" and found that 87% of criminal suspects on those television shows were associated with violent crimes.

Ironically, fictional programs on television treat violence more realistically than do so-called reality and news programs. When analyzing violence only in fictional programs, almost one third of all physical aggression is violent, whereas in television's "reality" programming almost two thirds of all crimes are presented as being violent. This is not to say that the fictional world on television treats violence in a realistic manner; it does not. Violence is over-represented in fictional programs compared with the real world, but the greatest distortion is in the genres of news and "reality" programming.

DISTORTION IN PORTRAYALS OF CHARACTERS

We can also examine how the people and characters who are involved in violence are portrayed. First, we will look at the gender patterns of the perpetrators and victims. Then we will look at the patterns of ethnicity. Third, we'll examine the portrayal of the relationship between the perpetrators and their victims.

Gender Profile

If the serious forms of aggression are realistic, the perpetrators and victims should be predominantly male. According to national crime statistics, among those arrested for violent crimes, 94% are male. This includes arrests for murder, where 89% are male; with rape, males account for 99%; robbery, 90%; aggravated assault, 80%; larceny and theft, 65% (FBI, 2001b). As for victims, typically 78% of murder victims are male (Maguire, Pastore, & Flanagan, 1993, pp. 390-391).

When we compare the real-world figures with the figures in the world of television, we can see some distortions (see Table 6.1). It is true that males are

Table 6.1   How the Violence Is Portrayed

		Television World	
Characteristic	*Real World*	*Fiction*	*Nonfiction*
Gender: female			
Perpetrator serious assaults	12	17	24
Perpetrator minor assaults	22	27	17
Perpetrator property crime	29	35	31
Victim serious assaults	22	27	51
Victim minor assaults	NA	33	26
Victim property crime	NA	41	53
Ethnicity: African American			
Perpetrator serious assaults	40	14	20
Perpetrator minor assaults	35	16	23
Perpetrator property crime	32	5	23
Victim serious assaults	50	11	24
Victim minor assaults	NA	13	23
Victim property crime	NA	8	6

more likely to be perpetrators and victims of violence compared with females in the television world, but there is still distortion. This distortion is most egregious in news programming, where females are greatly overrepresented as both perpetrators and victims of serious assaults. Again we see a pattern that the fictional portrayals in the television world are more in line with the real-world patterns than are the portrayals in the so-called nonfiction shows.

Ethnic Profile

If the serious forms of aggression are realistic, a high percentage of the perpetrators and victims should be African American. Almost half of those arrested for violent crimes are African American. This includes arrests for murder, where 52% are African American; rape, 37%; robbery, 54%; and aggravated assault, 35% (FBI, 2001b). As for victims, typically 50% of all murder victims are African American (Maguire et al., 1993, pp. 390-391). Only about 11% of the U.S. population is African American, so the real-world figures indicate that the rates of serious assaults are much higher among African Americans than among people of other ethnic backgrounds, but this is not reflected accurately in the television world.

In television entertainment programming, there is a very unrealistic picture of African Americans. For example, in the real world, 49% of those arrested for serious crimes are African American, but in the television world only 14% of all perpetrators of serious assaults are African American. This pattern of underrepresentation of African Americans holds across all categories of perpetrators and victims. This pattern of underrepresentation of African Americans also holds in nonfiction programming. In an interesting related study, Oliver (1994) found that among television police officers, African Americans were underrepresented in the TV world (9%) compared with the real world (17%).

Relationship of Perpetrator to Victim

In the real world, most victims of aggression know the perpetrators. With murder cases, among those in which police knew of the relationship between the perpetrator and the victim, one third were family members, about 40% were acquaintances, and only one quarter were strangers (Maguire et al., 1993, pp. 386-387).

Again, the television world provides a distortion. In our analysis of nonfictional television violence, we found that in the television world, the victim knew the perpetrator (close friend or family, self, or acquaintance) in fewer than 16% of serious assaults. With minor assaults, the figure is higher, at 30% (Potter & Vaughan, 1997). These figures are still far from the real-world figure of 75%.

DISTORTION OF CONTEXT AND MEANING

A fourth way to compare the accuracy of the television portrayals of violence with the real world is to look at contextual characteristics. The analysis of realism in this section focuses on two contextual characteristics: harm to victim and consequences to the perpetrators. Let's examine the patterns of these context factors, first in nonfictional programming, then in fictional programming.

Nonfictional Programming

On the issue of portrayal of harm, again the media present a very unrealistic picture. The NTVS (1998) reports that with nonfictional programming, about 30% of all violent instances are depicted with no harm. Interesting, the authors report that when harm is shown it is usually death. Thus the depiction of harm is either death or no harm at all.

The picture of harm came up as unrealistic in my analyses also. Over half (53%) of antisocial acts are portrayed with no harmful consequences to the victims (Potter et al., 1997). The highest rates of major consequences are with accidents and serious assaults, which is a positive indication that viewers are getting cues that antisocial activity results in harmful consequences. However, the number of antisocial acts shown without any consequences is also very high. So viewers are presented with a mixed message on this point.

There is a very intriguing, albeit complicated, pattern worth exploring in this area. On the surface, it appears that the television world is realistic in its portrayal of punishment. For example, only 23% of aggressive acts are depicted as being punished in news and "reality" programming (Potter et al., 1997). This seems like a very low number until we compare it to some real-world figures and find out that in real life, most serious acts of aggression also go unpunished. For example, in 1991 only 21% of all reported crimes were cleared by an arrest. Arrest rates are higher with violent crimes (44%) than with property crimes (18%), but still, most crimes remain unsolved, much less punished (Maguire et al., 1993, p. 452). So the low rates of punishment displayed in nonfictional programming correspond to real-world lack of punishment.

What makes this finding especially interesting is that the public thinks that the police are doing a good job of solving crimes. For example, 59% of Americans rate the police's record of solving crimes as excellent or very good (Maguire et al., 1993, p. 169). Where does the public get this misperception? In nonfiction television programming, less than one quarter of all antisocial acts are shown with any punishment. This figure climbs to about one third with serious assaults, but still this figure is far below what it should be to explain the public's trust in the efficacy of law enforcement. Again, where is the public getting this misperception? The answer might be from fictional programming.

Another example of a distorted picture of violence is in the way the media cover suicides. A recent report conducted by the Annenberg Public Policy Center at the University of Pennsylvania says that the press frequently sensationalizes a suicide, "describing the suicide method in detail, playing up the romantic or heroic elements of a suicide and misrepresenting troubled victims as healthy high-achieving people" (Gupta, 2001, p. A26). The report, which was endorsed by U.S. Surgeon General David Satcher as well as the National Institute of Mental Health, takes the position that the press does a poor job of informing people that mental illness is implicated in 90% of America's suicides and that a suicide should be treated as a failure in health, not as a dramatic story. Furthermore, the report says that the press also sends the wrong message with the use of terms such as *successful* and *failed* suicides.

Fictional Programming

One of the most distorted aspects of violence in fictional programming is the paucity of depictions of harm—even when the violent acts would be serious or even life threatening in real life. The unrealistic pattern of harm that we saw on nonfictional programming is even more unrealistic in fictional programming. The NTVS (1998) reports that in 43% of all violent acts, there were no depictions of any harm to the victim. The authors of the study report that in 54% of all violent acts, the likely harm to victims would be very serious, such as incapacitating or lethal. When they conducted their analysis of only those acts of violence that should be portrayed with serious harm, still about one third were depicted with no harm whatsoever to the victim.

In my analyses, fewer than one in six acts were shown with major consequences in the fictional world of television (Potter et al., 1995). This is due in large part to the fact that a relatively small percentage of the acts are serious enough to warrant such a portrayal. With most acts falling into the categories of verbal remarks, we should not expect a high percentage of major consequences. So the deviation of the contextual element of consequences from the morality play template does not provide a serious problem. However, the case with the reward contextual variable is quite different.

This pattern of unrealistic harm seems to hold for film also. For example, McArthur et al. (2000) analyzed the top 100 grossing American films of 1994 and found an average of 16 acts of violence per film. Although 80% of the violent actions were executed with a strong enough force to cause harm if done in real life, only 10% of all acts were depicted as showing any consequences to the recipient's body, and fewer than 1% of all acts showed the victim getting medical attention.

Another characteristic of unrealism is the lack of punishment for acts of violence. Based on my analysis of fictional television programming, only about one act in six is portrayed as being punished, and two out of six are actually portrayed as being rewarded. The NTVS (1999) study reports a similar pattern of low reward, with only about 20% of violent acts being punished. When we look at who gets rewarded and who gets punished, we see that the villains are more likely to be punished, whereas the heroes, who usually commit as much if not more violence than the villains, are almost never punished. Also, the punishment of villains comes at the end of the program, so although villains get away with dozens of acts of violence that go unpunished at the time, they eventually get punished at the end. Thus the counts of unpunished violent acts underrepresent the meaning of the overall message that villains do eventually get punished. This then explains why the public might think the police are doing a good job. But this pattern is unrealistic.

OTHER MEDIA

There is good reason to believe that the media-generated distortions of reality are even more serious than what has been presented thus far in this chapter. The analyses in this chapter are limited to television content. Although there are no systematic analyses of violent content in other media, there is reason to believe that violence pervades the other media. For example, recent popular novels by John Grisham, Michael Crichton, and Robin Cook—to name only a few respectable thriller authors—have in recent years depicted multiple grue-some murders in the U.S. Supreme Court, in corporate boardrooms, and at top teaching hospitals, but in the real world, murders happen in alleyways, tenements, and homes (Easterbrook, 1996). Thriller authors move murders to glamorous venues for obvious reasons, but then they add lots of realistic detail to make their stories plausible and to get readers to willingly suspend their disbelief. When we do so and let our filters down, we enjoy the entertaining nature of these books—but we also learn that the world is a violent place and there are no places free of violence.

Perhaps the worst synthesized realism is the obsession with serial murders and thrill killing. Dozens of contemporary movies and pop novels—Thomas Harris's Hannibal Lecter books, *Seven, Natural Born Killers, Copycat,* and many similar works present the perspective that everywhere you look, depraved psychopaths are torturing people to death for kicks. This sort of bru-tality occurs far more often in books and movies than in real life. According to Peter Smerick, a crime consultant who is a retired agent for the FBI's behavioral sciences division, there have been an estimated two "spree" or thrill killings per month nationwide in the United States over the last 15 years. Although this figure is far too high for a civilized society, it represents only one seventh of 1% of American murders. Serial killings are exceptionally rare. Almost all murders occur in the context of robbery or between acquaintances or family members. Today, on an annual basis, probably a greater number of serial killings are depicted on screen and on television than occur in real life.

Depictions of Hollywood-style "splatter-death" have even begun to infect literature, under the guise of "realism." For instance, the novel *Accordion Crimes,* by the serious writer E. Annie Proulx, offers a gory death on about every third page. The killings embody what Hollywood scriptwriters call "creative death"—something weird or graphic happens that helps make the crime spree even more horrible and hypnotic to readers.

IMPLICATIONS

If television producers set out to create fantasy, then of course they should be under no obligation to present characters, action, dialogue, or plots like those in the real world. Such is the nature of fantasy. But then media producers should not be allowed to claim that the violence they use to create that fantasy is simply a reflection of the real world. As the arguments in this chapter clearly demonstrate, fictional programming does not reflect the reality of violence in society either in frequency, type, character portrayals, or context.

Even more disturbing than the fantasy patterns in fictional programming is the distortion of violence in nonfictional programming. The world of television news presents the real world as having much more violence than it really does—violence that is much more violent in the media than it is in real life, violence involving women much more than it does in real life, violence perpetrated much less by African Americans than is the case in reality, and violence with consequences of harm to the victims much more sanitized than is the case in the real world.

Are these distortions important? If we view "importance" in terms of consequences to viewers, these distortions appear to be very important. The distortions have the effect of leading viewers to believe that there is much more violence than there is in reality. Furthermore, the distortions make viewers believe that the violence is much more serious (murders and rapes compared with minor assaults) than it really is, while at the same time presenting very little of that violence with harmful consequences to the victims or perpetrators.

Finally, the findings of this analysis raise a serious question about the value of nonfictional programming. If we rely on nonfiction programming to tell us about the parameters and nature of our society, then we are being seriously misled. Nonfictional programming is constructing narratives that are not particularly useful for the purpose of informing us about the nature of our world. Nonfictional television presents a very high rate of aggression, and the most serious forms of that activity (physical violence and crime) are presented at rates far above the rates in the real world. If we use the patterns in the news stories to tell us about the real world, then we become less informed the more we watch. Our continued exposure only reinforces false beliefs about how much violent crime there is and who is committing the violent crime.

Furthermore, the contextual cues in the portrayals are such that they serve to encourage the learning of aggression. That is, there is a low rate of punishment (less than one quarter of all violent acts) and a fairly high rate of lack of consequences (more than half). This pattern of context is fairly similar to the general context in which aggression is portrayed in entertainment programming (e.g., see Potter et al., 1995).

It appears that producers of nonfictional programming, even breaking news shows, are adopting many of the conventions of entertainment programs. As Bennett (1988) argues, news is a consumer good that is manufactured to be interesting to audiences. One of the elements in this manufacturing process is the use of drama: "Reporters and editors search for events with dramatic properties and then emphasize those properties in their reporting" (Bennett, 1988, p. 35). Drama requires conflict, and conflict is often triggered by violence.

Of course, it is understandable that producers of nonfiction programming would feel the same pressures to generate large, loyal audiences that producers of fiction feel. By itself, the desire to attract large audiences is not a problem, but it is a problem when informational programmers spend down their capital of accuracy and then credibility in order to buy those large audiences. Producers of nonfiction content have shifted their focus from the facts (the goal of getting the facts right so as to inform viewers about what they should know) to the market (identifying what viewers want to watch, then constructing those experiences for them in the most entertaining manner possible). From a financial point of view, producers have been successful with this shift. However, the public is not being enriched by this; instead, nonfictional programming is moving the public into a ghetto of misinformation.

SEVEN

MYTH 6

The media are only responding to market desires.

————◦•◦————

This is a myth promulgated by producers and programmers as a justification for their practice of providing so many violent messages to viewers. Their argument is based on the most simple of economic principles—that is, supply follows the demand. If only a few people liked violent programs, the market would not support this type of content. Because media markets continually support shows with violence, there must be a very large number of people who want to see violence.

This argument is valid—up to a point. It is of course true that businesses must supply what is demanded by consumers. But the myth blinds us to another, equally important, function of businesses, that is, media also shape demand. Businesses are not simply passive reactors to demand; they are also actively creating and reinforcing that demand.

This myth is misleading because it limits our thinking to only one function—satisfying existing demand. It tries to hide the other function—creating and reinforcing that demand. Let's examine both functions of the media businesses. First, we'll analyze the industry's belief that there is a demand for violent messages. Then second, we'll examine the conditioning function of media businesses.

THE DEMAND FOR VIOLENT CONTENT

People in the film and television production industries firmly believe that the public wants violence. For example, the president of the MPAA, Jack Valenti, said that if someone put Charles Manson on television, "everyone would tune in to [find out] how he felt when he stuck that knife into Sharon Tate's belly" (Lutterbeck, 1995). There is a belief that viewing violence is irresistible to humans. Peggy Charren, the founder of Action for Children's Television, observes, "If you're at a dinner party and there's fascinating conversation on both sides and somebody starts a fight, everybody will watch the fight" (Robb, 1991, p. 27).

Innate Attraction to Violence

Are human beings fundamentally attracted to violence? The prevailing thinking among scientists is that the human mind is hard wired to pay attention to violence. When something violent happens in a person's environment, he or she is programmed to notice it, and his or her body immediately reacts with physiological preparation to either stay and fight or flee the threat. Violence poses a threat to humans, and if we were not provided with a primal instinct to notice and react to it, we would long ago have been killed off by predators.

This survival explanation helps us understand why we would pay attention to violence once it occurs in our real-life environment. But why would we seek out violence when it does not occur? Some researchers answer that we find exposure to violence pleasurable. For example, Lorenz (1963) argues that the instinct of aggression in animals generates energy. This energy makes us feel active and alive. When we have this energy, our concentration level is very high, and we feel powerful. Thus the release of hormones in our bodies in this fight-flight reaction results in a pleasurable experience. Agreeing with this explanation are other scientists, such as Lenore Terr, a psychiatrist at the University of California at San Francisco who has studied the effects of violence on children for years; she described her research in the book *Too Scared to Cry*. Dr. Terr says, "There's probably some brain release of potent neurotransmitters" that causes the feeling of slowing time and the vivid remembering of detail during traumatic events (Robb, 1991, p. 27).

Attraction to Violence in the Media

If the scientific explanations are valid, then people should be continually seeking out violence in the media. If exposure to violence is indeed pleasurable, violent shows should have high ratings, but this is not always the case. Scientific analyses of television programming are equivocal. Although some of these studies do indicate that higher ratings are associated with the more violent programs, others do not. For example, the average rating for shows on the Parents' Television Council's 10 Best Family-Friendly Shows is 6.9%, compared with a 7.6% rating for shows on its Top 10 Most Offensive Shows. Violent movies are popular, especially among young children. Thomas Radecki, an Illinois psychiatrist who heads the National Coalition on Television Violence, says that in a recent survey of randomly selected children aged 5 to 7 years of age, 20% were found to have seen *Nightmare on Elm Street,* and 89% of 11-year-olds had seen it.

There are also many indications that violence in programs does *not* attract the largest audiences. For example, Diener and De Four (1978) examined 71 prime-time episodes for elements such as suspense, emotion, sex, humor, action, and violence over more than a three-month period. The occurrence of none of these elements was related to program popularity as determined by the ratings of the shows. Similar findings are also reported by Himmelweit, Swift, and Biberian (1980), who conducted a study in which they found that ratings of violence were not related to ratings of enjoyment. Gerbner (1994) compared average Nielsen ratings for violent and nonviolent shows from 1988 to 1993 and found that nonviolent shows in general had a higher mean rating (13.8 vs. 11.1). Among Finnish television viewers, Mustonen and Pulkkinen (1993) found no correlation between the audience size for a program and the rate of brutality of aggression. They said the "most popular programs such as quiz shows, news, and family serials did not contain aggression at all or were only mildly aggressive" (p. 181).

There are even studies that conclude that violence in movies is associated with *lower* ratings and box office volume. A recent study of 2,380 major movie releases from 1988 to 1997 reports that there were 17.4 R-rated movies for each G-rated movie. Yet a G-rated film on average was more than eight times as profitable as an R-rated film. The profitability of films was found to be inversely related to the rating, with G films having the highest profitability per film, followed by PG, then R, and finally NC-17 (Williams, 1999).

Another study analyzed Hollywood movies from 1984 to 1993 and reported that R-rated movies grossed an average of $10 million less than PG-rated films (Paul Kagan and Associates, 1994). Also, Levine (1998) points out that the film *Forrest Gump* grossed $300 million, whereas the latest *Nightmare on Elm Street* brought in only $18 million. Most recently, a survey research company called MarketCast conducted a telephone survey in the country's top 200 markets and asked people which movies they planned to see. MarketCast reports that out of 37 R-rated movies that earned more than $5 million during their opening weekends, at least 15 of these movies would have attracted one third more viewers if they had had a PG-13 rating (James, 2001).

The results of carefully conducted scientific analyses are equivocal on the issue of whether the most violent programming attracts the largest audiences. Sometimes a high degree of violence attracts a very large audience, and other times it fails to attract many people. There is not a simple and consistent relationship between amount of violence in a media story and the size of its audience. If there is a relationship between violence and popularity, it is a complex one.

There are several reasons why this relationship is complex. One is that the public's taste for violence may be cyclical. For example, Clark and Blankenburg (1972) analyzed prime-time programs on three commercial networks from 1956 to 1969 and found a strong correlation (r:0.49) between the ratings for violent programs in one year and the number of high-violence programs in the following year. Thus the industry appears to respond to the public's taste by increasing the number of high-violence programs for next year when the high-violence programs get high ratings the current year. In some years, the public's attraction to violent programs drops, and programmers respond with fewer violent programs the next year. This explains the cyclical nature of rates of violence on television. In Gerbner's annual counts of violence over 22 years, regular cycles of about 6 to 10 acts of violence per hour were found (Gerbner & Signorielli, 1990).

Another reason for the complexity is that attraction is not determined by violence alone. Factors such as interesting plots, popular actors, exotic locations, fancy clothes and costumes, intriguing sound tracks, and so forth all contribute to attractiveness. When all of these elements work together along with violence, audience members feel pleasure, and the size of the audience is likely to be large. But when violence appears in an unattractive context, it does not foster pleasure, and the audience is likely to be small. So the key to understanding audience size is the content's ability to evoke pleasure—not how much violence appears in the content.

What is very disturbing is that most people in the media industries are convinced of the value of violence as an audience attractor. There are examples of research that they can cite in support of their belief, but because they are unwilling to look at a broader spectrum of that research, their belief is faulty. Even so, many producers and programmers make decisions on the basis of this faulty belief and continue to present a high amount of violence year after year. This serves to narrow our viewing choices and channel us into a situation where we are conditioned to expect violence—then to demand it—in our media messages.

THE CONDITIONING FUNCTION

Not only do the media supply programming to respond to demand, they also shape that demand over time by conditioning us with the messages they supply—and with those they fail to provide. Conditioning is a process that links violence to feelings of pleasure.

Some scholars believe that the public's taste for violence is traceable almost entirely to conditioning. For example, George Gerbner (1994) uses an analogy of cigarette smoking. He says that TV and movie violence literally may cause nausea in many people when they first see it, but they come back for more, and the more they see the less they are affected. In his experiments conducted at the University of Pennsylvania, Gerbner finds that adults who view violent horror or slasher movies daily quickly become accustomed to the violence, and it no longer upsets them (Robb, 1991).

In their book *Stop Teaching Our Kids to Kill,* David Grossman and Gloria DeGaetano (1999) argue that in nature, intraspecies killings are rare; instead, species kill outside of their species. Humans also have an aversion to killing other humans. That is why the military must train soldiers to kill in war, and even with this training only a small percentage of soldiers ever kills anyone. Police officers rarely draw their guns. And yet the general population is becoming more violent. This is due to the "training" they are getting from violent television, movies, and video games. The heroes used to be Mickey Mouse and Davy Crockett. Today the heroes are Mighty Morphin Power Rangers, X-Men, and Spider Man.

Research has shown that conditioning is a useful explanation for preferences of violence in the media. For example, in one study, Diener and Woody (1981) found that people who watched a lot of television liked all kinds of shows, especially violent ones. However, among people who seldom watched television, the violent shows were rated as significantly less pleasurable than nonviolent shows were. Of course, it could be argued that the interpretation of the authors of this study, which measured people at only one point in time, is wrong—that is, viewing preferences determine amount of viewing, rather than amount of viewing influencing preferences. But remember, what I am arguing in this chapter is that we need to look at the bigger picture of cycles and not fixate on only one part of a cycle. Over years of television viewing there are likely many instances in which preferences will increase or decrease the amount of viewing and where the amount of viewing will shape content preferences. This is the process of conditioning.

Amount of television viewing has been found to be related to attraction to violence. Heavier viewers "watch violent television programs with more absorption but—ironically enough—with more detachment as well" (Van der Voort, 1986, p. 336). He explains that although viewers' enjoyment of violence keeps them absorbed in the program, so that they continue to watch without interruption, these same viewers can also be detached—that is, they don't get drawn into strong identifications with particular characters or feel strong emotional reactions—because they have become jaded by so much exposure to media violence. These heavier television viewers also enjoy violence more, have a clear preference for it, and are more likely to regard violence as justified.

In the extreme case of conditioning, people can become addicted to violence. Several people have been complaining that the public has become dependent on the media to provide them with violence. For example, *New York Times* columnist Frank Rich says people like watching the mayhem on the *Jerry Springer Show* and the mindless violence covered by local news organizations. According to Rich, the public has become addicted to it, and the media are just giving the public what it wants (Rich, 1998). He complains that the public is too addicted to back up their criticisms of the media with even the mildest acts of protest, such as boycotting the programs that they feel are the most offensive. He says that people complain about sex and violence on television but refuse to monitor their children, cancel pay-cable channels, or even turn off their sets. That sounds like addiction and denial.

How do the media condition us to tolerate and then search out violence in the media? They condition us both physiologically and cognitively.

Physiological Conditioning

Psychologists have known for a long time that certain behaviors can be linked with particular changes in brain chemistry. When those changes in brain chemistry evoke a pleasant feeling in an animal, the animal will become conditioned to manifest those behaviors that are associated with the changes in brain chemistry and hence feelings of pleasure. In animal studies, researchers implanted electrodes in the brains of cats and monkeys and taught the animals that by pushing a button they would stimulate their limbic system—the brain's control center for emotion, aggression, and memory. Once the animals learned the connection between the button and a feeling of pleasure, they repeatedly pushed the button, leading scientists to conclude "there are neurochemicals in the brain which actually are associated with reward," says Bruce S. McEwen, a neuroendocrinologist who heads the Laboratory of Neuroendocrinology at Rockefeller University in New York (Robb, 1991, p. 27).

Dr. Lenore Terr explains that people have been conditioned to experience the thrill of arousal when they see violence presented in a vicarious manner. She says that bloody horror films are big at the box office because "there's a thrill connected with terror in the same way there's a thrill connected with sex," says Terr. "I think audiences get titillated about the aggressive drive, not just their sexual drive" (Robb, 1991, p. 27).

The media present violence in a vicarious manner and make it pleasurable to viewers. When people watch a serial killer stalk a victim with whom they identify, they feel the thrill of strong emotions without actually being in danger themselves from the killer. They get a physiological arousal, and this is pleasant. Himmelweit, Swift, and Jaeger (1980) explain that "the enjoyment of a program depends on the kind of arousal it evokes" and that "the arousal is associated with enjoyment when it is moving, absorbing, and exciting, but unpleasant when it is disturbing, brutal, and unpredictable" (p. 94).

Over time, viewers come to associate the pleasant feeling of arousal with exposure to media violence. Thus they become conditioned to seek out violent episodes in the media in order to evoke those pleasant feelings.

Cognitive Conditioning

In addition to the physiological explanation of conditioning, there is also a cognitive process of conditioning. With the cognitive process of conditioning, we make mental associations and do not rely on brain chemistry. One of the associations we learn to make when viewing violence is to feel a sense of power and control. When we get to determine when and where we will experience the thrill of violence rather than having it happen randomly to us, we feel in control. Also, by playing violent video games, we feel a sense of ultimate power. Joseph Gold, a child psychiatrist who practices at Westwood Lodge, a private psychiatric hospital, says, "One of the traditional ways of handling our fear has been to try to chew off a bite-sized piece," he says. "A violent movie can give us a satisfying sense of having faced the dragon and survived" (Robb, 1991, p. 27).

Power also comes from witnessing other people in danger while we are safe. "There's a certain satisfaction and pleasure that people get in seeing the misfortunes of others," says psychiatrist Judith L. Herman, director of training at the Victims of Violence Program of Cambridge Hospital and an associate clinical professor of psychiatry at Harvard Medical School. It is, she says, a form of sadism. For children, the pleasure of violent movies, TV, and stories may come partly in hearing the truth of their environment acknowledged. "I think kids, who are powerless, are very aware of the malevolence of the world around them and like stories that talk about that," says Herman (Robb, 1991, p. 27).

Although the process of conditioning affects us all, some of us are conditioned more than others. These differences in conditioning can be explained in terms of certain factors that vary across people. These factors include mood, self-concept, motivation, long-term exposure to violence, and political attitudes. As for mood, anger (Freedman & Newtson, 1975) and stress from unhappy or irritating experiences (Munakata & Kashiwagi, 1991) have been found to be related to attraction to violence. Also, a poor self-concept was found to be related to attraction to violent video games (Dominick, 1984; Donnerstein et al., 1994). People who are depressed seek the boost that arousal can give them. People who are powerless or angry seek an outlet to express their negative emotions and to experience power. Therefore, violence in the media can be a tool to deliver pleasure to viewers.

Enjoyment varies across people—that is, not all types of people would find a particular portrayal of violence equally enjoyable. For example, Oliver and Armstrong (1995) conducted a random telephone survey of adults to determine why people like to watch crime shows. They found higher enjoyment of reality-based crime programs with viewers who watched more television in general and those with lower levels of education. Also, enjoyment was related to punitive attitudes about crime, higher levels of racial prejudice, and higher levels of authoritarianism.

The physiological and cognitive conditioning processes work together. The physiological component provides the arousal, and the cognitive component provides the awareness of pleasure (Zillmann, 1978, 1982). Himmelweit and her colleagues (1958) say that children like being frightened, but only up to a point. When their fear is increased up to a moderate level through suspense and then relieved, children find this very pleasurable. In repeated surveys, children have consistently said they like to be frightened by media programs. Early research found that among third graders, 86% recalled instances when they were very frightened by media presentations, but 82% of these children also said that they liked being frightened by movies (Blumer, 1933). In a later study, 80% of adolescents and over 50% of elementary school-aged children said they liked scary movies and television shows, and the same results were found in several samples by Wilson et al. (1987). Adults also exhibit an attraction for horror (Zillmann, Weaver, Mundorf, & Aust, 1986) and crime (Oliver & Armstrong, 1995).

There is evidence that the media industries begin this conditioning at an early age by creating advertising campaigns aimed at children. In the summer of 2000 the Federal Trade Commission (FTC) had suspicions that some of the media industries with self-regulatory codes against marketing violent products to children were not following their own guidelines. The FTC commissioned a study to examine the marketing practices of the motion picture, recorded music, and electronic game industries. The FTC report, which was released in September 2000, concluded that

> while the entertainment industry has taken steps to identify content that may not be appropriate for children, the companies in those industries still routinely target children under the age of 17 in their marketing of products that their own ratings systems deem inappropriate or [to] warrant parent caution due to violent content. (FTC, 2000, p. 1)

The report commended these three industries for labeling their products so that parents could know which were not appropriate for children under the age of 17, but the report was critical of the industries for not following through and preventing children's access to the violent messages in products that those very industries had labeled as being unsuited for them. Specifically, the report found that children are frequently able to buy tickets to R-rated movies without parental accompaniment. Their survey found that half the movie theaters admitted children ages 13 to 16 to R-rated films, even when they were not accompanied by an adult. Also, 85% of the time, children ages 13 to 16 who were unaccompanied by an adult were able to buy both explicit recordings and electronic games that were rated M ("Mature").

Furthermore, the FTC study found evidence that not only were the companies in these three industries lax in preventing children from buying products unsuitable for them, but also many companies were actively marketing these unsuitable products specifically to children. They found many instances of marketing and media plans that expressly targeted children under 17. For example, 70% of electronic games with a Mature rating for violence were being targeted to children under 17, and 80% of R-rated movies were targeted to children under 17. Many of these companies conducted promotional and advertising campaigns for their violent products in media outlets most likely to reach children under 17; marketing plans for 64% of these movies contained express statements that the films' target audience included children under 17.

The music industry responded to the FTC report and its threatened legislation to fine media outlets that sell adult-rated material to children by saying that it might have to terminate its rating system (Garvey & Leeds, 2001). Jack Valenti, president of the MPAA, said that if the proposed legislation became law, he would recommend that studios abandon the film ratings system that he helped create 30 years ago to inform parents about which movies may present content unsuitable for children (Garvey, 2001b). Of course, doing away with the ratings would be one way of avoiding the situation in which they could be found to be marketing violent material to children and allowing those children to gain admittance to violent films and buy CDs with violent lyrics. Without the ratings, the industries would not be admitting that they sell products that are not for children, so they could then sell to children with impunity. But one has to ask: How responsible are industries that suggest such a change in practices in order to avoid possible fines? Furthermore, how sensitive are such industries to the public's well-being when they announce this pettiness so publicly?

Media companies that sell violent products have maintained that when they put their products out into the marketplace they cannot control who buys those products. According to media providers, it is up to parents to read the warning labels and decide for their children what products they should have. But the FTC report shows that this is a smokescreen. These companies carefully craft marketing plans to get their advertising appeals before children. Also, advertising campaigns for many of these highly violent products have the goal of using children as their target audience.

The FTC commissioned a follow-up report in early 2001 to examine whether the three industries (film, recordings, and electronic games) had made progress in not marketing their violent products to children (FTC, 2001). The report found that the motion picture and electronic game industries had made some progress both in limiting advertising in popular teen media and in providing rating information in advertising. However, with the music recording industry, it was found that advertising for music recordings labeled for explicit content typically appeared on popular teen programming. This was the case with all five major recording companies.

The media industries are very sophisticated and enormously profitable. The most profitable of them acquire so much revenue that they have the means to acquire more media assets, which in turn brings them more revenue and the need to acquire still more assets. Since 1983, Benjamin Bagdikian has been monitoring ownership and control patterns among media businesses. In the sixth edition of his book *The Media Monopoly,* he says that "six firms dominate all American mass media. Each is a subsidiary of a larger parent firm" (Bagdikian, 2000). These parent firms are General Electric, Viacom, Disney, Bertelsmann, Time Warner, and Murdoch's News Corp. These six have more in annual revenues than the next 20 firms combined. The interests of these six companies are interrelated: They own stock in each other, they cooperate in joint media ventures, and they sell products to one another. In 1983, when Bagdikian first conducted his analysis, he concluded that 50 corporations dominated most of every mass medium. Also, at that time, the largest media merger in history was for $340 million. The strategy of those 50 firms was to dominate in one medium, such as newspapers, books, or movies. Seventeen years later, his analysis concluded that the figure had been reduced over 80% to just six firms, each with a strategy to dominate all media. Now the largest media merger is the AOL Time Warner $350 billion merger.

IMPORTANCE OF STORY FORMULA

The media companies know how best to attract and hold our attention with violence. They do this repeatedly and thus condition us to seek out violence. What has helped them be so successful at this is that they have developed a storytelling formula. This formula is simple, so it is easy for writers and audiences to follow. The formula is continually repeated, so it is familiar and thus requires little mental energy to tune in and out of the story at any point without becoming confused. Finally, the formula delivers a satisfying thrill to viewers, so it keeps viewers coming back for more.

Stories that use this formula begin with some easy-to-recognize bad guys stirring up conflict. Their actions are selfish, brutal, and unjustified, so we, the audience members, quickly start to hate them. The good guys are drawn into the action either as victims or as the protectors of the victims. These heroic characters usually have one or two highly attractive traits, such as being very strong, smart, sexy, or witty. The audience is led to identify with the heroes and the victims so that the audience can feel the thrill of danger. Of course, the audience knows from the formula that the heroes will eventually prevail—there is no suspense about that. The suspense is sustained in the audiences' minds as they wonder how bad the villains are going to be and how the heroes will ever be able to subdue them. As the plot progresses, we crave that the good guys will render their justified revenge to teach the bad guys a well-deserved lesson. Finally, in the climactic scene, the heroes fight fire with fire and get the better of the villains.

Media theoretician Dolf Zillmann (1998) explains that the media story-tellers know how to make the presentation of violence highly pleasurable. "There can be little doubt, then, that righteous violence, however brutal but justified by the ends, will prompt gloriously intense euphoric reactions the more it is preceded by patently unjust and similarly brutal violence" says Zillmann. He continues,

> In other words, *displays of monstrous gratuitous slaughter and the distress they evoke are a necessary prelude to the portrayal of righteous maiming and killing that is to spark euphoric reactions.* Without such prelude, violence cannot be righteous and, hence, is rendered unenjoyable—at least for non-sadists, who should constitute the vast majority of the drama-consuming public. (Zillmann, 1998, p. 208, italics in original)

This formula evokes a pleasurable experience in viewers while skirting around images that might evoke a negative feeling. The presentation of violence elicits few feelings of empathy, sadness, or guilt, says Ervin Staub, a professor of psychology at the University of Massachusetts at Amherst who has studied the roots of aggressive behavior. By ignoring these consequences, he says, TV links violence with "a sense of power, identification with the right cause, serving justice," feelings that enhance self-esteem. Unfortunately, it also teaches that the world is full of enemies and that "the normal way to deal with conflict is aggression" (Robb, 1991, p. 27).

Over time the industry has employed the violent formula so much that it is the easy and safe thing to use. According to Simon, violent programming flourishes because it "is an easy, simple, uncreative way for people to make money" (quoted in Lutterbeck, 1995).

When a formula works, everyone wants to copy it. This is seen most recently in the computer game market, where of the top 20 best-selling games (as measured by PC Data, a market research company in Reston, Virginia) more than half have violence, combat, or warfare at their core. The main reason for this saturation of violence in the video game market is the phenomenal success in 1993 of Doom, a very violent game "filled with satanic imagery that just happened to become one of the most successful in computer history," noted Chris Charla, editor in chief of *Next Generation,* a respected computer and video-gaming magazine. Charla explains,

> As soon as 'Doom' came out, everyone decided that the way to be successful was to make their games satanic and violent, too. What you have in the computer industry is that every innovation is followed by years and years of slavish copying. (quoted in Kent, 1997)

The same can be said for all media.

CONCLUSIONS

People in the media industries get frustrated by criticism from those who do not recognize that the media companies are businesses and that the purpose of those businesses is to construct audiences that can be rented to advertisers. Therefore, programmers are under pressure to select material that will meet the greatest demand. Programmers believe there is a great demand for violence.

The media also create and shape the demand for violence. They do this by using a storytelling formula that is simple to follow and that provides pleasure to the audience members. Over time, the use of this formula conditions viewers to become attracted to violence. Violent stories excite viewers and thus provide them with a pleasurable set of physiological responses and cognitions.

Once we understand that the storytelling formula conditions viewers, the focus of attention can shift to a debate about what should go into the formula.

People in the industry feel that violence is an essential element in that formula, but that is faulty thinking. The key ingredient is arousal. Without arousal, viewers cannot become engaged in the action and cannot feel the pleasure of strong emotions.

Arousal is essential, but violence is not the only tool that can be used to arouse audiences. Danger can arouse. For example, viewing a character crawling over a rotting rope bridge across a deep canyon can increase a viewer's heart rate and blood pressure. Also, production features can increase arousal—fast cuts, loud music, sudden sound effects, lots of motion within a scene, fast dialogue, and so forth. These tools are often linked with violence, and the package can be very arousing. Producers who are creative can remove violence from this package without reducing the arousal.

EIGHT

MYTH 7

Violence is an essential element in all fiction.

———•◦•———

Each year the top 60 television broadcast and cable networks present over half a million hours of programming. Violence is typically found in all of those networks, across all days and day-parts, and across all types of television programming. Why? There is a general belief among programmers that violence is an important and even an essential element in telling stories.

This is another myth that the media industries use to defend themselves from criticism. Again, it is misleading because of what it fails to address. Of course it is true that violence is a useful tool in telling some types of stories, and there are some stories that cannot be told without some violence. But that is not to say that storytelling per se requires violence. The essential element in all good stories is conflict, not violence. Violence is only one of a variety of tools that can be used to generate and heighten conflict, but many other tools are available to storytellers.

STORY FORMULAS

Why do so many producers rely on the single tool of violence to generate conflict? It appears that a good answer to this question is that the use of violence has become a convenient habit, and it has been a habit for a long time in the television world. For example, almost three decades ago, in the first Surgeon

General's Report on Violence and Television, one producer said, "violence and drama are almost synonymous" (quoted in Baldwin and Lewis, 1972, p. 303). Another producer said, "Good drama is based on conflict which erupts in violent emotion" (p. 303).

The habitual use of violence follows typical storytelling formulas. Producers and writers must learn these storytelling formulas, especially when they want their stories presented on television. Writers must generate some action very quickly to capture the attention of an audience with lots of viewing options. The writer must heighten the action on a very strict timetable that allows for a two-minute interruption (for commercial breaks) every ten minutes and must tell the entire story within a 30-, 60-, or 120-minute time period. These formulas are very rigid and very elaborate. Writers who do not understand and write to the formula do not get their scripts produced.

Violence Formula

Part of the television storytelling formula deals with violence. The basic structure of this formula is to introduce a life-or-death conflict situation using violence early in the story. As the story progresses, this conflict gets more serious and more widespread as it involves more characters. Tension builds among the characters—and in the experience of the audience members—until the conflict reaches a high point; then is resolved, which is the climax. Within this storytelling structure, there are three popular ways in which violence is used in the telling of the story: the bad-guys/good-guys formula, the who-done-it formula, and the aftermath formula.

With the bad-guys/good-guys formula, violence is used early in the story to generate the primary action. Then additional violent incidents are portrayed in order to heighten the conflict; throughout this middle part of the story, the bad guys are very active and have the upper hand. The story is told from the good guys' point of view so that the audience will identify with the heroes and crave revenge against the villains. When the audience's need for revenge is at its highest point, the good guys get stronger by "fighting fire with fire" and using violence themselves. This escalates quickly to a climax in which the good guys subdue the bad guys in a scene in which both types of characters use violence. After the climax, the remaining characters appear happy, because the bad guys have once again been removed from society, and the world is put back in order.

An example of this bad-guys/good-guys formula is *Walker, Texas Ranger.* Each week there are clearly identifiable villains who cause some trouble and continue to act violently throughout the program. Ranger Walker, who is the hero, is drawn into the action when victims seek his help. Often, Walker and his partner or friends are also personally victimized by the villains. Eventually Walker gains the upper hand and subdues the villains, usually by dispensing violence of his own as retribution. This "justified" violence is the climax: The villains are removed from society, tension is reduced, and the conflict is resolved.

With the who-done-it formula, a violent act appears very early in the plot. However, this violence is hardly ever shown on the screen; instead, evidence of this violent act is shown (e.g., a dead body), or else someone tells us about it. Throughout the middle of the story, the hero gathers clues and uses deduction to solve the crime. The climax comes not in a violent scene but instead when the hero solves the crime and explains who did it and how the crime was perpetrated.

An example of the who-done-it formula is *Murder, She Wrote.* Unlike *Walker, Texas Ranger,* this show almost always keeps the violent acts off-screen. Once the crime is introduced, Jessica Fletcher, the main character, goes about trying to solve the puzzle of "who done it." Although the story is told from Jessica's point of view, the audience does not feel a growing need for revenge; instead, the increasing tension comes from the audience members' growing desire to have Jessica solve the crime and reveal who the perpetrator is. The audience is kept in suspense as they are invited to sift through the clues with Jessica and see if they can figure out who did it. This suspense builds until the very end, when Jessica exposes the identity of the murderer.

Finally, there is the aftermath formula. With this formula, the story begins much like the who-done-it. Although this formula follows a who-done-it structure as the police search for the perpetrator, the story is really about the consequences of the violence. There is a strong focus on the suffering of the victims—the friends and family of the person murdered. The tension is heightened as the perpetrator is discovered and tries to avoid responsibility for his or her actions. The audience is held in suspense as we wait to see if the perpetrator will get away with the crime. The climax comes when the suspense is resolved, usually with the perpetrator facing (or being forced to face) the consequences.

An example of the aftermath formula is *Law and Order,* which usually begins very similarly to an episode of *Murder, She Wrote.* We enter the plot after a violent act has taken place. The police undertake a who-done-it for the first half of the show, but in this search for the perpetrator we are shown the suffering of the victim or of people close to the victim. In the second half of each episode, the perpetrator tries to avoid responsibility. The plot highlights the harmfulness of violence—emotionally, psychologically, financially, and physically—both to the victims and the perpetrator.

Although violence appears in all three formulas, there are major differences in terms of the way violence is used to tell the story, the meaning of that violence, and its effect on viewers. There is also a big difference in skill required to use the alternative formulas. The easiest formula to use is the bad-guys/good-guys formula. The plot is very simple: Any time writers want to heighten the action and tension, they simply drop in more violence. Characters are one-dimensional and have very simple motivations. Villains are greedy and want to have their way regardless of whether they hurt other people or not. Heroes are good in their motivation to protect the weak and society in general, even when the heroes use violence—and even when the heroes use more violence than the villains. Writers who use this formula are telling viewers that violence can create a fast-paced, exciting, attractive lifestyle if one lives the villain's life. Also, violence enacted by heroes is always highly desirable and always justified. Because these stories are told from the heroes' perspective, audiences identify with those heroes and thereby learn to use violence themselves whenever they feel they are wronged.

Using the aftermath formula is a more challenging task, because plots are more complicated and characters are multidimensional. There are also many more forms of conflict. For example, the perpetrator is in conflict with the police. Often the police are in conflict with legal restrictions on the way they gather and use evidence. Once caught, the perpetrators are often in conflict with their lawyers and the district attorneys. Perpetrators are also shown in conflict with their own moral principles as they try to justify their actions and mitigate their punishment. Sometimes a character who is wrongly charged is in conflict with the true perpetrator. Finally, the victims are in conflict with the police (impatience with solving the crime), the district attorneys (anger over plea bargains), and with the perpetrators themselves. The meaning of violence in this formula is that violence always sets off very harmful shock waves in all directions. Viewers who follow these shows learn that violence is a poor way to solve problems. Thus, not all violence in the media is equally harmful to viewers. With some stories—such as episodes of *Law and Order, NYPD Blue,* or *ER*—the use of violence can have a positive effect on viewers, *because the violence is shown to have a very negative effect on the victims in the story.*

It is much more difficult to tell a good story using the aftermath formula. However, there are examples of this formula's being successfully applied. An episode of the Fox TV show *Roc,* for example, dramatically brought into focus the tragic aftermath of violence and delivered a strong antigun message without showing the murder that proved Roc's warning that "the only answer to a gun is a bigger gun." The NBC cop show *Homicide: Life on the Street* kept the focus squarely on the consequences of violence in an episode in which guest star Robin Williams played a tourist whose wife is killed during a robbery. The audience never sees the shooting but deeply feels the pain of the victim's family and, ultimately, of the perpetrator, who is portrayed not as a stone-cold killer but a young boy who took a gun away from his friend to protect others from violence, then found it all too easy to use the gun himself in the course of the robbery ("Alternatives to Violence," 1994).

Writing Challenges

The use of violence in the aftermath formula requires more talent from the people telling the story. It is easier to attract viewer attention and hold it if there are fast cuts, loud music, and sound effects with characters shooting at each other and bombs going off, so less talented writers can get by with the typical good-guys/bad-guys formula. But this is not to say that only writers with the lowest level of talent can use this formula. It is possible for more talented writers to use the good-guys/bad-guys formula and in so doing to elevate the formula with a higher level of creativity, that is, to expand the conflict beyond the violence in some way to involve the audience even more. There are some examples of talented writers being able to do this. One example is the CBS true-crime drama *Armed and Innocent.* In this story, an 11-year-old boy kills two men who break into his house while he is home alone. Both his community and his father, who had taught him how to shoot, treat him as a hero. But rather than leave this as a revenge story with the boy as a one-dimensional hero, the writer shows the boy trying to hide the guilt and fear he feels. The audience is led to identify strongly with the boy. However, the identification does not involve a feeling of revenge, where we cheer the boy on to committing violence; instead, we feel the boy's confusion, remorse, and shame. Only the intervention of a Vietnam veteran who can empathize with him enables the boy to come to terms with the horror of having killed a human being and, by the end of the movie, to confront a potentially violent situation unarmed ("Alternatives to Violence," 1994). The boy's internal struggle—not his use of violence—is what pulls viewers into the story. Audiences recognize this struggle. They can realize that harnessing the contentious thoughts, feelings, values, and beliefs that guide behavior often takes more strength than a Walker, a Terminator, or a Rambo has ever shown.

Portrayals that show the strength of standing up to a culture of violence can also have tremendous emotional appeal. Consider Steven Spielberg's *Schindler's List,* which is set in Nazi-occupied Poland and tells the story of Oskar Schindler, a businessman and bon vivant out to mine the opportunities of war for personal gain. But Schindler is portrayed experiencing moral conflict between his quest for riches and his treatment of his workers as well as between his personal risk of protecting his workers and his growing friendship for many of them. The movie is so engrossing because it intertwines many forms of conflict. There is also a good deal of physical violence in the movie, but Spielberg does not glamorize the violence, nor does he portray the consequences in a trivial manner.

WHY SO MUCH VIOLENCE IN STORYTELLING?

It has been a strong belief among television programmers that they must present programs that appeal to the lowest common denominator in the audience. Thus programs must be very simple and avoid being offensive. This belief may have had some validity several decades ago when the "Big Three" television networks targeted their programming to the entire U.S. population and together shared more than 95% of the viewing audience. But now the top four commercial television networks account for less than half the viewing audience, and the networks are becoming more niche oriented in their programming. There are many different audiences looking for entertainment, and each one has a different preference in programming. The same is true with other media, especially books, magazines, recorded music, and video games.

There is no longer a shared common denominator. Although there may always be an audience for the revenge formula with one-dimensional characters, there are likely to be many other audiences that want different forms of programming. Producers who are creative will take the risk of splitting off different audiences by creating different types of programming. This, of course, will be risky, because not all innovations in storytelling will work well. But the bigger risk is continuing to believe that there is a chance to create a mass audience for a program by using an old formula that is believed to appeal to the lowest common denominator in the viewing population.

If there is no common denominator and if violence is only one of many tools that can be used to create conflict, why is it still used so often? The answer is that the use of violence is easy, requires little creativity, and is profitable. These factors have not changed.

Easy Formula

Over time, the media industries have developed easy-to-follow formulas for telling their stories, and those formulas more often than not contain violence as the generator of conflict. We, as viewers, are trained at a very young age to follow stories according to these formulas. When we listened to stories such as *The Three Little Pigs* and *Little Red Riding Hood,* we learned how to follow the action and know that there will be violence. The media, especially television, have used this simple formula to create many of the stories required to fill thousands of hours of programming each week. The use of the formula is so common and widespread that all viewers instantly recognize the structure and thereby have a very easy time following the stories.

Requires Little Creativity

For a writer, one of the easiest and simplest ways of generating conflict is to use violence. It takes only one line of stage direction ("Harry threatens Mo with a loaded gun") to plunge characters into a life-threatening conflict. It requires a much more talented writer to move the action along through dialogue that deepens the conflict and makes it more dramatic. For actors, it is much easier to portray the high-profile emotions of anger and fear than the more subtle emotions of peevishness and wariness.

This low level of creativity has plagued television for decades. Richard Powell, a former president of the Writers Guild of America, observed three decades ago that action shows are so vacuous and unrealistic that they have "nowhere else to go" except for violence. By the late 1990s, the situation had not changed, according to Matt Groening, creator and executive producer of the TV hit *The Simpsons,* who said, "Most TV, most movies, really, are less pernicious than tedious and boring. What's bad for kids is bad storytelling. Tell better stories" (Krasny, 1993).

Some writers lack the talent to develop believable characters in depth and put them in conflict situations that do not include violence. Instead, to these writers, creativity means little more than imagining a new form of violence. John Leo observes a trend toward more shocking violence in the guise of creativity. "In the dreadful Mel Gibson movie *Payback,* a nose ring is yanked off, bringing some of the nose with it. A penis is pulled off in the new alleged comedy *Idle Hands*" (Leo, 1999b, p. 16). For these writers, creativity means finding a new body part to destroy. When the audience sees this gruesome portrayal, they immediately experience a strong emotion and sense of arousal. Generating the same strong emotions in the audience without the use of violence requires a great deal more talent.

As creativity is defined by the escalation of graphicness over time, movies and television shows have changed. The film critic Mark Crispin Miller observed that earlier movies such as *The French Connection* (1971) and *Bullitt* (1968) were very violent, but they suppressed the viewer's urge to join in. By the 1990s, however, "screen violence now is used primarily to invite the viewer to enjoy the feel of killing, beating, mutilating" (Medved, 1992). We are inside the mind and emotions of the shooter, experiencing the excitement. This is violence not as a last resort but as deeply satisfying lifestyle. And those who use films purely to exploit and promote the lifestyle ought to be called on it, says Miller. When Keanu Reeves slaughters his enemies in *The Matrix,* the action is presented as a beautiful ballet. Thousands of shells fall like snow from his helicopter and bounce in romantic slow motion off walls and across marble floors. This scene makes gunning people down seem like a wonderfully satisfying hobby, as if a brilliant ad agency had just landed the violence account. In this film, the expression of creativity is not in finding alternative forms of conflict; instead, creativity is in pushing the line of glamorizing the violence itself.

If the industry is really interested in creating art, then it is hard to see how these products in general are really artistic expressions by creative people. Most mainstream movies and television programs seem to be assembled by technicians who execute minor variations on a formula. Those variations do not require much artistic ability or much creativity. The formula focuses on unusual people in atypical situations. Producers rely on the formula for creativity (being different) and get away with superficial treatments.

There is a difference between art and artificiality. Art requires creativity to bring forth the essence of the human existence. Creativity is what makes real people interesting and real situations compelling. This is what makes the great artists great. We can see this difference across television programs. For example, *NYPD Blue* is art and *Walker, Texas Ranger,* is artificial.

If the industry were indeed driven by a desire for creativity and the production of art, it would encourage more writers and producers to break from the simplest violence formula—or at least to provide much more of a range of variation when dealing with it. But this does not seem to be the case. Violence fits the formula, and the formula appears to be more important than creativity or quality. To illustrate this point, consider the results of a study conducted by James Hamilton at Duke University. Hamilton (1998) analyzed movies shown on 32 television channels over a 12-month period to see how critics rated those movies on a four-star rating system for quality. Among the 5,030 movies that had program indicators for violent content, only 2.8% received a four-star rating.

The poverty of ideas among "creative" people is also seen in the video game industry. For example, the creator of "Doom," John Romero, sees the violence as equal to other kinds of activities at the center of different games. "Mario 64 is a pure exploration game," he said.

> You run around and you collect things and you explore. Shooters basically add shooting on top of that. It's basically adding a couple of new things. I'm sure that we can probably come up with something else to do, but shooting things is pretty fun. (Kent, 1997)

As Romero phrased it, "Going around shooting things is something that you can't do in real life unless you want to go to jail for a long time" (Kent, 1997).

Instead of art or quality, it appears that the industry sees its locus of responsibility as a business one. The formula rules. Breaking with the formula is a risk, and producers do everything they can to reduce the risk that they will not appeal to large audiences. But art is about risk. Art is about showing people things they may not want to see in order to make them more aware about more facets of their world.

Maximizing Revenues

The media need to create large audiences in order to generate enough revenue to cover the high cost of producing programs. Taking a chance on a program that follows a new formula is a risky business, because audiences might not like the innovation and therefore avoid the show. For television series, a single rating point over the span of a year could be worth $90 million, so there is a huge incentive to increase the size of the audience and to avoid content that may reduce the potential for a large audience.

The medium of film is also a high-risk business. Top-of-the-line Hollywood movies now average about $50 million to produce and are backed by another $50 million in promotions and advertising. Therefore, a film must earn $100 million just to break even. Of the 350 films Hollywood releases each year, only about 10% earn back their costs of production and promotion at the box office in this country.

Because most movies do not usually do well in American box office receipts, movie studios have had to cultivate other streams of revenue—such as foreign distribution. For many Hollywood movies, the difference between a profit or loss is how well a film will do in other countries, and it is a common belief among producers that violent stories export well. For example, let's look at the recent movies of one studio, Fox. In 1996, *Independence Day* earned $306.2 million in U.S. revenue and another $507.2 million overseas. In 1997, *Speed 2* earned $48.6 million in U.S. revenues and an additional $113.9 million in overseas distribution; *Volcano* earned $49.3 million in this country and another $80.7 million in foreign markets. In 1999, *Star Wars: Episode I, The Phantom Menace* earned $431.1 million domestically and another $494.5 million in foreign markets. The highest-grossing film of all time was *Titanic,* which earned $1.8 billion—two thirds of it from foreign markets (Eller, 1999). Also, in the summer of 2000, 91% of the box office receipts in France were for American movies, especially *Gladiator, Mission Impossible 2,* and *X-Men*—all violent movies (Dahlburg, 2000).

Clearly, the international marketing of American media products is important from a financial point of view. Many movies (such as *Speed 2*) would not make back their production costs with U.S. revenue alone; it takes the foreign revenue to make the movie profitable. Because more than 90% of the world's population lives outside the United States, Hollywood cannot ignore the potential revenue from this huge international market, but we should challenge the assumption that the international language is violence.

CONCLUSION

On the surface, this myth appears to be a reasonable argument for why there is so much violence in storytelling and why there will always be a great deal of violence. But upon closer examination, this myth really tells us more about the talent level of our storytellers than about the nature of storytelling.

When the industry is criticized for an element in its formula, it becomes very defensive for several reasons. First, the industry knows its formula is successful and wants to preserve it. Changing it could cost marketers billions of dollars in lost revenues. Second, the industry is composed of many talented people who have learned the craft of telling stories on television, and these people are offended when amateurs seem to tell them what they can and cannot do.

We need for the industry to get beyond its defensiveness and think about providing alternatives to the typical violence formula. But in order for this to be successful, the public needs to ask for alternatives in its selection in the way it spends its time and money on entertainment.

NINE

MYTH 8

Reducing the amount of violence in the media will solve the problem.

———•·◦·•———

E ven if we substantially reduced the amount of violence in the media, there would still be a serious problem. The solution does not lie in simply reducing the amount. Keeping score of the problem of media violence is *not* as simple as playing golf, where getting better means lowering our score.

With the problem of media violence, getting better means changing the way violence is predominantly portrayed. Our risk of experiencing negative effects is influenced primarily by what the portrayals tell us about violence. The frequency of violent portrayals is a secondary concern. If the context of the portrayal posed no risk, then the frequency would have no influence on risk. Only when the context poses a risk does frequency matter.

To illustrate the importance of context, let's consider two scenarios. In the first scenario, a teenage boy swaggers into a convenience store. The clerk insults him, so he physically assaults the clerk and takes the money from the cash register in retaliation. Later we see him partying with his friends as he tells them about his adventure. His friends treat him as a hero, saying that the clerk has always been nasty to all of them and deserved the beating.

In the second scenario, the teenager is insulted and physically assaults the clerk, but this time he is subdued and arrested. While sitting in jail, he is scared and thinks about how stupid his actions were. We see that the clerk has painful bruises and that the teenager is suffering a broken hand from the assault.

The setting, the characters, and the violence are the same in both scenes, but the meaning of the violence is very different. In the first scene, the violence is portrayed as justified and successful, and the teenager is shown as a happy hero. In the second scene, the violence is unsuccessful, the teenager is remorseful, and the participants are shown in physical pain.

The meaning of violence is very different in the two scenarios. Viewers who watched a great deal of the first type of portrayal would come to believe that violence is often justified and can therefore be an acceptable—even a rewarding—way of solving problems. Viewers who watch many examples of the second kind of portrayal would come to believe that violence should be avoided, because it is very harmful to both the perpetrator and victim.

Context is important, because it provides people with information about how the violence should be interpreted. Therefore, our primary concern about the influence of media violence should be focused on context instead of frequency.

PREDOMINANT CONTEXT

Is there a predominant pattern of context in the portrayals of violence? Although there is a wide variety of contextual patterns, one of those patterns seems especially prevalent, especially in Hollywood action-adventure films and television series. This formula for storytelling begins the show with some exciting violence in order to capture the attention of audience members and get the plot moving as quickly as possible. This initial violence is perpetrated by some interesting villains who victimize innocent people and continue to cause mayhem throughout the middle of the show. The hero is pulled into the action and is also victimized by being shot at, blown up, forced into car wrecks, and hit with objects intended to knock him out. Rarely is the hero shown with physical harm, and when he is, the harm is nowhere near commensurate with the beating he took. The victimization of the hero serves to accelerate his anger into a justified rage that propels him into the climactic scene, in which he uses highly violent means to subdue the villains. Once subdued, the villains are quickly removed from the action. Throughout the show,

Table 9.1   Context of Violent Content on Television

Glamorized

- Seventy-four percent of all violent acts go unpunished.
  - Good characters are rarely punished when they use violence.
  - Bad characters are usually punished, but only at the end of the program.
- Seventeen percent of all violent scenes showed the violence as being rewarded.
- Twenty-eight percent of all violent interactions are portrayed as justified.

Sanitized

- Forty-three percent of all violent interactions portray no observable harm to victims.
  - Lack of harm is even more prevalent in children's shows (54%).

Trivialized

- Forty-two percent of all violent scenes are presented in humorous context.
- Forty-five percent of violent acts are presented in fantasy context.
  - In the genre of children's shows, 87% of violent acts are fantasy.

SOURCE: Figures from the NTVS (1997).

the audience is manipulated into identifying with the hero, who is portrayed as being highly attractive either physically or in terms of his personality.

This formula treats violence in a very particular way—that is, violence is typically glamorized, sanitized, and trivialized (see Table 9.1). Because of these patterns, viewers are at an especially high risk of negative effects. If violence were not so glamorized, viewers might not be attracted to it so much, or, if attracted to the action, viewers might not identify with the characters to such a degree. If the violence were not so sanitized, viewers would not become desensitized to the physical, psychological, and emotional harm to victims and society. If the violence were not so trivialized by humor and fantasy, viewers would be able to see its seriousness. Let's look at each of these three characteristics in more detail and examine their negative effects on viewers.

Glamorized

Producers glamorize their characters when they hyperbolize certain qualities of those characters. Thus villains are shown as ultrasadistic, stunningly ugly, enragingly arrogant, or displaying a super-genius IQ. Heroes look like supermodels and exhibit the physical abilities of Olympic athletes. This glamorization of characters serves to lead viewers to identify strongly with the heroes and intensely hate the villains.

What makes a character attractive? For younger viewers, physical appearance is especially important. As people age, the judgment of attractiveness shifts from physical characteristics to personality characteristics such as kindness, cruelty, and so forth (Hoffner & Cantor, 1985). So although younger children perceive the villains as those characters who are ugly, older children begin recognizing villains in terms of their degree of cruelty. The formula of attractiveness is so entrenched and obvious that even young children can easily tell the difference between heroes and villains. For example, research clearly shows that kindergarten through fourth-grade children were able to distinguish between protagonists and antagonists and that "the superheroes are compelling, attractive, and evidently above reproach, making their actions highly visible and favorable for generalized imitation" (Liss, Reinhardt, & Fredriksen, 1983, p. 184).

When viewers identify with characters who are rewarded for using violence to get what they want, viewers vicariously learn that violence is a good thing (Anderson, 1983; Comstock, 1989; Comstock et al., 1978; Dorr, 1981; Hicks, 1965; Huesmann, Lagerspetz, & Eron, 1984; Leyens & Picus, 1973; McLeod, Atkin, & Chaffee, 1972; Perry & Perry, 1976; Tannenbaum & Gaer, 1965; Turner & Berkowitz, 1972). Thus, reward (and punishment) is a powerful contextual factor, because it provides viewers with information about which actions are acceptable.

Viewers also make judgments about how justified the violence is. These judgments can increase viewers' risk for a negative effect (Ball-Rokeach, 1972). How do viewers make this judgment? Viewers are influenced by the apparent motives of the perpetrators in assessing the meaning of the violence. It appears that retaliatory motives, such as revenge, are the strongest in leading to negative effects. When a motive legitimates the violence, that violence is regarded as justified, and viewers are more likely to learn that violence is a good thing. When violence is presented as legitimate, characters' behaviors "are rewarded by others with praise, acceptance, status, etc. They can also see themselves as moral, responsible, and good people because their behavior is so regarded by themselves and others" (Ball-Rokeach, 1972, pp. 101-102).

When viewers are exposed to violent acts that are portrayed as being justified, they are more likely to behave more aggressively (Bryan & Schwartz, 1971; Comstock, 1989; Comstock et al., 1978; Comstock & Strasburger, 1990; Hearold, 1986; Meyer, 1972; Rule & Ferguson, 1986). For example, Bryan and Schwartz observed that

> aggressive behavior in the service of morally commendable ends appears condoned. Apparently, the assumption is made that moral goals temper immoral actions. . . . Thus, both the imitation and interpersonal attraction of the transgressing model may be determined more by outcome than by moral principles. (p. 58)

Finally, viewers judge the violence on appropriateness. People assess the appropriateness of aggressive acts, especially those that are in retaliation for previous aggression (Brown & Tedeschi, 1976; Kane, Joseph, & Tedeschi, 1976). For example, Tedeschi and his colleagues conducted experiments in which subjects took turns administering electric shocks to each other as a form of feedback in learning tasks. The researchers found that when subjects administered a degree of shock similar to what they had received, such retaliation was not regarded as violent. However, acts of retaliation that were stronger (in terms of number of shocks) than an initial act of aggression were regarded as much more violent. The researchers reported that people's judgments of violence were attributable much more to the appropriateness of the retaliation than to the actual number of shocks administered. Therefore, the judgment of violence does not rest solely with the type of act performed but is also keyed to the context of surrounding events.

Sanitized

When producers glamorize the violence, they run the risk of offending audiences and triggering complaints. To counterbalance this threat, producers frequently sanitize their portrayals of violence. Sanitizing the violence means limiting the portrayal to the action itself and not showing the harm to victims. For example, producers want to excite and arouse audiences, so they might include a fistfight between a villain and a hero. The fight escalates into hitting each other with pieces of wood, then pipes, then rocks, then wrestling down a steep embankment while careening off tree trunks and rolling through briar patches and into a river—where they try to drown each other—and finally the hero feeds the villain to a passing crocodile. We never see the villain again, and the hero shows no serious physical harm other than some minor abrasions.

When portrayals are sanitized, viewers—especially children—can get the wrong idea about how harmful violence is. Research studies continually find that when violence is portrayed with no consequences (lack of pain, suffering, sorrow, or remorse), viewers are not likely to feel inhibited from performing aggressively, and their levels of aggressive behavior usually increase. For example, in an experiment, Goranson (1969) showed people one of two versions of a film of a prize fight; in one version, there were no consequences, but in the other version, the loser of the fight received a bad beating and later died. The people who did not experience the negative consequences were more likely to behave aggressively after the viewing. This same pattern has been found in other experiments, and reviewers of this set of research are convinced that consequences of the violence are associated with effects (Comstock, 1989; Comstock et al., 1978; NTVS, 1997).

A key element in the consequences is whether the victim shows pain, because portrayals of pain inhibit subsequent aggression (Baron, 1971a, 1971b, 1979; Sanders & Baron, 1975). For example, Baron (1971a, 1971b) found that when the victim in a program shows pain and suffering, the strength of the attack's effect on viewers is significantly decreased.

There is a range of harmful consequences; writers need not be limited to showing the victims in physical pain. Mees (1990) states that three types of harm can be distinguished: (a) harm from distress (one's freedom from physical-mental harm is interfered with), (b) legal harm (violation of an accepted standard of social interaction), and (c) harm from moral guilt (someone disregards the moral aspects of people's fundamental attitudes).

Some producers have been bothered by this sanitizing of the violence. For example, a chief censor for one of the networks said,

> I would like to see more of the painful consequences of violence (hurt and after effects on people) but find it difficult to explain. If I were to put that into a memorandum to producers, I would be in trouble. (quoted in Baldwin & Lewis, 1972, p. 346)

Some producers do get this point. One said that the aftereffect of the violence "has more dramatic impact than showing the violence" (Baldwin & Lewis, 1972, p. 345). However, most producers disagree with the claim that it is better to show more harm. One producer said, "We caution writers and directors against unnecessary exhibition of repulsive material. To make a heavy seem ruthless, you don't have to have him eviscerate someone and eat his vitals. To sicken the audience is not drama" (Baldwin & Lewis, 1972, p. 345).

Trivialized

When violence is presented in a humorous and fantasy context, it is trivialized. Think of an episode of *The Three Stooges*. The plots of these shows present repeated acts of physical violence, but the audience is expected to laugh at each instance. This is slapstick comedy, so we don't take it seriously.

In general among effects researchers, there are two conflicting predictions about the role of humor with violence. One prediction is that when humor is used with violence, the humor serves to *reduce* or eliminate the negative effects of violence. The other prediction is that humor serves to *increase* the negative effects of violence. Let's examine both of these positions.

Some scholars have demonstrated that humor serves to reduce a viewer's risk of a disinhibition effect of exposure to violence. Humor is thought of as being able to displace aggression through distraction or catharsis. Freud (1960) theorized that hostile humor can often serve as a form of disguised attack against a target, thus providing the person making the joke with an opportunity to release emotional tension or purge hostile impulses. Also, Berger (1988), in an essay speculating about humor, says that the thing humor does particularly well is "to help break set—that is, change one's assumptions about something, gain a new perspective, escape from a previously held pattern of beliefs and expectations" (p. 246). He also points out that humor has social and cultural value and helps people collectively to deal with anxieties and stress. He says that "comedy emphasizes survival; tragedy leads, almost inexorably, to death and destruction" (p. 247).

In reviewing the experimental literature on the relationship of humor and aggression, Baron (1978) says that exposure to nonhostile humor reduces subsequent aggression by previously angered persons. The explanations for this are (a) humor serves to induce emotions incompatible with aggression, and (b) humor serves to shift attention away from a person's prior annoyance. Some humor interrupts violence, whereas other humor is linked with the violence itself. When humor is used to interrupt violence, it has been found to reduce the effect of violence (Lieberman, 1975). When humor is linked to violence, it has been found to lower inhibitions toward committing acts of aggression by subjects in controlled experiments (Baron, 1978; Berkowitz, 1970).

Other people argue that humor is an enhancer of negative effects of exposure to violence. Baron (1978) says that exposure to hostile humor actually enhances such behavior. Zillmann (1979) argues that humor can increase a viewer's arousal, which leads to a greater probability of behaving aggressively in real life. Thus humor can be regarded as a facilitator of aggression through heightening arousal.

From the research studies on humor just presented, it should be apparent that humor can serve different roles in the risk process. If the humor is non-hostile and deflects attention away from violence, then it can reduce the risk of a disinhibition effect, but if the humor works together with the violence to create higher arousal in viewers, then it can increase the risk of a disinhibition effect. What has not been tested thus far is the role of humor in altering risks of other types of negative effects, especially desensitization.

As for the contextual factor of realism, there is high agreement that the more real a portrayal is, the more seriously viewers take the action. When violence is portrayed in a fantasy setting, viewers tend to discount or even ignore the violence (Atkin, 1983; Berkowitz & Alioto, 1973; Berkowitz & Geen, 1966, 1967; Donnerstein & Berkowitz, 1981; Eron, 1982; Feshbach, 1976; Geen, 1975; Huesmann, Lagerspetz, & Eron, 1984; Jo & Berkowitz, 1994; Thomas & Tell, 1974). Also, a viewer's belief in the reality of a violent portrayal can affect the fear reaction (Geen, 1975; Geen & Rokosky, 1973; Lazarus, Opton, Nomikos, & Rankin, 1965). For example, Lazarus and colleagues found that showing gory accidents to adults served to arouse them physiologically less when the viewers were told that the accidents were fake. This effect has also been found with children (Cantor & Hoffner, 1990; Cantor & Sparks, 1984; Sparks, 1986).

Determination of reality is a judgment that viewers must make, and this judgment is a multidimensional one (Hawkins, 1977; Potter, 1988). The judgment usually begins with assessing whether a portrayal actually happened, but there is more to it than this. Viewers—especially when watching fictional content—make assessments about whether something could happen as portrayed. That which could never happen is considered as fantasy. So the judgment must move beyond the actualities of occurrence and consider the possibilities that different characters could be people encountered in real life and that different situations could occur.

Viewers also look for cues in the portrayal that mimic real life—a victim with the same name or traits as someone in real life whom the viewer dislikes

(Berkowitz & Geen, 1966, 1967; Donnerstein & Berkowitz, 1981). Furthermore, Gunter (1985) has shown that viewers' discriminations between portrayals become more refined when the portrayals are perceived as more true to life and when viewers feel a greater familiarity with their own settings.

Yet another answer deals with how the characters are presented. Violence performed by human-type characters leads to more intense responses than violence performed by cartoon characters or puppets (Osborn & Endsley, 1971; Surbeck, 1975). For example, Osborn and Endsley found that viewers responded more emotionally to the violence, especially when human characters were involved. The human violence was also rated as the most scary, and viewers recalled more details from it. Cantor (1994) says that children are especially sensitive to the similarity of depicted characters to real-life people, so that when human characters perform violence, children are much more likely to experience a fear effect.

MULTIPLE FACTORS, MULTIPLE EFFECTS

Context is a complex issue. Remember that there are many elements in the creation of a portrayal that glamorize violence. There are also multiple elements that create portrayals that are sanitized and trivialized. Also, some elements contribute to more than one characteristic, such that a portrayal of violence can be glamorized and trivialized at the same time. Many combinations of portrayals are possible, and therefore many different effects are possible—often countereffects occurring at the same time. Let's examine these issues in a bit more detail.

Multiple Portrayals

It might seem contradictory that violence is typically portrayed in a glamorized and at the same time trivialized manner. How is this possible? By *glamorized,* I mean that the violence is committed by attractive characters with whom the viewers identify and the violent action is justified and rewarded. By *trivialized,* I mean that the humor and fantasy contexts make the violence seem like no big deal. Think of a cartoon in which a heroic action figure is blown up by a huge bomb in a spectacular explosion, but then the character quickly shakes it off, and as we watch this, we are expected to shake it off too with laughter that keeps us in a comfort zone—knowing that this could never happen in real life.

Multiple Effects on Viewers

How is it possible that when violence is glamorized and at the same time trivialized, such a portrayal can lead to a negative effect? Wouldn't the two characteristics somehow cancel each other out? At first, it would seem that the two would be acting in opposite directions. If violence were glamorized, it would seem to turn on viewers' emotions, thus attracting them into believing that violence is something they might want to try in order to make their lives more exciting, successful, and vibrant. But if violence were also portrayed as trivial, it would turn their emotions down into boredom. The solution to this seeming conundrum is that there is more than one negative effect. Some elements in the portrayal can be increasing the probability of one type of effect, whereas some other elements in the portrayal are increasing the probability of second type of effect (rather than canceling out the first type of effect).

Look at Table 9.2 to see what media researchers have found to be the key contextual elements that increase the probability of three negative effects. Let's examine the disinhibition effect first. So far, researchers have identified seven major contextual variables that have been shown to increase the likelihood of this effect.

Next, consider the fear effect. Cantor (1994) says that a fear reaction is enhanced by three sets of factors. First, fear is enhanced when there is a similarity between the elements in a portrayal and the characteristics in a person's own life. For example, live-action violence triggers more fear than animated violence; also, portrayals of real events lead to greater fear than portrayals of fictional events. If the viewer believes that the portrayal has consequences for him or herself, then the fear reaction can be heightened. Second, if a person's motivation to view violence is for entertainment, he or she can employ a discounting procedure to lessen the effects of fear. Third, fear requires arousal. Arousal can come from nonviolent or nonviewing factors, but when people are aroused, they are at more risk for fear.

Notice how some factors work in opposite directions. For example, an attractive villain will tend to reduce the probability of a disinhibition effect but at the same time increase the risk of a fear effect. Also, when there is little blood and gore (low graphic harm), the risk of a disinhibition effect increases while at the same time the risk of fear and desensitization effects decrease.

Table 9.2   Research Findings: Context Factors That
                     Increase Risk of Three Effects

Increasing Risk of Disinhibition Effect

   No harmful consequences to victims are portrayed.
   Perpetrators of violence are rewarded or at least not punished.
   Perpetrators are attractive.
   Villain is unattractive.
   Viewers are made to identify with the perpetrators.
   Violent action is portrayed as being justified.
   Violent action takes place in realistic settings.

Increasing Risk of Fear Effect

   Target of violence is portrayed as being attractive.
   There is high graphicness.
   There is high realism.

Increasing Risk of Desensitization Effect

   There is high graphicness.
   Violence is presented in humorous context.

BREAKING THE FORMULA

The starting point for working beyond the faulty belief in this myth is to realize that not all violence in the media is the same. For example, Bok (1998) points out that Shakespeare's *King Lear* or *Macbeth* or Homer's *Iliad* all contain many acts of violence, but they are helpful because they realistically teach us about violence. These works of literature help us understand the role of violence in our own lives by showing us what happens to victims and perpetrators. Bok criticizes current media treatment of violence because

> programs now literally assault viewers and are intended to excite viewers and to make them buy what's being advertised on the program. To make people thrilled about violence, to make them find it very exciting, that's entirely different from literary works which deal with violence. (Bok, 1998)

Some producers realize the differences in types of violence. For example, Mastrosimone, who wrote *Bang, Bang, You're Dead,* denounced Hollywood's "strident silence" toward needless violence. "I'm not against violence. I'm against gratuitous violence. The violence where there is no remorse. Violence that is made to look like fun, filmed in slow-motion, lighted beautifully and adorned with glib lines and uncaring heroes" (Puig, 1999, p. 1D).

After the Littleton, Colorado, massacre, a group of screenwriters and producers debated the topic "Guns Don't Kill People, Writers Do." Veteran writer Sy Gomberg said, "We who create entertainment must honestly acknowledge and urgently address the responsibility we all have to eliminate excessive or gratuitous or unpunished violence. Otherwise, children will continue to kill children" (Puig, 1999, p. 1D).

There is growing recognition among producers that they have a duty to use violence responsibly. For example, Andre Morgan, executive producer of the TV drama *Martial Law* and cocreator of TV's *Walker, Texas Ranger,* says he and his partners have discussed what their responsibilities are. "The one continuing lesson we teach is that crime will not pay. But you also have to show that force will be met with force" (Oldenburg & Snider, 1999, p. 1D). This producer has it half right. It is good that he does not show criminals getting away with violence. But his heroes, who subdue the criminals with force, do get away with their violent actions. Heroes are never punished for their brutal assaults; to the contrary, they are rewarded. They are also glamorous role models for viewers. So while viewers are learning that crime does not pay, they are also learning that violence is often justified and successful. To be truly responsible, producers need to show heroes as well as villains experiencing great harm and remorse for their violent actions.

Some producers are truly creative in breaking with the formula now and again. In *Schindler's List,* Steven Spielberg told a story using violence that was *not* glamorized, sanitized, or trivialized. This movie was a critical and commercial success. But for every *Schindler's List,* there are scores of movies and TV series that use the old formula.

It is also ironic that if producers decided to unsanitize their portrayals of violence, they would be increasing the graphicness in order to show the terrible harm to victims who, for example, are cut deeply with a knife or who have a bone shatter as a bullet tears through their flesh. Graphicness is the one criticism that producers (or at least standards and practices departments) have responded to over the years—showing sensitivity not to offend audiences. So increasing the graphicness in portrayals in order to unsanitize them would elicit more public criticism, and this would increase the risk of losing audiences.

Producers want to avoid such a risk, so it is unlikely that they will move substantially toward showing the realistic harm to their victimized characters. Thus by continuing with the old violence formula and avoiding their risk of offending us, they are implicitly asking us to accept the ever-increasing risk of becoming desensitized.

CONCLUSIONS

Expecting a substantial reduction in the frequency of violent portrayals in the media is not a realistic expectation, nor is it a useful goal.

It is not realistic to believe that there are arguments powerful enough to get producers to abandon what they believe is the most successful way of telling action stories, especially when their business is so competitive and the cost of change so high in terms of risking the loss of substantial revenues.

Even more important, a reduction in the frequency of violence in the media is not a very useful goal. This becomes clear when we understand that context is more central to changing risk levels than is frequency. If our purpose is to reduce the risk of negative effects among viewers, then our strategy should be focused on altering the context of the portrayals much more so than trying to reduce their frequency.

The concern over media violence is generated by the fear that viewers will experience negative effects. The risk of negative effects is keyed to how people interpret the meaning of the violence they see. When violence is presented as glamorized, sanitized, and trivialized, the risk for many negative effects is high.

The violence formula that has dominated so many stories over the decades tells us that violence is associated with attractive characters as well as an exciting life where you get what you want. If you justify the violence, there is no need for remorse. Good guys are always justified in their violent actions, and we, the viewers, also learn to feel justified as we identify with those heroes. Besides, the victims are rarely harmed. When something is portrayed with such a big upside and such a minor downside, what are the lessons being taught to viewers? An honest answer to this question is the key to dispelling the myth that the problem of media violence is limited to frequency.

TEN

MYTH 9

The First Amendment protects the media from restrictions on violence.

———————

Media businesses usually invoke their freedom of expression whenever they feel criticism pushing them into a corner with threats of content regulation. When all other arguments fail, freedom of speech is used as the ultimate line of defense. Observes Deborah Lutterbeck (1995), writing in *Common Cause Magazine,*

> The industry players know the script. They know when to hang their heads while lawmakers preach at congressional hearings. But they also elicit agreeable nods when they talk of the dangers of censorship, of a cultural backlash that could crack the very pillars of democracy.

This defense usually works, because the public strongly supports this freedom—at least in principle.

Of all the myths, this one is arguably the most manipulative and the most misleading. It is manipulative because it equates criticism of media violence with censorship and cynically plays on the public's fear of big government taking away individual freedoms. Therefore, anyone who argues *for* censorship is not only un-American but also dangerous. The myth is misleading because it deflects our attention away from the commercial nature of the marketing of violent products and tries to reinforce the assumption that media violence is "speech" that should be afforded absolute protection from any limitation.

ANALYZING THE ARGUMENTS SUPPORTING THE MYTH

Let's analyze this claim that media violence is speech that is protected by the First Amendment. When we look more closely at this claim and how it is used, we can see that it is based on three arguments. The first argument is that critics of violent media messages are asking for censorship of the media and that this is a very un-American thing. The second argument is that the First Amendment is absolute, so there is no basis for limiting the industry's freedom of expression. The third argument—the one lurking under the other two but rarely discussed directly—is that media violence qualifies as speech. In the following discussion, I will show that all three of these arguments are faulty.

Critics Want to Censor

When people in the media industries feel threatened by critics of their content, they polarize the issue by treating the critics as censors who want to eliminate all the violence in the media. However, serious critics of media violence are not asking for the total elimination of all violence in all stories and in all news programs. When critics complain about violence in the media, they are essentially saying either: (a) *reduce* the amount of violence from its persistently high level, (b) *shift* the highly violent programs into time slots where children are not as likely to see them, or (c) present the violence in a *different context* so that its harmful risks to audiences are reduced.

None of these is an argument for the total elimination of all violent portrayals in the media. With "a," the critics are saying that in a movie, perhaps the producers can do the same character development with 10 acts of violence rather than 50. With "b," the critics are saying that programmers can present the same amount of violence, just concentrate it in particular time periods. With "c," critics are saying that violence can be presented in all programs and even at high rates if its context is changed.

None of these three requests is intended to limit the expression of producers; to the contrary, critics are actually asking for producers to be more creative and expand their variety of expression. When asking for a reduction in the number of violent acts, critics are not asking for producers to eliminate conflict in their stories but instead to move away from their strong dependence on violence for generating conflict and to use other forms of conflict. When asking that highly violent shows be scheduled at times when large numbers of children are not in the audience, critics are not asking producers to limit their expression but instead to provide a wider variety of programs so that there are more alternatives in the earlier parts of prime time. When asking producers to change the context in portrayals of violence, critics are asking producers to break away sometimes from their slavish dependence on the violence formula, in which the violence is typically glamorized, sanitized, and trivialized.

However, many producers are incapable of understanding the criticism as anything except censorship. These producers try to stigmatize the critics by tarring them as censors. For example, John Carpenter, the horror film director whose work was blamed years ago for a killing in England said to be inspired by his movie *Halloween,* complains about public criticism and equates the public's expression as censorship:

> This is a moan I've heard since I was a kid. I first heard about it in relation to comic books. . . . Then in the late '50s it was the violence in foreign films—the neo-realists films with their non-Hollywood endings. We went through Elvis and rock 'n' roll music. And on and on and on it goes. It's a basic compulsion in human beings to censor. We've always had it. (Harrison, 1999, p. F1)

As long as producers can characterize the critics as censors, then the producers become the "good guys" and the critics become the "straw men" who can be easily destroyed.

This strategy of equating criticism with censorship can be seen in the 1990s, especially in the aftermath of the shootings in Littleton, Colorado, in 1999. In response to strong criticism from the general public, a few members of Congress proposed legislation using a variety of means to attempt to control media violence. When those bills faltered, Jack Valenti, president of the MPAA, hailed this as a victory over censorship, saying, "Those votes mean that it has been confirmed that conservatives and liberals, Democrats and Republicans, treat the First Amendment with great regard." Some members of Congress bought the industry's argument. For example, Rep. Maxine Waters (D-CA) said, "We are not going back to burning books, we are not going to lock people up for artistic expression. We cannot violate the Constitution in the name of wanting to do something about violence." But none of those bills addressed content in books—or in any medium except television. Also, few of the bills had any penalties for noncompliance, and those that did specify penalties were limited to fines; none of the bills included a jail sentence. It appears as if Rep. Waters had not read any of these bills—or perhaps she was speaking metaphorically. But if her rhetoric was metaphorical, her poor choice of imagery could serve only to mislead and scare the public rather than to lead the public to a better understanding of the problem.

The more *mis*information that is introduced into the debate, the more easy it is to become confused. For example, even the American Civil Liberties Union (ACLU) showed some confusion and appeared to have lost its way in February 1992, when it took out a full-page ad in *Daily Variety* warning of an apocalypse in the form of "a list of moral rules that would return us to the 1950s." What stimulated their reaction? Cardinal Roger Mahony of the Los Angeles diocese had published an editorial in the *National Review* in which he expressed his opinion that it would be a good idea for the television and motion picture industries to develop a voluntary code to limit sex and violence in mass entertainment. Mahony was not asking for the elimination of violence and sex in the media, nor was he asking for any legislation or governmental restrictions. He was only suggesting that the film and television industries act more responsibly by considering self-regulation. It is interesting to contemplate what must have been the decision-making process of ACLU leaders. On one side of the controversy was the powerful film and television industries, which were marketing violence as speech in their unfettered drive for profit. On the other side was a man who was using his freedom of expression—which he had to pay for when buying the ad in the newspaper—to ask an industry to act more responsibly.

An example of how far some people in the industry will stretch the idea of freedom of expression came about as a response to "Turn Off the TV Day" in November 1992. The president of the Network Television Association objected to this day on the grounds that "participating in national boycotts is an infringement of the networks' First Amendment Rights" (Minow, 1995). Also, in 1954, in one of the earliest Senate hearings on TV violence, Senator Hendrickson suggested that it might be a good idea to appoint a "TV Czar" to review children's programming. Immediately broadcasters labeled this as censorship.

Another example of the industry's distortion of the concept of freedom of expression is their claim that being asked to label their programs is an act of censorship. They claim that for government to require television programmers to provide more information about their programs infringes on their rights *not* to provide such information; therefore, it is a violation of their First Amendment rights. Even though the federal government has given the programmers themselves total freedom to develop their own rating system and to rate their own programs, the programmers say that the very idea that they must provide any information about their programs infringes on their freedom of expression.

Some people are arguing that the media industries seem to use the First Amendment to protect a wide range of their business practices and that their interpretation is a distortion of the meaning of the idea of freedom of expression. Constitutional scholar at Stanford Law School Lawrence Lessig says that media companies are using the First Amendment to stifle competition, circumvent antitrust rules, and gain a stranglehold on emerging businesses. One of the many examples of this is AT&T, which owns many cable systems. When Broward County, Florida, required the AT&T-owned cable provider to lease its high-speed Internet wires to rivals, AT&T claimed that this was a violation of its First Amendment rights (Sanders, 2001). Broward County was not telling AT&T to change any content; instead, the county wanted to protect competition by asking AT&T to share (for a fee) its clear lines.

Who is more in favor of censorship—that is, imposing limits on information and ideas? Is it critics who are asking for a wider range of expression in the form of different kinds of conflict beyond violence, a wider variety of context, and more information from programmers about their shows? Or is it producers who resist program labeling, who are adverse to the risk of using a wider range of formulas in telling stories, and who do not provide their speech free but instead charge the public for it?

The First Amendment Is an Absolute Protection

Producers cloud the issue when they argue that the First Amendment is a guarantee of free speech. This is a widespread misconception. The First Amendment is not a *guarantee* of anything. The First Amendment *prevents* the federal government from making any law abridging the right of free speech to any individual. It does not prevent nongovernmental entities—such as parents, teachers, professional associations, or businesses—from limiting your expression. If an organization or an individual prevents you from speaking, they are limiting your freedom of expression, but they are not violating the First Amendment. This is why you cannot use the First Amendment as a basis for forcing a newspaper to publish your letter to the editor. The newspaper has the right to censor you, that is, to reject your letter for publication or to publish their edited version of your letter.

Even though the First Amendment says that the federal government will make no law abridging the freedom of expression, the federal government has done just that on several occasions. Furthermore, these exceptions have been upheld in the U.S. Supreme Court when the court felt that another right was in conflict with the right of freedom of expression and that the other right was more important. Examples of these exceptions are slander, libel, invading the privacy of a private individual, and when expression creates a clear danger to the safety of the public (such as yelling "Fire!" in a crowded theater when there is no fire).

The U.S. Supreme Court has also limited rights to free speech when the harm of that speech is likely to be great and the value of the speech is small. Such is the case with obscenity. The court reasoned that obscenity had so little social value that it deserved no protection. People argue that if obscenity is not protected, then violence should certainly not be. The groundwork is being laid to treat violence as speech with little value and therefore outside the absolute protection of the First Amendment. Three possible rationales have been used to justify the possible regulation of violence in the media. First, courts have already held in two cases (*FCC v. Pacifica Foundation*, 1978; *City of Renton v. Playtime Theatres*, 1986) that speech may be regulated to prevent secondary effects of the speech unrelated to freedom of expression (e.g., to prevent violent and criminal acts). In these cases, of course, the rulings concerned indecent and obscene content, but there may be a compelling case for defining violent content as indecent (*Hearings on H.R. 1391*, 1989). Second, the federal government can make a case that there is a compelling interest to protect children from the effects of television violence (*FCC v. League of Women Voters*, 1984). In this case, such regulation would be given only special scrutiny, which sometimes permits content-based regulation of speech (Hearings on Television Violence Act, 1989).

Former Attorney General Janet Reno has argued in favor of governmental regulation of violence in the media. In a scathing attack on television violence in 1992, she told a Senate committee that "regulation of violence is constitutionally permissible." She was talking about broadcast violence, and she was relying, she said, on the Supreme Court's 1978 decision in *FCC v. Pacifica Foundation,* which upheld government limits on hours for "indecent" radio shows (Denniston, 1993). Also, even democracies with strong protections for political and religious freedom—such as Canada, Sweden, and Holland—have statutes limiting violent pornography and hate speech (Bok, 1998).

Producers continue to argue from an absolutist position. They try to make us fear noncategorical thinking by warning us of a "slippery slope." For example, Andre Morgan, executive producer of the TV drama *Martial Law* and cocreator of TV's *Walker, Texas Ranger,* says,

> Where do we draw the line? Do we ban CNN from showing the effects of bombing in Kosovo? Do we ban live TV of police chases? Is it OK if Wolf Blitzer is giving the narrative, but not OK if Chuck Norris is? (Oldenburg & Snider, 1999, p. 1D)

These are indeed knotty issues, but their difficulty alone is not a good enough reason for not trying to deal with them.

Violence Is Speech

There are two fundamental rationales for protecting speech. One rationale is that the free flow of ideas is essential to a democracy. A second rationale is that artists need to be afforded full latitude of expression. When we examine carefully these bases for freedom of expression, we can see that violence in the media largely falls outside the scope of this reasoning.

In a democracy, the power is in the hands of the public, and the public needs access to all ideas so people can make up their own minds about which ideas are good or bad, accurate or faulty, useful or harmful. If the government is allowed to screen the flow of ideas, then the power is no longer in the hands of the public, and the public then becomes conditioned to believe what the government wants the public to believe. Bok (1998) reminds us that the First Amendment was designed to protect political and religious expression— thereby ensuring that the population would be exposed to as many viewpoints as possible. Bok points out that countries have had a long history of banning storytellers. Plays and books have been banned, but those stories that were banned were not banned because of their violence. They were banned because their messages threatened people who ran political or religious institutions.

Media violence is almost never a form of political or religious expression. For example, what are the important political or religious insights conveyed by movies such as *Terminator, Rambo,* and *Lethal Weapon* or by television shows such as *Walker, Texas Ranger?* Would the political or religious discourse in this country be impoverished by a lack of input from these media products? Programmers do not use violent stories to advance their political or religious positions. Instead, programmers simply want to entertain. If the form of that entertainment were restricted, it would not alter their ability to present political or religious points of view—or any new point of view. All it would do would be to perhaps limit their revenue by reducing the size of their audiences, but even this is in question. It is not at all clear that audience size would be reduced if the amount of violence were reduced or if its portrayals were altered to present a different message (recall Myth 7). So the industry is really motivated by a fear (not a reality) of lower revenue (not a fear of restricted range of expression). Also, if we set the economic concern aside for a moment and ask who would really be harmed if there were less violence on television, we would probably have to say audience members whose access to more violence is being limited. But we have not heard from anyone in the public who feels that the amount of violence is too small for their tastes.

The second rationale for freedom of expression is to provide artists with the greatest latitude. There should be no bounds on creativity. Artistic expression should push the boundaries of society in order to stimulate our understanding of our world.

Is media violence art? Oliver Stone says that *Natural Born Killers* is art rather than an attempt to profit from murder and mayhem. He says it is a satirical—and gory—look at social violence, a send-up of the way the tabloid press exploits violence. "The whole purpose of drama [is] to uncover the social truth, uncover in a sense the taboos, to explain the society to itself." If this expression is censored, he believes, key elements of truth are lost. But critics are skeptical of this claim. For example, Lynne Cheney, a fellow at the American Enterprise Institute, said that Stone's claim would be a lot more convincing if Stone would contribute to charity the multimillion-dollar profits the movie earned.

Producer Rick Rubin said his responsibility is to "support great art." "The arts reflect what is going on in our culture," he said, and that is why there is so much violence in the media. But the task of documenting what exists is journalism, not art. Art requires the expression to allow us to see the everyday in a new way or to increase our range of emotional reaction.

There is a difference between art and artificiality. Art requires creativity to bring forth the essence of human existence. Creativity is what makes real people interesting and real situations compelling. This is what makes the great artists great. In contrast, there are the technicians who execute minor variations on a formula. Those variations do not require any artistic ability or much creativity. This is why *NYPD Blue* is art and *Walker, Texas Ranger* is artificial. The producers of *Walker, Texas Ranger* put stereotypical characters in one-dimensional situations in order to elicit a narrow set of emotions (outrage against the villains and satisfying revenge). In contrast, the producers of *NYPD Blue* continue to develop their characters in many dimensions, tell stories about crimes from many points of view and narrative arcs, show the unfolding of consequences to the police as well as to the victims and perpetrators, and evoke a very wide range of emotions in viewers.

We need to keep clear the distinction between freedom of expression and quality of expression. The public is asking for a more responsible quality of expression from the media industries, and this does not necessarily mean limiting the industry's freedom of expression. For example, Ira Teinowitz (1999) made this point in an *Ad Age* article in which he wrote,

> Those who defend freedom of expression have an obligation to promote quality of expression as well. Defending bad books may be necessary . . . Larry Flynt may have every right to publish *Hustler*, but the world is not necessarily a better place because he does. Readers can refuse to buy it and writers can refuse to write for it without anyone's freedoms being compromised.

Is media violence speech? The fair answer is to say yes, it is. But it is also a commercially marketed product. It is both. To ignore either of these characteristics is faulty. Not all messages of violence in the media are the same in terms of their contributions to the political discourse, to art, or to the risk of negative effects. The important questions then become: (a) to what extent does a particular portrayal qualify as speech—created primarily for the benefit of society? and (b) to what extent does it qualify as a commercial product—manufactured primarily to generate revenues for producers? Some portrayals exhibit qualities of both, but other portrayals are merely commercial products with little value as art or to help us think more broadly or compellingly about political or religious issues.

BATTLEGROUNDS

Whenever the federal government considers imposing regulations on the presentation of violence in the media, a strong opposing force fights back. Over the past 60 years, this battle has been fought many times, and the battleground has shifted from focusing on the public's interest, to morality, and now to product liability. The different battlegrounds provide critics with different rationales that would allow the federal government to remove violence from the category of protected speech. Thus far, the media have been the superior force in each of these battlegrounds.

As for television, the first battleground was the public's interest. The 1934 Communications Act granted broadcasters free access to the airwaves in return for the broadcasters' promises that they would provide programming in the public interest. However, the idea of public interest has many different definitions, and there has been little agreement as to what constitutes the public interest. Broadcasters argue from a marketing perspective, claiming that the public interest is defined by how people spend their time and what they buy in the marketplace. Because the public spends a lot of time watching media violence and buying violent CDs, violent video games, and tickets to violent movies, the public is therefore interested in violence.

In contrast, the government sees its role as a caretaker of what is best for the public, and this suggests the need for a very different kind of programming. This difference is rather like parents trying to guide a child's selection of foods at a restaurant. The parents would pick out foods low in fat and high in nutrients, such as green, leafy vegetables, but the child is more interested in desserts and if forced to eat vegetables would prefer french-fried potatoes and tomato ketchup.

In 1961 Newton Minow, then head of the FCC, said, "To those few broadcasters who would evade the nation's needs and cry 'Censorship! Oh where will it end?' there can only be one answer: Responsibility—when will it begin?" He reasoned that when broadcasters are granted a license by the federal government, they must accept the responsibility to serve the public trust.

Over time, the battleground shifted to morality. As religious leaders became involved, the issue became avoiding violence—along with sex and bad language—because these story elements should be offensive to the moral code of religious people. The Judeo-Christian code of morality is based on the principle idea of "Do unto others as you would have others do unto you" and has as a commandment "Thou shalt not kill." Therefore, when television shows constantly dwell on people mistreating each other and even the violation of this commandment, something must be done.

The problem with using morality as a battleground is that there are many different moralities in play in the American culture. Furthermore, moralities are rules set by religious bodies, and the First Amendment guarantees freedom of religious expression. So with all moralities protected, no one morality could be used as a standard to judge the acceptability of portrayals.

The battleground is now shifting into product liability. Media messages are now being regarded less as speech that adds variety to our information base or uplifts us with artistic, challenging images. Instead, they are being regarded as products that are marketed primarily for profit. If these entertainment messages are commercial products, then perhaps they need to be held to the same expectations as other commercial products are. Manufacturers of defective products that cause harm to their users are held accountable. Some major media companies are currently being sued on these grounds for the influence of their violent content on the minds of adolescents who emulated the content and killed fellow classmates or others.

Over the years, some victims of real-world violent acts that may have been stimulated by media violence have been suing the producers of particular violent movies. As is traditional, the producers call the claims silly and cite their First Amendment rights to make the movies they choose. However, recently some plaintiffs in these cases have been claiming that the producers have made defective products that have resulted in their harm, so they are seeking remedies from those producers.

The family of a Louisiana woman who was left a quadriplegic after being shot during a convenience store robbery filed a lawsuit against Warner Brothers and producer Oliver Stone. The suit claims the assailants were inspired to embark on a crime spree after repeated viewings of Stone's 1994 film *Natural Born Killers* (Stern, 1999a). Best-selling author of courtroom thrillers John Grisham suggested that Stone and Time Warner be subject to a new kind of charge: a product liability suit alleging that the film was not speech but a product that had caused injury, just like breast implants or cigarettes (Douglas, 1999).

Grisham's claim was characterized as "preposterous" and "a nonstarter" by Martin Garbus, a noted First Amendment attorney. At stake here is whether a movie like *Natural Born Killers* is the kind of speech that lacks First Amendment protection. The plaintiffs are hoping to show that Stone's film falls into the category of unprotected speech as outlined in *Brandenburg v. Ohio* (1969). The requirements for meeting the Brandenburg exception are high: Plaintiffs must prove that the speech was intended to produce "imminent lawless action" and that the producers of the speech knew that the speech was indeed likely to produce such behavior. "It is impossible to believe that the plaintiffs will discover anything that will prove that Stone wanted to produce lawlessness," notes First Amendment authority Floyd Abrams. Joseph Simpson admits that Stone "is never going to admit that he intended to cause these murders." But Simpson cites a quote from the *New York Times* in 1996 in which Stone said "the most pacifistic people in the world said they came out of this movie and wanted to kill somebody." In other words, says Simpson, "it looks like he knew people would kill" after seeing the film (Douglas, 1999). In 1999, the U.S. Supreme Court cleared the way for a lawsuit to proceed against Warner Brothers and producer Oliver Stone (Stern, 1999a).

A lawsuit was filed in Paducah, Kentucky, against several major entertainment companies including Time Warner, Seagram, and Sony. The suit alleges that movies and video games produced by the defendants had a direct role in inciting 14-year-old Michael Carneal to go on a deadly shooting spree at his school. Carneal says he was inspired by New Line's film *Basketball Diaries.* In that movie, a character played by Leonardo DiCaprio fantasizes about shooting up his high school, including students and teachers.

A suit was filed against Paladin Press, publisher of a self-help book entitled *Hit Man: A Technical Manual for Independent Contractors,* which is a manual on how to kill someone. The suit alleged that the manual provided crucial instructions to James Perry, who was hired by Lawrence Horn to kill three people: Horn's ex-wife, their 8-year-old paraplegic son, and his nurse. At Perry's trial, prosecutors itemized 22 points of similarity between the book and the crime (Douglas, 1999). The Paladin case is quite different from that against *Natural Born Killers,* but both try to make causal connections between speech and subsequent criminal behavior.

Another example of a product liability approach is a lawsuit filed by the parents of a 15-year-old girl, Elyse Phaler, naming as defendants the heavy metal band Slayer and its Sony-financed American Recording label. The girl was stalked, then choked, stabbed, killed, and raped by three teenage boys who said they were obsessed with the rock group Slayer, whose lyrics depict acts of devil worship, human sacrifice, and necrophilia. The boys were convicted of murder and are serving long prison terms. The suit claims that the band's lyrics inspired the three teenage boys to torture and kill the plaintiffs' daughter. It claims that the defendants unlawfully marketed and distributed harmful and obscene products to minors. The suit claims that Slayer's lyrics served as an instructional manual for disturbed adolescent fans to behave violently. Sony hired the noted free speech attorney Floyd Abrams to argue that Slayer's music is protected by the First Amendment. Elyse Phaler's father remarked,

> This case isn't about art. It's about marketing. Slayer and others in the industry have developed sophisticated strategies to sell death metal music to adolescent boys. They don't care whether the violent, misogynistic message in these lyrics causes children to do harmful things. They couldn't care less what the fans did to our daughter. All they care about is money. (quoted in Philips, 2001, p. C7)

Even governments are getting involved with filing lawsuits. For example, in June 2000, New York City filed a lawsuit against the firearms industry, joining 30 other cities and counties that have sued gun makers. The suit alleges that gun makers have created a public nuisance by selling products that eventually are used to commit crimes ("New York City Plans," 2000).

Thus far the product safety arena has not been a fruitful one for critics of media violence. As of this writing, none of these lawsuits has been successful. The difficulty in making the case for product liability is linking particular media products with harmful consequences. It is rather like a person with health problems and on several medications who eats dinner at three restaurants, suffers what he or she believes is food poisoning, and then wants to sue one of the restaurants. To make such a case the person would have to present convincing evidence that the sickness was not a result of prior ill health or medications; also, he or she would have to demonstrate that the bad food was served at the restaurant being sued and neither of the other two. This is a very difficult case to make. For this reason, the product liability battleground is not as useful an arena as a public health perspective would provide. With a public health foundation for an argument of harm, the focus on negative consequences are on the society and not on any particular individual. That is, we know that the context and frequency of violence being pumped out of the media businesses and into our culture raise the risk of harm for everyone. The public health perspective can be supported by the body of scientific evidence that clearly shows that exposure to media violence increases the risks of all sorts of negative effects to large aggregates of people. The limitation of this evidence is that it focuses on patterns rather than risks to individuals, that is, we can predict the probability of negative effects' occurring in the aggregate, but we cannot know which individuals will experience those effects. When we take a broader, cultural view, we can work to reduce the risk for everyone, and when we all accept the idea that reducing the risk for all people is more important than protecting the marketing of harmful products by the media, we can be comfortable with the idea that violence should not be automatically assumed to be protected speech.

In April 2001 three senators introduced the Media Marketing Accountability Act, which would hold entertainment companies liable for their own voluntary marketing guidelines. By the summer of 2001, the House introduced its version of the bill, and Congress began holding hearings. The proposed bill would hold companies accountable for following their self-proclaimed marketing guidelines. For example, a company that claimed it did not market violence to children but then was found to do so would be fined up to $11,000 per day. The backlash from producers was swift and strong, again claiming First Amendment protection. As a result Jack Valenti, president of the MPAA, said that if Congress were to pass this bill, he would advise his industry to dismantle the film ratings system. The Recording Industry Association of America withdrew its promised marketing guidelines system because it feared being held accountable for it (Garvey, 2001b).

CONCLUSIONS

The First Amendment has a populist foundation. It was designed to prevent a few people in power from depriving the general population from the full spectrum of ideas, especially those expressions that may be critical of those in power. As such, it says that the public's well-being is far more important than protecting the power of a few. The irony in media programmers' using the First Amendment as a shield is that they are in essence saying that the power (to market products and make money) of those few people is far more important than the well-being of the entire public.

The difference between the industry and the public is the perspective from which the two groups view what speech is and what protections it should be afforded. The public views the freedom as a window that should be opened as wide as possible to let in more speech, not less. Public criticism of media violence is really a call for the industry to provide more information in the form of program labels and to be more creative by presenting alternatives to violence.

In contrast, the media industries regard the freedom as a shield to protect the status quo. They label criticism as calls for censorship in an attempt to frame the debate in a way to force the public to allow the continuation of violence as a lesser evil than the more horrible alternative of eliminating the right of free expression.

Clearly producers want speech to be free for them and expensive for us. For the public, this expense is both on the front end (in terms of the price of admissions and subscriptions) as well as on the back end (in terms of paying for the harm to society). The industry treats the First Amendment more as a shield than an open window. To the people in the industry, freedom of speech does not mean the opening up of expression. To the contrary, it means freedom to control expression to a narrow realm of storytelling and the freedom to provide no information in the form of labeling.

The debate about media violence needs to be treated in a more respectful fashion than the simpleminded fear over censorship. We need to think about the media businesses' claim that they have a right not to speak, that is, not to provide information about their products. We need to think about the extent to which violence in the media is speech designed to broaden the knowledge of the public and not a packaged product designed to deepen the pockets of a profit-oriented industry. We need to balance the industry's right to transmit its messages freely against the potential harm those expressions may be creating throughout society.

I am not arguing for censorship. I abhor that. The point I am trying to make is that making allegations of censorship is a very weak argument for defending the current state of violence in the media. It has a grain of truth to it, but the industry should be less duplicitous and defend itself on something more honest, such as an economic argument.

ELEVEN

MYTH 10

The rating systems and V-chip will help solve the problem.

———•———

E ver since televisions became a staple in American living rooms, the public has been pressuring Congress and the FCC to do something about the violence pouring into their homes every day. Congress has been holding hearings on this complaint for over 50 years but doing very little to effect a remedy—or even a change. There have been a few instances of Congress pressuring the industry to alter some of its practices, but these have been largely unsuccessful. Then in 1996, the V-chip (for "violence chip") was swept into law on the coattails of the Telecommunications Act. Many hail this as a major breakthrough in the problem of media violence. I am not one of them. In fact, I think this is a major failure, as I will show in the following analysis of this myth.

BUILDING TOWARD THE V-CHIP

Throughout the past decade, both Congress and the public grew more fixated on a ratings system as a solution to the problem of media violence, while alternative proposals were falling by the wayside. For example, in the early

1990s, Congress was considering as many as 10 bills dealing with violence on television. These bills were generally one of three types: family viewing hour, ratings system, and blocking devices.

Family Viewing Hours

One set of proposals put forth since congressional debates began in the 1950s is the idea of a "safe harbor," a time when programming would be appropriate for the entire family. This type of legislation is designed to prohibit the airing of violent content during hours when children are reasonably likely to make up a substantial portion of the audience ("Violence on Television," 1993). The NAB Broadcast Code contained such a restriction until its abandonment in 1988 ("Voices Against Violence," 1994), so throughout the 1990s many people were working to get the programmers to create safe harbors or violence-free periods of the day when children are most likely to be viewing.

On the surface the safe harbor, or "family viewing hours," appears to be a good idea. But this is an unworkable proposal, because there is no time when children are not viewing television in large numbers. For example, 9 p.m. is usually regarded as a safe harbor border, that is, it is assumed that children drop out of the prime-time audience at 9 p.m. Thus it is safe to program exclusively for adults at 9 p.m. Apparently the supporters of this proposal do not have children, or if they do, their children are in the minority as far as bedtime. When we look at the data from the A. C. Nielsen Company, we see that among children 2 to 11 years of age, there is a drop at 9 p.m., but that drop does not mean that children disappear from the viewing audience. The drop is from 12 million to 10.8 million children. Does a 12% shrinkage in the size of the children's audience qualify as a signal to start the safe harbor period? I think not. Young children are viewing in large numbers during all day-parts. At 11 p.m., when prime time is over, there are still 3.2 million children viewing television; this figure is even higher than the 3.0 million adolescents (13 to 17) viewing at this same time. How small does the children's audience need to get before we can consider the harbor safe for violence? Any number but zero would be an arbitrary—and indefensible—answer to this question. It is disingenuous to embark on a quest to protect children from risk and then to be satisfied with a proposal that ignores the risk to more than 10 million children.

Ratings and Report Cards

There were two notable bills designed to provide viewers with information about violent content on television. One measure, the Children's Television Violence Protection Act of 1993, would have required the broadcast of advisory messages before violent programs (with the exception of shows aired from 11 p.m. to 6 a.m.). The second bill, the Television Violence Report Card Act of 1995, would have required programs to be rated for violent content so that broadcasters and advertisers may be included in public reports on televised violence ("Violence on Television," 1993). Neither of these bills was passed, because attention shifted toward a more technological "solution"—blocking devices.

Blocking Devices

Several bills sponsored by Rep. Edward Markey and Sen. Kent Conrad (among others) called for mandatory installation on all sets of a so-called V-chip, which would use the vertical blanking interval portion of a TV signal to transmit program information to viewers' homes. With this technology, viewers could block out violent or other offensive programming. One of these bills was incorporated into the Telecommunications Competition and Deregulation Act, which was passed in 1996. Part of that law required that all television sets with screen sizes of 13 inches or larger must have the V-chip technology if they were to be sold in the United States beginning January 1, 2000. The passage of the law was hailed as a major victory in the war against media violence.

V-CHIP SOFTWARE PROBLEMS

The V-chip is only a piece of hardware. In order to work at all, it needs to be programmed with information about the programs to be aired. In order to work well, it needs to be programmed with information that is accurate, detailed, and keyed to the risks of harm to the viewers.

There are some significant challenges to developing good software for the V-chip. In rising to those challenges, we have gotten off to a very poor start, particularly in five areas. First, the industry was allowed to develop its own system. Second, the system that the industry designed provides as little information to viewers as possible. Third, the industry was permitted to assign ratings to its own programs and to do so with no oversight. Fourth, the ratings are misapplied, so that two very different shows can get the same rating. And fifth, most people do not understand the ratings, nor do they use them. This set of problems is characterized by George Gerbner with the following analogy: "It's like the major polluters saying 'we shall continue our profitable discharge into the common cultural environment, but don't worry we'll also sell you gas masks to protect your children and have a free choice!'" (Martin, 1998, p. 7).

Programmers Develop Ratings System

The first barrier in the way of a meaningful solution was erected when Congress allowed the television programmers to develop their own ratings system. In order to circumvent the industry objections to the V-chip, Congress left it up to the television networks to establish their own rating system and to put it in place by January 1997. From a political point of view, this was a success. Although many people in the industry complained and dragged their feet, almost everyone got on board by 1997 (one exception was NBC).

From a problem-solution point of view, this concession to the industry was not a success. The process the television industry used to develop its own ratings system was highly controlled by industry insiders, thus ensuring that the resulting system would be crafted primarily for the industry's benefit. Programmers began this process by putting together an advisory board headed by Jack Valenti, president of the MPAA and one of the designers of the motion picture rating system.

The advisory board at first appeared to be concerned about getting input from many concerned parties. Although the board went through the motions of talking to people outside the industry, there is no evidence that they were influenced by any of the opinions that the industry did not already hold. For example, Valenti said he talked to some members of the clergy

> to tell them that when we have something that seems to be reasonable by way of a ratings system, we'll run it by them. But we will not be running it by them for veto purposes. We're going to keep this within the television industry. (quoted in Biddle, 1996, p. 59)

In any event, this process was a public relations success: The industry portrayed itself as acting very responsibly even in the face of being manipulated by an oppressive federal government.

The ratings system that was developed for television was based on—and looks very similar to—the MPAA ratings system. The developers knew that the MPAA ratings system was palatable to the film industry and that producers knew how to manipulate the ratings for marketing advantages.

The MPAA system was established in 1968 to ward off government intervention. It started with four categories (G, PG, R, and X); in 1984, PG-13 was added. In 1990, the X designation was changed to NC-17. The MPAA ratings are assigned by a ratings board consisting of parents in the Los Angeles area. The members of this board, whose names are kept secret, are appointed by the film industry. Valenti explains, "I don't have any child behavioral experts on that panel. I just want ordinary people." Although standards are arbitrary and often unclear, illicit drug use automatically warrants a PG-13, as does a single sexually derived obscenity, and if the obscene word is used in a sexual context, it warrants an R (Morris & Silver, 1999).

The television ratings advisory board began with the MPAA system and made some minor adaptations by moving to six age-based categories: two for children (TV-Y and TV-Y7) and four for general audiences (TV-G, TV-PG, TV-14, and TV-MA) (see Table 11.1). The television industry grudgingly agreed to this rating system, and it was first instituted in January 1997 (Mifflin, 1998).

Although Valenti headed the development of the TV ratings system, he said he did not want the television system to resemble too closely the MPAA system of G, PG, PG-13, R, and NC-17. His reasoning was not that the content in television is different from content in movies and therefore two different systems are warranted. Instead, Valenti said, "I don't want to diminish their effectiveness as ratings for motion pictures, nor would I want to diminish their effectiveness on television" by making them interchangeable (Biddle, 1996, p. 59). This is very curious reasoning. Apparently Valenti believes that a certain kind of violent portrayal may be appropriate for a 7-year-old in the movies but not at home, or vice versa.

Immediately, this system was criticized for being an age-based system, not a program content-based system (Cantor, 1998b). The age-based system relies on the assumption that all children of the same age are the same as far as their ability to handle different television content. All parents can recognize

Table 11.1   Television Industry-Developed Program Rating System

---

Age-Based Ratings

TV-Y: Program is designed to be appropriate for all children.

TV-Y7: Program is designed for children age 7 and above.

TV-G: Most parents would find this program suitable for all ages.

TV-PG: Program contains materials that parents may find unsuitable for younger children.

TV-14: This program contains some material that parents would find unsuitable for children under 14 years of age.

TV-MA: This program is specifically designed to be viewed by adults and therefore may be unsuitable for children under 17.

Content-Based Ratings

FV: Fantasy violence in children's programs

V: Violence

S: Sex

L: Coarse language

D: Sexual dialogue and innuendo

---

this as a faulty assumption. To this criticism the industry responds that the age ratings are meant to be suggestive, that is, they are merely guidelines that parents must use in their individual families. This is a fair response to the criticism. But this then leads to the question: If the age-based ratings are only suggestive, where do parents get the rest of the information they need to make good decisions? Clearly parents need more information about the content in the shows.

In response to the criticism, the industry group amended the rating system nine months after their initial adoption to add some information about the content of their rated programs. The revisions were essentially five letter ratings (FV, V, S, L, and D) to indicate whether the programs contained violence, sexual situations, or bad language (see Table 11.1). Although this system appears to provide information about the content of programs, that information is almost meaningless. The ratings are categorical and provide no sense of the extent of negative elements. For example, a rating of V means there is some violence in the program, but that could be 1 act or 60 acts—there is no way to tell from the rating of V. More important, the content ratings are missing a sense of context. A program marked with a V could be very harmful to viewers (i.e., containing violence that is glamorized, sanitized, and trivialized), or it could teach valuable lessons (i.e., violence is portrayed with a highly remorseful perpetrator and victims in great physical as well as emotional harm). Risk of harmful effects to viewers lies in the context of the portrayals—that is, where viewers construct their meaning—but the people who developed the television ratings system have been unwilling to provide meaningful information to people who want to make good choices about whether to watch a violent program.

System Is Designed to Provide as Little Information as Possible

The second of the problems with the V-chip system is that the system developed by the networks is designed to provide viewers with very little information through ambiguous labeling. The low information content of the symbols allows the programmers to present the ratings in a harmless (to the show) manner. Furthermore, if programmers are clever, they can manipulate certain symbols to achieve a "forbidden fruit" kind of attraction. Prohibiting children and adolescents from doing something often makes them regard that something as highly attractive. Research clearly shows that the more restrictive movie ratings entice many children to seek out media content that is labeled as being inappropriate for their age group (Cantor & Harrison, 1996). For example, when a movie is rated R, many children find the movie more attractive than if that same movie were rated G.

Are programmers using this information about forbidden fruit attractiveness to their advantage? It is a little early to determine whether this is the case with television, but there are critics who argue that this is the case with film. These critics argue that the film ratings are used more as a marketing tool than as a sincere attempt to convey good information to the public. For example, Andrews (1995) contends that systems such as the MPAA ratings for film are often used to generate marketing publicity for films with questionable content. Also, the well-known film critic Roger Ebert says that the ratings do not help parents shield children from objectionable material but instead allow more sex and violence than many 17-year-olds should see.

It is important to note that researchers have found that labeling the content does not create a similar forbidden fruit attraction (Cantor & Harrison, 1996). Although labeling a movie with an R or NC-17 makes the movie more attractive to adolescents, the labeling of that same movie with a V for violence does not increase attractiveness. So age ratings can be manipulated to attract more viewers, but content information can only scare viewers away. This is a reason why the programmers have accepted the age-based ratings and resisted using the content information ratings.

Also, the age-based system requires the raters, who are not experts in child development, to make important judgments about the appropriateness of certain shows for different age levels of viewers. However, not all people develop their understanding of stories and their experience with life at exactly the same age. Not all 12-year-olds are the same. Also, not all households are the same. Some have a higher tolerance for violence but no tolerance for sex or bad language. When the ratings system does not provide a description of the content, it is impossible for parents to make an informed decision.

MPAA president Jack Valenti admits that the ratings system is flawed but chooses not to change it, because, he says, "we can't draw the lines that precise" (Morris & Silver, 1999). But Valenti, as well as critics, are missing the point. The system is flawed *not* because the MPAA is unable to draw more precise lines between age groups but because the MPAA is not providing more information about content. Consumers do not want the MPAA system to draw more age-based lines or to defend their lines as being nonarbitrary. The public wants more information so that individuals can draw their own lines. My child might not be ready for a PG-13 movie when she is 13 or even 14, but your child might be ready at age 11. How can we tell? We need to use the information we have about our children and put that together with information about television programs in order to make informed decisions. In surveys, parents continually say they prefer ratings that give information about content over those that provide age recommendations (Cantor, 1998b; Cantor, Stutman, & Duran, 1996). Most parents prefer content labels, that is, they want warnings about whether violence, sex, bad language, and so forth are in particular shows. However, the industry has resisted such labeling. Valenti deflects such criticism by saying that parents need to take more responsibility for what their children see (Morris & Silver, 1999), but the irony here is that parents who are trying to be responsible in making better viewing decisions for their children need more information from programmers. However, the industry's response to such a request is to lay the blame on parents for not being more responsible.

The most serious shortcoming of media businesses' providing little information is that consumers are provided with no sense of risk. Even when networks agree to label their violent programs with a V, people have no way of knowing if that means one act or wall-to-wall violence. Also, no distinction is made between a show that portrays violence in a morality play and those shows that portray it as a glamorous and successful way of solving problems. Recall from Myth 9 that the context of the portrayal is much more important than the frequency when trying to understand how harmful the exposure to particular violent occurrences might be.

Let's consider the different options available to people who are entrusted with labeling programs (see Table 11.2). For purposes of keeping the illustration simple, I have organized this into five types. Notice that as we go from Type 1 (no labeling) to Type 5 (risk ratings) the benefits to viewers greatly increase, but the cost of the system also goes up. Also, as we move up the types, the program providers lose control over the ratings. This is why it has been such a struggle to go from Type 1 to Type 2 and also why there is little hope at this time that there will be any further progress to higher types.

Programmers Assign Ratings to Their Own Programs

Only the programmers themselves are permitted to give their own shows the ratings. To most readers, this shortcoming is intuitively obvious. It is putting the fox in charge of guarding the henhouse. In a public opinion poll taken at the end of the first year of the new program ratings systems, parents were found to be very skeptical of the networks' providing useful information they can use to guide the viewing of their children (Jones, 1998).

Industry insiders defended the application of their system by saying that all the networks had their own broadcast standards and practices departments and that they had worked well in the past (Biddle, 1996). "We've had a very productive standards and practices department," said Martin Franks, senior vice president at CBS. He continued, "This is a point we've been trying to make for five years. . . . We have producers bitching and moaning about what cuts they have to make. We're looking at each script anyway." Franks argues that the very fact that censors approve a given episode suggests its suitability for general audiences. He also points out that the networks have been placing warnings of violence in front of certain programs for years. For example, CBS occasionally aired warnings about violence before episodes of *Walker, Texas Ranger,* and ABC airs a sober warning that is "this is an adult drama" before each episode of *NYPD Blue.*

Table 11.2   Different Types of Media Content Labeling Systems

Type 1: No Labeling

Advantage: This requires no effort from program providers.
Disadvantages:

- Consumers have no way to know the violent content of a program ahead of viewing unless they can find a critic who has previewed the program and written a detailed account of it.
- If there are a lot of critical reviews of shows published in local newspapers and magazines, then there is a concern about uniformity in judgments across different critics reviewing different shows.

Type 2: Age-Based Labeling

Advantages:

- Program providers get credit for labeling while providing as little information as possible.
- Program providers can use "forbidden fruit" labels to attract larger audiences.
- These are relatively easy for viewers to understand, because they are already used to the system from the MPAA.

Disadvantages:

- Labelers must make two very sophisticated judgments: (a) content judgments about the level of maturity needed for someone to understand, appreciate, and not be adversely affected; and (b) viewer judgments about how people of different age groupings would process the information and be affected by it.
- Not all people in a certain age group are the same in terms of maturity or risk of negative effect. Many 13-year-olds are able to handle PG-14 shows, whereas many 14-year-olds are not.

Type 3: Categorical Content Labeling

Advantage: More information is provided to viewers and their parents.

Disadvantage: The system is categorical, that is, if a show has violence it gets a V, and some V shows can be wall-to-wall violence, whereas others present only one act.

(Continued)

Table 11.2 Continued

Type 4: Content Synopsis

Advantage: This provides lots of information so viewers can make more informed
decisions.

Disadvantage: This system is very labor intensive.

Type 5: Risk Ratings

Advantage: This type of system puts the focus on the meaning of violence portrayed
and how that meaning can change the probability of harming viewers.

Disadvantage: We do not have enough research findings at the present time to make
good risk ratings.

What Franks fails to address is that if the broadcast standards and practices departments have been doing their jobs well in the eyes of the public,
why is there so much criticism? Of course, it is possible that the standards and
practices departments *have* been screening out unacceptable portrayals of violence. Because we never see what is screened out, we must take it on faith that
the networks are in fact toning down violent content. So let's give them credit
for the situation's not being worse, but we must also give them the blame for
the situation's being as bad as it is.

Not all television networks have standards and practices departments.
UPN, which has been a major television network since 1995, does not have a
department or even a single person whose primary job is to monitor content
and identify material that may be unsuitable to present. Instead, this function
is shared by Adam Ware, the chief operating officer, and David England, the
chief financial officer (Stanley, 2001). This may be one reason why studies
have shown that UPN is usually ranked first in terms of rates of objectionable
material. For example, a study by the Parents Television Council found 18.1
acts of objectionable material per hour on UPN; this was much higher than the
rates on any of the other broadcast networks (Garvey, 2001a).

The locus of the problem with allowing the networks to rate their own
programs is not with whether they have a broadcast standards department but
instead with their motives. Because programmers have a very different motive
than do consumers, it is important that an independent body assign ratings
so that one group's motives do not supercede the motives of the other. The
motive of the programmers is to use the ratings to increase audience size.

From the programmers' perspective, when ratings can be used to increase audience size (such as attracting new viewers through a forbidden fruit effect), they are useful, but if the program labeling highlights risk to viewers, this might have the effect of scaring potential viewers away, and this is bad for programmers.

Parents who try to make responsible decisions about their children's viewing are not asking for advertising or for "forbidden fruit" temptation to lure their children; instead, these parents want enough information about the upcoming programming so they can assess the degree to which their own children might be at risk from viewing the program. If consumers already had this information or if they could get reliable information from other sources, there would be no reason to ask for it. But such information does not exist for television shows; the situation is different with theatrical films: People can read a variety of reviews from their most trusted critics to help them make the decision about whether to see the movie. The only reviews available about television shows appear after the shows have already been broadcast, and then the review is more about the series than about a particular episode.

The media industries have a very different perspective on the V-chip. Programmers do not want to provide information about their shows *unless they can control that information in order to attract large audiences to their programs.* The television networks are highly competitive businesses whose primary purpose is to maximize profits and thus increase the value of their businesses. Their motivation is to protect themselves, not the viewers. If their motivation were to protect viewers, they would be making very different deci-sions about what gets screened out. In fact, if they were primarily concerned with the welfare of their audiences, they would be much more likely to keep highly graphic content—even though it has a high probability of offending many viewers—because they would be concerned that sanitizing the violence would increase the risk of desensitizing viewers (see Myth 9).

Ratings Are Misapplied

When we analyze the content of certain films or television shows and then look at their ratings, several other problems clearly emerge that indicate that the ratings are not being applied in a uniform or meaningful manner. There are examples of very different shows being given the same rating as well as very similar shows being assigned different ratings. For example, Roger Ebert points out that a film with occasional profanity such as *Limbo* received an R rating—the same rating as *8mm,* a film about the hyperviolent world of snuff films. Ebert complains that the R rating covers too much territory and has therefore lost its meaning.

Joe Zanger, managing editor of a Web site (pg14.com) and newsletter aimed at giving parents information on choosing movies, says the problem with the ratings system is that the line between R and PG-13 has become "hopelessly blurred." Zanger cites *The First Wives' Club* as an example. "The theme of that movie was divorce and revenge. That's pretty grown-up stuff. But that film pulled a PG rating. Not even PG-13!" (Oldenburg & Snider, 1999, p. 1D).

Some films are clearly violent but are still marketed as family entertainment. For example, within two weeks of the release of the movie *Karate Kid,* a violent film that was rated as family fare, pediatricians had seen numerous children who were injured by their playmates while imitating the action portrayed in that film (Robb, 1991).

Just because a film has a G rating does not mean it is suitable for all ages. Movie ratings typically don't rate for fear. Something might be rated G and produce a lot of fear for kids. Accordingly, KidScore has warnings on such popular fare as *The Hunchback of Notre Dame,* because it presents some fantasy violence, illegal and harmful acts, and scenes that have the ability to cause fear. KidScore warns that this video should be viewed with caution by young children. Likewise, KidScore warns parents about *Toy Story,* again because of the nature of the violence as having the ability to scare young children (Churnin, 1998).

In a study published in the *Journal of the American Medical Association,* Fumie Yokota and Kimberly Thompson (2000) reported the results of an analysis of all G-rated feature films released in theaters between 1937 and 1999. They found at least one act of violence in all films, and these acts of violence consumed anywhere from 6 seconds to 24 minutes, with the duration getting longer in more recent films. Furthermore, the majority of the violence (55%) depicted good characters using violence as a successful means of dueling with the bad characters. Also, they found that in G-rated animated films in 1940, there was an average of 6 minutes of violence per movie, and by 2000 there were 11 minutes per movie (Morris, 2000).

The use of the television ratings system earned a mixed grade in an analysis of the television networks' revised ratings system one year after it was implemented. The good news was that the age-based ratings were generally applied fairly (Kunkel et al., 1998). As for the age-based ratings, among all TV-G-rated shows, 20% contained violence, but usually the level of intensity was low, and there were an average of only two acts of violence per show. As for the TV-PG shows, violence was found in 55% of them. In the TV-14 programs, 70% contained violence.

The bad news was that the content information was largely missing. For example, only 21% of the shows with violence were marked with a V, and only 19% of children's shows with fantasy violence got an FV rating (Kunkel et al., 1998). Remember that it is the content ratings that are more valuable to TV viewers and risky for the networks.

Most People Do Not Understand or Use the V-Chip

Do people, especially parents, use the new system? The answer is no. The ratings system began in January 1997. In May 1998, the Kaiser Family Foundation commissioned a survey to assess the reaction of parents to the age-based and content-based programming warnings. This was after the system had been operational for 16 months. The survey found that a little more than half (54%) of the parents surveyed reported they at least sometimes used the industry-imposed TV content ratings to help them decide what their children should watch. A little less than half (46%) said they pay scant or no attention to the warnings printed in the *TV Guide* listings and briefly superimposed on the upper lefthand corner of the TV screen. A companion survey of children ages 10 to 17 reported that just over one third of them (36%) said they decided not to watch a program based on its rating, for reasons ranging from avoiding the wrath of parents to avoiding the shame of watching a program aimed at younger children. Later study by the Kaiser Foundation found that only 28% of parents said they use the television ratings regularly, and only 17% of parents with a V-chip in their television said they program it (Johnson, 2001). Also, parents in the poll said the ratings often are confusing, and their 15-second duration at the beginning of a program is not long enough (Jones, 1998). Also, according to a 1998 poll by the Annenberg Public Policy Center, only a small percentage of parents understood and used the onscreen ratings that accompany TV shows (Barnhart, 1999).

A large part of the problem is that parents do not understand what the ratings are or what they mean. For example, in a Kaiser-funded study, Dale

Kunkel and his colleagues (1998) found that 61% of parents who used the ratings believed that shows that are rated TV-Y are not supposed to contain any violence, but an analysis of those shows revealed that 55% did in fact contain violence.

Another problem is that parents find that programming the V-chip is not simple, so many parents are put off by the task. Even experts sometimes have trouble. At a Senate committee hearing, one manufacturing executive was unable to successfully demonstrate the technology (Mundy, 1995).

Parents need to be taught how to program the hardware of the V-chip and how to understand what the ratings mean. Where were parents supposed to go to get the needed information? They were supposed to get the information from broadcasters themselves. When the V-chip legislation was enacted, the commercial television networks agreed to educate users by presenting public service announcements (PSAs) in their programming to explain the rating codes. But by the summer of 2000, a survey found that 39% of parents still had never even heard of the V-chip. It appears that this problem of lack of knowledge in the public can be traced to broadcasters' not following through on their mandate to educate the public. From January 2000 to August, the big four commercial television networks had run a combined total of only 59 PSAs on the V-chip, and 54 of these (92%) were run by CBS. That means that CBS ran its PSA about twice each week; Fox and NBC aired their PSAs once every 15 weeks; and ABC aired its PSA only once in the 30-week period (FCC, 2000). This poor performance from the commercial networks prompted FCC Commissioner Gloria Tristani to question the degree of commitment the networks have to educating their viewers about their system. During that 30-week period, each of the networks scheduled more than 30,000 30-second slots (called avails) for ads, program promos, and PSAs. In this more than 1,000 hours of avails, less than 30 minutes of time total across the four networks was set aside for V-chip education. This prompted Tristani to send a letter to the major broadcast networks asking them to do more in educating the public about the V-chip and the ratings systems.

Many people in the industry are satisfied with the ratings system, and they shift the burden of responsibility back on to parents. For example, Maryann Grasso, vice president and executive director of the National Association of Theater Owners, says that the way to improve the current system of movie ratings "is for parents to take a strong position with their kids and say, 'I don't want you to see this movie'" (Oldenburg & Snider, 1999, p. 1D). Also, director

Barry Sonnenfeld (*Men in Black* and *Wild, Wild West*) thinks that the existing rating system is sufficient. "It lets parents and children know what kind of movie they are seeing. No more is necessary," he says (Oldenburg & Snider, p. 1D).

Valenti argues that it is purely the fault of parents if the MPAA system is not working well. "We can't have policemen with bayoneted guns in front of every household [to get them to follow the ratings]," Valenti says. Of course Valenti can't control the parents of America. But it also appears that Valenti has no control over the people who work in his own industry. A recent FTC report revealed that children are frequently able to buy tickets to R-rated movies without parental accompaniment. The FTC survey found that half the movie theaters admitted children ages 13 to 16 to R-rated films, even when they were not accompanied by an adult. Also, 85% of the time children 13 to 16 who were unaccompanied by an adult were able to buy both explicit recordings and electronic games that were rated M (mature) (FTC, 2000, p. 1).

Valenti also said, "We can only put the ratings out there—that is the most we can do in a democratic society." Again Valenti misses the point. There are good labeling systems that have lots of information about potentially harmful content in movies, and there are poor systems that are based on intuitive judgments made by people on a secret board that believe all 12-year-olds are the same and that all 13-year-olds are much more mature than all 12-year-olds. Some systems are simply more useful than others. It is disingenuous to provide parents with a weak system and then blame those parents for not using the system more, especially when the industry has done so little to follow through on its promise to educate the public about the V-chip and the ratings.

CONCLUSIONS

It is a myth that the V-chip and its program ratings system will help solve the problem of media violence. Television programmers have kept control of the development and use of the system, so it is not surprising that the system is crafted to serve their needs—not the needs of the viewers. Recall that the ratings are not assigned to shows by experts who understand the nature of risks to viewers. To the contrary, Valenti brags that ratings for films are assigned by a board that specifically excludes social scientists. Furthermore, ratings of television shows on at least one network are assigned by people primarily concerned by the company's finances, not the well-being of the viewers the company is affecting.

Furthermore, programmers have done little to educate the viewing public about how to use the V-chip. As a result, many people are still unaware of this device and how to use it. Also, many people who consider using the system find the age-based categories not very helpful and the content letters confusing. If the ratings system were to evolve into one that provided much more information about the amount and nature of violent content in shows, it would be much more useful. But given the current motives of the television industry, there is little chance that such a system will evolve.

⊰ TWELVE ⊱

MYTH 11

*There is nothing I can do to
make an effect on reducing the problem.*

———•◦•———

Now that you have read this far, you may have become a strong believer in this myth. After all, the problem seems so large and so persistent. But if you accept this last myth, then you give up and become part of the problem. Giving up is a mistake, because giving up will leave you in the dark, where you will continue to accept the myths and therefore will continue to be vulnerable to all the negative effects.

It is also a mistake to expect government to solve the problem. The government can provide forums for discussion and can keep the issue on the public agenda, but the government can do very little to effect meaningful change.

Change must come from individuals. Although you cannot solve the entire problem by yourself, you can make changes in your own life that will make the problem less risky for you and for the people around you. There are some personal strategies you can begin using right now. Also, there are things you can do of a more societal nature—such as working to influence institutions.

PERSONAL ACTION

Become More Media Literate

Movement toward any meaningful solution begins with personal responsibility, and your first responsibility is to get accurate information. This book can help in that task. There are other books you could read. Some of these deal specifically with the problem of media violence (see Table 12.1), and others address the larger issue of media literacy (see Table 12.2). There are also organizations from which you can get more information by visiting their Web sites, calling them, or writing to them (see Table 12.3).

Without a firm grounding in what the real dangers are and how the effects processes work, it is not very helpful to view with other people and expect that you will have many useful things to say other than "Isn't that violence awful?"

Help Others Around You

There are many things you can do to influence the thinking and behavior of others—friends, coworkers, family members, and others. Perhaps the most important "other" people to influence are children, especially if you are a parent. Children are vulnerable to certain negative effects from exposure to media violence because they have less experience with the media, but this does not mean that adults are not also vulnerable (remember Myth 4). So although many of the suggestions articulated in this section come from techniques aimed at helping children, they all can be applied to people of any age.

What should you do to help others? I outline five strategies. One of these strategies is to limit exposure to media violence. Notice that I present this as the fifth—or last—strategy on the list. The other four strategies are much more important and should be tried first, but it is not always possible to do the first four. In that situation, the fifth strategy is the one of last resort.

1. View actively with others. Every set of media literacy guidelines encourages parents to be there when their children are exposed to violent portrayals in the media, but there is more to it than simply being there to hold their hands. Parents must be active. They need to talk to their children and point out certain things during the viewing. The goal of active viewing with children is to make them more aware of what is happening on the screen and more aware of how

(Text continues on page 195)

Table 12.1   Books on Media Violence

Bok, Sissela. (1998). *Mayhem: Violence as public entertainment.* Reading, MA:
Addison-Wesley. (195 pages with endnotes and index)
   Bok traces the public's fascination with violent entertainment from the days
   of the Romans. She provides an overview of the effects that have resulted
   from such exposure, then discusses the dilemma of censorship. Her book
   concludes with some recommendations about what people can do to protect
   themselves from the harmful effects of media violence.

Cantor, Joanne. (1998a). *Mommy, I'm scared: How TV and movies frighten children
and what we can do to protect them.* New York: Harcourt Brace. (249 pages with
notes; no index)
   This is a very readable book written by one of the foremost experts in the
   area of effects of the media on children. Cantor explains the social science
   research in a way that enables readers to use the findings to protect their
   children from unwanted effects. The book builds to an insightful critique of
   the ratings systems currently in use by movies and television. She argues for
   a better ratings system, one that would inform parents about the content of
   the programs rather than simply indicating age levels for which the movies
   may be appropriate.

Cooper, Cynthia A. (1996). *Violence on television: Congressional inquiry, public
criticism and industry response.* New York: University Press of America. (201
pages with index, references, and appendices)
   Cooper traces the history of the public debate on the issue of television
   violence over a 60-year period, focusing primarily on congressional hearings
   as the forum for that debate. She examines how policy was made and not
   made over the past 40 years. She examines policy as the negotiation among
   six participants: the FCC, Congress, the broadcast industry, citizen groups,
   the courts, and presidential administrations.

Glassner, Barry. (1999). *The culture of fear: Why Americans are afraid of the wrong
things.* New York: Basic Books. (276 pages, including 66 pages of endnotes and
index)
   Glassner argues that Americans are fearful of many nonrisky things while
   ignoring the risks of many other things that deserve more attention. He deals
   with the topics of crime, health, plane wrecks, aliens, and others.

(Continued)

Table 12.1 Continued

Grossman, Dave, & DeGaetano, Gloria. (1999). *Stop teaching our kids to kill: A call to action against TV, movie & video game violence.* New York: Crown. (196 pages with index)

> This is a strong indictment of media violence, especially video games, television, and films. The authors present evidence to show that video games in particular are literally teaching children to kill through operant conditioning. Also, the flood of violence is weakening their natural violence "immune system" and thus making them desensitized to the violence around them. The book builds to suggestions about what parents can do and provides a list of resources where they can get help.

Levine, Madeline. (1998). *See no evil: A guide to protecting our children from media violence.* San Francisco: Jossey-Bass. (290 pages with index, notes, and resource directory)

> Written by a child psychologist and mother of three sons, this book presents a good deal of information about what researchers have found out about how exposure to violence in the media affects children. Levine presents strong arguments about how irresponsible the people in the media have been. The book concludes with two chapters about what parents and others can do to protect children from this problem.

Potter, W. James. (1999). *On media violence.* Thousand Oaks, CA: Sage. (304 pages with references and index)

> This is a book written primarily for scholars and researchers. First, I review the set of research on media violence in the areas of content, effects, and theories. Then I present a critical analysis that reconceptualizes the ideas of violence, context, levels of analysis, development, effects, risk, and the industry's perspective. I present a critique of the methodologies used to generate the existing research base. Finally, I synthesize these critical ideas along with the existing literatures to formulate what I call "lineation theory," which provides an explanation for the nature of violent content in the media, why the industry presents such content, how viewers process such content, and how the violent content affects individuals as well as society.

Surette, Ray. (1998). *Media, crime, and criminal justice: Images and realities (2nd ed.).* Belmont, CA: Wadsworth. (318 pages with index)

> Surette argues that the media are a cause of crime and also a means of combating crime. Not only do we learn about crime from the mass media, we also learn how to live with it. He uses a social construction of reality approach to explain how people use information from the media to construct beliefs about the real world.

Table 12.2   Books on Media Literacy

Bianculli, David. (1992). *Teleliteracy: Taking television seriously.* New York:
Continuum. (315 pages with indices)
Bianculli was a TV critic and columnist for 15 years before writing this book,
which is a defense of television. Admitting that 90% of TV content is "crap,"
he nevertheless feels that there is also a great deal of value there. He presents
a manifesto of 10 points, all intended to generate more respect for television.

Neuman, Susan B. (1991). *Literacy in the television age: The myth of the TV effect.*
Norwood, NJ: Ablex. (230 pages)
Neuman treats literacy mainly as a skill needed to understand the printed
word, then she lays out the arguments that television has reduced literacy
because of four reasons: displacement, information processing, short-term
gratification, and interest stimulation. She shows that the empirical evidence
does not support any of these explanations, that is, the criticism that the
media have hindered literacy is unwarranted.

Potter, W. James. (2001). *Media literacy (2nd ed.).* Thousand Oaks, CA: Sage.
(423 pages with index)
I argue that media-literate people need a strong set of knowledge structures
and skills. The book introduces the essential knowledge structures about the
media industries, their content, and the effects those messages have on us and
our institutions. The book also provides exercises to help readers increase
their skills of analysis, comparing and contrasting, evaluation, synthesis,
abstracting, and generalizing.

Silverblatt, Arthur. (1995). *Media literacy: Keys to interpreting media messages.*
Westport, CT: Praeger. (340 pages including index)
This is a mass media book that presents some chapters with information
about what is needed as far as knowledge about the media. It has the feel of
a textbook for an introductory-level course. The first section of the book,
called "Keys to Interpreting Media Messages," lays out a method of critically
analyzing the process, context, framework, and production values of the
mass media. The second section, called "Media Formats," presents exercises
to show students how to analyze print journalism, advertising, and American
political communications. The third section—the smallest at under 40
pages—briefly raises some critical issues such as violence in the media,
children, social change, and global communications.

Table 12.3   Organizations That Can Provide
                   Information on the Problem of Media Violence

Americans for Responsible Television
P.O. Box 627
Bloomfield Hills, MI 48303
Telephone: (313) 963-8000

Center for Media Education
Kathryn Montgomery, President
1511 K Street NW, Suite 518
Washington, DC 20005
Telephone: (202) 628-2620
Fax: (202) 628-2554
Web site: www.cme.org/cme

Center for Media Literacy
Elizabeth Thoman, Founder and President
4727 Wilshire Boulevard, Suite 403
Los Angeles, CA 90010
Telephone: (800) 226-9494
Fax: (213) 931-4474
Web site: www.medialit.org

Center for Media and Public Affairs
2101 L Street NW, Suite 405
Washington, DC 20037
Telephone: (202) 223-2942
Fax: (202) 872-4014

Children Now
Lois Salisbury, President
1212 Broadway, Suite 530
Oakland, CA 94612
Telephone: (510) 763-2444
Fax: (510) 763-1974
Web site: www.childrennow.org

Citizens for Media Literacy
Wally Bowen, President
34 Wall Street, Suite 407
Asheville, NC 28801
Telephone: (704) 252-0600

Table 12.3 Continued

Coalition for Quality Children's Media
112 West San Francisco Street, Suite 305A
Santa Fe, NM 87501
Telephone: (505) 989-8076
Fax: (505) 986-8477
Web site: www.CQCM.org

Cultural Environment Movement
P.O. Box 31847
Philadelphia, PA 19104
Telephone: (610) 642-3061

Fairness and Accuracy in Reporting (FAIR)
130 West 25th Street
New York, NY 10001
Telephone: (212) 633-6700
Fax: (212) 727-7668

Families Against Violence Advocacy Network
4144 Lindell Boulevard #408
St. Louis, MO 63108
Telephone: (314) 533-4445
e-mail: ppjn@aol.com
Web site: http://members.aol.com/ppjn

Freedom Forum Media Studies Center
2950 Broadway
New York, NY 10027-7004
Telephone: (212) 280-8392

Foundation to Improve Television
60 State Street, Suite 3400
Boston, MA 02109
Telephone: (617) 523-5520
Fax: (617) 523-4619

Maryland Campaign for Kids' TV
300 Cathedral Street, Suite 500
Baltimore, MD 21201

(Continued)

Table 12.3 Continued

Media Action Research Center
475 Riverside Drive, Suite 1901
New York, NY 10115
Telephone: (212) 865-6690
Fax: (212) 663-2746

Media Education Foundation
26 Center Street
Northampton, MA 01060
Telephone: (800) 659-6882

Media Research Center
113 South West Street
Alexandria, VA 22314
Telephone: (703) 683-9733
Fax: (703) 683-9736

Media Watch
P.O. Box 618
Santa Cruz, CA 95061
Telephone: (408) 423-6355
e-mail: mwatch@cruzio.com
Web site: www.mediawatch.com

Mediascope
12711 Ventura Boulevard, Suite 280
Studio City, CA 91604
Telephone: (818) 508-2080
Web site: www.mediascope.org

Mothers Offended by the
    Media (M.O.M.)
P.O. Box 382
Southampton, MA 01073
Telephone: (413) 536-9282

Table 12.3 Continued

National Alliance for Nonviolent Programming
Whitney G. Vanderwerff, Ph.D., Executive Director
122 North Elm Street, Suite 300
Greensboro, NC 27401
Telephone: (336) 370-0407
Fax: (336) 370-0392
e-mail: NA4NVP@aol.com

National Association for Family and Community Education
Children's Television Project
P.O. Box 835
Burlington, KY 41005
Telephone: (606) 586-8333
Fax: (606) 586-8348
Web site: www.nafce.org

National Coalition on TV Violence
5132 Newport Avenue
Bethesda, MD 20816
Telephone: (301) 986-0362
e-mail: nctvmd@aol.com

National Council for Children's TV and Media
32900 Heatherbrook
Farmington Hills, MI 48331-2908
Telephone: (810) 489-3177

National Institute on Media and the Family
Founded by David Walsh, Ph.D.
606 24th Avenue South, Suite 606
Minneapolis, MN 55454
Telephone: (888) 672-5437
Web site: www.mediaandthefamily.com

National Telemedia Council
120 East Wilson Street
Madison, WI 53703
Telephone: (608) 257-7712
Web site: danenet.wicip.org/ntc

(Continued)

Table 12.3 Continued

Parents' Choice
119 Chestnut Street
Newton, MA 02164
Telephone: (617) 965-5913

Strategies for Media Literacy
1095 Market Street, Suite 617
San Francisco, CA 94103
Telephone: (415) 621-2911
Fax: (415) 255-2298

The Cultural Environment Coalition
c/o Dr. George Gerbner
The Annenberg School for Communication
University of Pennsylvania
3620 Walnut Street
Philadelphia, PA 19104

The National Alliance for Non-Violent Programming
1846 Banking Street
Greensboro, NC 27108

Concerned Primarily With TV and Movie Ratings
Classification and Rating Administration
Motion Picture Association of America
15503 Ventura Boulevard
Encino, CA 91436-3103
Web site: www.mpaa.org

OKTV (Alternative TV Ratings)
c/o Gaffney-Livingstone Consultation Services
59 Griggs Road
Brookline, MA 02146
Web site: www.aacap.org (American Academy
    of Child and Adolescent Psychiatry)

TV Parental Guidelines Monitoring Board
P.O. Box 14097
Washington, DC 20004
e-mail: tvomb@usa.net
Web site: www.tvguidelines.org

the violent portrayals are affecting their feelings about what is acceptable behavior.

To build screen awareness, talk about what is happening and make frequent value judgments about who is acting bad and who is acting good. Point out when bad actions are punished. If a violent act is not punished in the media portrayal, ask your child how he or she would feel as the victim and ask if the perpetrator should have been punished.

Focus on the plot and help children see how consequences of violence unfold. Also, focus the child's attention on the motives of the perpetrators. Then help children see the connection between bad motives, bad behavior, and eventual punishment. Children, especially younger children, have difficulty making these connections on their own.

When characters use violence to solve their problems, ask your children if they can think of other ways the characters could have solved the problem. Then get the children to talk about how those alternative ways would play out in terms of consequences for all the characters.

Get children to think about the feelings of characters. Ask them to think about why a character behaved a certain way. Ask the child how he or she would feel if he or she were in the same situation as a particular character.

Help children be aware of the lessons the violence is teaching, such as "might makes right," "only the strong survive," "keep a stiff upper lip," and "big boys (and girls) don't cry." Then challenge those lessons.

Help children understand their own feelings as they react to violence in the media. Think of feelings as an index to our inner needs. The more entries in our emotional index, the more precisely we can identify our needs and the more likely we are to find appropriate solutions. A character who realizes that jealousy is fueling the rage he unleashes on his stepson, for example, may be better able to refrain from beating the boy than one who has no insight into his own emotions. When he can also talk about his jealous feelings with his wife or a trusted friend, he may begin to gain more control over his rage and violent behavior ("Alternatives to Violence," 1994).

Develop empathy, which is the ability to feel someone else's emotions as if they were your own. The capacity for empathy begins to develop in childhood when a child receives empathy firsthand and sees it modeled by a loved one. It evolves as individuals learn to distinguish between their own emotions and those of others; to take another's perspective; and to share another's emotional state, if only for a moment, by drawing on personal experience.

A character who can feel the pain another feels when slapped may refrain from hitting. A viewer who is empathic with the anger or fear within someone who is ready to lash out may be able to defuse the emotions and prevent the violent act.

Finally, don't underestimate how media literate your children may already be. "First-graders can be incredibly astute at looking at their shows and critiquing them" (Malcolm, 1999). So when you talk to your children, try not to be condescending or patronizing. Also, listen to what your children tell you; they may help you increase your own media literacy.

2. Teach the right lessons about violence. What are those lessons we need to teach? We need to teach children—and others—that violence in the real world is very different than it appears in the media world. Real-world violence is not glamorous or desirable. Instead, it is very serious and harmful. Thus there are three lessons.

First, violence hurts people. It has serious consequences for both the victims and the perpetrators. Real-life violence is not sanitized like it is typically shown in the media. Second, violence is not a good way to solve problems. Real-life violence is not a glamorous, successful tool for getting what you want as it is portrayed in the media. If you behave in a violent manner, once you calm down you will feel bad. Third, violence in the media is not real. Characters in fiction are made up to look and act scary. Plots exaggerate our risk of being involved in violence.

If parents can instill these simple lessons in their children, they will not have to be fearful of most negative effects when their children are exposed to violent portrayals. The children will be better able to handle those exposures in a way that helps them avoid negative effects.

3. Model good behavior. A majority of Americans—81%—believe that the best solution to the problem of violence is having parents teach their children to be nonviolent (Diamant, 1994). "You first learn violence at home," explains Leonard Eron, Ph.D., a psychologist at the Institute for Social Research at the University of Michigan in Ann Arbor (Diamant, 1994, p. 40). In one study, Eron discovered that the children whose parents used the harshest disciplinary methods—spanking, hitting, and abusive language—were more likely to start fights with other children (Diamant, 1994). These children had picked up from their parents the message that hitting was acceptable. Similarly, if you allow your children to watch violence either on television or in video games and don't counter what they see with your opinions, you are also supporting the message that violence is cool, funny, grown-up, sexy, and normal.

Elizabeth Thoman, founder of the Center for Media Literacy in Los Angeles, says the question of what parents are watching is overlooked. Of particular importance are young fathers. "How does a young man who has grown up with action movies and video games suddenly change his viewing habits when he has a 2-year-old boy?" she asks. Although he may think that he grew up watching violence and turned out OK, he needs to question if the violence in the media and the culture is the same today. "Does entertainment satisfy him without shocking him? Does he go for ever more adrenaline-rushing images?" (Malcolm, 1999, p. 14). When the people to whom an individual turns for guidance and the subgroups to which he or she belongs (be they gangs, cliques, or political groups) mirror this "I'll-show-you" ethos, learning to resolve conflict without violence becomes much more difficult.

4. Plan your viewing. Be selective in what you watch. If you feel there is not anything worthwhile on television at a particular time, turn it off. One of the worst things you can do is to use the TV for background noise. This will guarantee that violent sounds and images will flood into your house on a continual basis. Instead, make television viewing a special event—either for entertainment or to learn something fun.

Once a week read the television guides and movie listings for the coming week. Circle the shows you really want to see, then find out some information about each of those shows. Read the reviews. Talk to people who have already seen the show. Check Web sites (see Table 12.3).

Make the viewing a family event. Be there with your children and be active. If the show airs at an inconvenient time for you to do this, tape the show and watch it when you can.

Try to use the industry labels, but if these are not useful to you, find information from nonindustry sources. One such source is KidScore, available at www.mediaandthefamily.com, in which parents rate videos and other media products based on violence, fear, sexual content, nudity, language, and depiction of illegal or harmful acts (Churnin, 1998).

The Coalition for Quality Children's Media publishes an annual *Kids First! Directory* that is accessible at www.CQCM.org. To be listed in the directory, videos can contain no gratuitous violence or sexual behavior; no physical or verbal abuse; no bias in terms of race, gender, culture, or religion;

no condescension toward children; and no unsafe behaviors. However, be cautioned that, unlike KidScore, *Kids First!* has a tie-in with video sellers.

Unfortunately, most parents don't even try to control their children's TV viewing. Carol Rothwell, community relations director for Time Warner Cable in Kansas City, holds regular "critical viewing" seminars with parents. Although most say they are concerned about what their children watch, only about 1 in 10 actually monitors the family's TV habits, and only a small percentage of parents understood and used the onscreen ratings that accompany TV shows, according to a 1998 poll by the Annenberg Public Policy Center. So it is likely that young viewers will continue to see violence on television unless the networks reduce their reliance on violent programming (Barnhart, 1999).

5. Limit exposure time. The simplest thing to do is to cut back on time spent with the media, especially television. In the summer of 1996, the American Medical Association released a set of guidelines to each state's attorney general and to 60,000 doctors, primarily pediatricians, to help combat the effect television and movie violence has on children. The guidelines urge parents to know what their children are watching and to limit the amount of television their children watch. The American Academy of Pediatrics also recommends that parents limit their children's viewing time to one to two hours per day (Diamant, 1994).

If you do this, make sure you do it in a way that does not stimulate rebellion. There are two things you can do to reduce the probability of heated arguments with your children. First, give your children some control over when they can watch. Present the limitation as a weekly television allowance that your children can spend. By making their own decisions, they do not feel as powerless. Also, they may even develop a sense of partnership with you in this endeavor. Second, plan something fun to take the place of television viewing. When their time is up, immediately shift their attention into a fun activity. If you do not do this, they are likely to sit around the house and feel bored and resentful, because they believe they have lost the most exciting activity in their lives, and they are tempted to sneak back to it.

Limiting exposure has its difficulties. Most households have a parent working outside the home. Even two-parent households frequently have both parents working away from home. Therefore, much of children's viewing is unsupervised. Also, children who have their access limited at home can always go to a friend's house to view television. There is no way to insulate children from violent media images. Patricia Holland (1994), writing in the *New Statesman,* says that violent videos are part of playground subculture. They circulate informally, and if they're forbidden at one house, they can be seen at another.

An unexpected problem is that when you limit access to a medium such as television, you end up reducing positive exposure as well as risky exposures. The problem of media violence is better addressed by making good choices than by eliminating media exposure altogether.

SOCIETAL ACTION

Although it is important to educate yourself about media violence and to help those around you, the problem will still persist at the societal level. "My concern with media literacy is that it shifts the onus onto the viewer," said Kathryn Montgomery, president of the Center for Media Education in Washington. "Yes, you have to be responsible as a viewer, but companies have to be responsible too" (Barnhart, 1999, p. A1).

What can we do on the societal level? Most people will think of grand schemes, and these seem too big for any individual to undertake. But there are other societal things you can do. One thing is to support the efforts of institutions that are already trying to address the problem. Another is to keep pressure on the media. A third is to create your own consumer activist group.

Support Efforts of Institutions

There exist institutions that can do more to address this problem. These are educational, religious, and medical institutions. There are things we can do as individuals to influence these institutions to be more visible on this issue.

Educational Institutions. Ask schools to teach media literacy. Learning about the biases and distortions of television as well as the other mass media should be an essential part of public education. The purpose of the public school system is to teach students the basic knowledge and skills they will need to function in the world. However, much of people's knowledge is provided by the media, and much of this information is a distortion from the real world.

Each year it becomes even more important that the educational system provide students with accurate information so they can continually assess the value of information coming at them from the media. The skills of reading, writing, and arithmetic are important but no more so than the skills incorporating media literacy (for more detail on this topic, see Potter, 2001). There are many good materials available that could be used in schools (see Table 12.3).

Religious Institutions. There have been some religious leaders who have spoken out on the issue of media violence and who have tried to bring about change. The most preeminent of these people is Pope John Paul II, head of the Roman Catholic Church. During his 1993 tour in America he spoke out against America's urban violence, and he called on all segments of society— but particularly the media—to accept responsibility and find solutions (Hutchinson, 1993).

Others have written that the Roman Catholic Church should be even more active in condemning media violence. Teresa Malcolm (1999), writing in the *National Catholic Reporter,* argued that Catholics should be writing letters to media outlets, setting up discussion groups in dioceses, and also initiating dialogues with media and business leaders.

A recent update of a 1993 document from the U.S. Catholic Conference's Committee, *Family Guide for Using Media,* also outlines ways for parents to examine the values being promoted in the media in light of Catholic teaching and asks parents to look at ways the media manipulates or shows bias (Malcolm, 1999).

Deborah Lutterbeck (1995), writing in *Common Cause Magazine,* explained that members of fundamentalist and evangelical Christian groups set up the Family Research Council with the purpose of creating an environment in which children are safe. The Reverend Billy Melvin, executive director of the National Association of Evangelicals, said, "Let us build a climate where it is so compelling that we will want to do better." Melvin reasons, "If I saw a woman being raped I would not walk away, [and] this is the same kind of thing" (Lutterbeck, 1995).

Not everyone is sanguine about the idea of religious institutions' becoming involved in the media violence issue. For example, Catherine Besteman (1996) published an article in *Cultural Anthropology* in which she expressed ambivalence about religion getting involved. "Recently I was mulling over this question and meditating on possible nonviolent campaigns," she said.

I began to wonder whether Catholics couldn't be organized in order to collectively boycott the offending media and thereby exert social pressure. Suddenly it hit me: Good grief, you're trying to reinvent the Legion of Decency! What an irony! We used to loathe and despise being commanded to stand up in church and repeat an oath not to go to immoral movies. . . . But on second thought, why not rehabilitate this church effort to influence the media by using the more acceptable method of petition? Signing petitions and protest might make a difference. If we just passively stand by and don't try to do anything, we are surely guilty of letting our country decline and fall without a struggle. (Besteman, 1996)

Religious institutions have a moral power. People look to them for guidance, so when they do not speak out against something that is harmful to the way their adherents view life and the way they should treat other people, members of those institutions will likely learn that the problem is not important, but this *is* an important problem. Religious institutions need to act on their responsibility here, but in doing so, they need to act in unison. The Catholic, Protestant, Jewish, and Muslim communities should form coalitions to combat any mistaken idea that only splinter groups object to media exploitation, argues Sister Mary Walsh, spokesperson for the Catholic bishops in the United States. She explains that with large corporations controlling much of the media, "The ordinary person feels powerless. I can turn my television off, but is there some way of saying that these are public airwaves?" Walsh said churches are in a position to mobilize public opinion, particularly as an interfaith effort.

Medical Community. Over the years, medical groups have become more active in denouncing media violence and have even gone so far as to develop guidelines to help people avoid media violence and thereby avoid risks to their health. For example, the American Academy of Pediatrics has urged movie, television, and music producers to do more to portray the consequences of violence and has asked TV networks to agree to a one-day moratorium on violent programming. They also called on parents to be more responsible about their children's TV habits. They say parents should see that their kids don't watch more than one or two hours of TV daily, instead of the three or more hours typical for American children.

The doctors' precise recommendations may be less significant than the fact that the doctors are adding their voices to the controversy. Physician groups traditionally have stayed out of public debates not specifically about medicine. But Vic Strasburger said that pediatricians now feel that violence has become such a threat that they have to speak out. The pediatricians' group is calling for voluntary changes rather than new laws, Strasburger said, because changing the law would "get into politically motivated agendas and statements."

Keep Pressure on the Media

The television industry is enormously profitable, and it believes it has been successful in developing the right formulas to keep people entertained. Anyone who challenges those formulas is a great threat to them. Pushing the television and film industries to change the way they tell stories is a very difficult challenge. It is also a worthwhile challenge. Unless the public forces the media companies to view their responsibility to something beyond their immediate profits, the industry will continue with business as usual. You may want to contact media companies or government agencies (see Tables 12.4 and 12.5).

Fortunately, there are some important people in the media industries who recognize their responsibility to the health of the public, and they are speaking out. For example, Ted Turner, founder of TBS, TNN, and CNN, told Congress, "Unless you keep the gun pointed at [television executives'] heads, all you'll get is mumbly, mealy-mouthed BS. They just hope the subject will go away" (Lutterbeck, 1995). Don Hewitt, executive producer of *60 Minutes,* has an interesting suggestion. He says that concerned people should call and write the wives of top movie studio executives and say, "If you're worried about kids in school, maybe you should talk to your husband. Wives get things done" (Oldenburg & Snider, 1999, p. 1D).

Because the media industries are businesses, their primary vulnerability is the bottom line on their balance sheets. Thus strategies that send a financial message to the decision makers in the industries are likely to be the strongest. This is why boycotts of products advertised on highly violent programs can be so effective—and are so feared by people in the industry. However, in order to work, a boycott must be highly organized. If only a small number of people stop buying certain products in protest, no one will notice.

Also, boycotts need to be led by someone who is acting from principle, not from a selfish desire for power. This last characteristic is sometimes

Table 12.4   National Television Networks

ABC, Inc.
2040 Avenue of the Stars
Los Angeles, CA 90067
Telephone: (310) 557-6655
Web site: www.abc.com

CBS Entertainment
7800 Beverly Boulevard
Los Angeles, CA 90036
Telephone: (213) 460-3000
Fax: (213) 653-8266
Web site: www.channel2000.com

Fox Broadcasting Company
P.O. Box 900
Beverly Hills, CA 90213
Telephone: (310) 369-1000
Web site: www.fox.com

NBC Entertainment
3000 West Alameda
Burbank, CA 91523
Telephone: (818) 840-4404
Web site: www.nbc.com

Public Broadcasting Service
1320 Braddock Place
Alexandria, VA 22314
Telephone: (703) 739-5040
Fax: (703) 739-5295
Web site: www.pbs.org

Turner Broadcasting System
1 CNN Center
Atlanta, GA 30303
Telephone: (404) 885-4291
Web site: www.turner.com

Table 12.5 Government Sources of Information

Federal Communications Commission
1919 M Street NW
Washington, DC 20554
Web site: www.fcc.gov/vchip

Federal Trade Commission
Attention: Marketing Practices
Room 238
6th Street and Pennsylvania Avenue NW
Washington, DC 20580
Fax: (202) 326-2050

U.S. House of Representatives
Subcommittee on Telecommunications and Finance
2125 Rayburn Building
Washington, DC 20515
Telephone: (202) 225-2927
Web site: www.house.gov/com

U.S. Senate
Subcommittee on Communications
227 Hart Senate Office Building
Washington, DC 20510
Telephone: (202) 224-5184
Web site: www.senate.gov/~commerce/

missing in high-profile boycotts, and this provides the industry with an easy opportunity to stigmatize them. For example, in the early 1980s, Donald Wildmon, a minister from Tupelo, Mississippi, put together what he named the National Coalition for Television, which was composed of about 400 civic and religious organizations. Wildmon's group identified the shows with the highest amounts of violence and put them on a hit list for boycotting. The boycott got a lot of attention and started to work, but then Wildmon went too far. On one of NBC's talk programs, a guest inadvertently used an expletive on the air. Wildmon wanted NBC to discipline the guest, but NBC refused. In retaliation, Wildmon doubled-counted the violence, sex, and profanity on NBC during their next counting period. This had the effect of moving NBC from the least-offending network in terms of bad acts to first place. Wildmon's motives were revealed when he said, "Now I have the clout. After three years of wandering in the wilderness, I've found a road to the Promised Land" ("The New Right's TV Hit List," 1981).

A strong backlash started against Wildmon. The press labeled Wildmon as the "ayatollah of the airwaves" (Cooper, 1996) because of his ego-inspired tactic. ABC president Frederick Pierce told the Association of Advertisers, "We cannot hand over [industry regulation] to self appointed judges intent on selecting what we watch, read, study and ultimately think" (Van Horne, 1981). Peggy Charren, president of Action for Children's Television, characterized the boycott as a dangerous form of censorship, and NBC president Fred Silverman referred to the campaign as "a sneak attack on the foundation of democracy" (Stein, 1981, p. 23).

Wildmon reappeared in the mid-1990s with a new organization named the American Family Association. Using this group, Wildmon headed a boycott again. This time, Wildmon tried to discourage corporations from advertising on *NYPD Blue*. Despite the boycott, *NYPD Blue* continued with very high ratings and strong advertiser support, yet Wildmon claimed victory, saying, "We have been extremely successful with that, we have really hurt them in their pocketbooks" (Cooper, 1996).

There are examples of successful boycotts. With endorsement from U.S. Surgeon General David Satcher, among others, an estimated 6 million Americans took part in TV-Turnoff Week in April 1999 (Barnhart, 1999). Also, 25 years ago, a group called the National Citizens Committee for Broadcasting monitored TV shows for levels of violence. The committee, led by former FCC member Nicholas Johnson, then published a list of the "10 Bloodiest Corporations"—companies that advertised most often on violent TV shows. Johnson, now a law professor in Iowa, said violence levels measurably declined after that list came out. He recalled one company receiving 300,000 letters as a result of making the list. "Ad agencies were telling their clients that they were losing as much as 5 percent of their market share as a result of our doing this," Johnson said. "Companies don't care about violence. They care about not looking bad for any reason" (Barnhart, 1999, p. A1).

Boycotts usually start out small on the initiative of one individual, but if that person can influence others, the boycott can grow. For example, the Women of Hadassah at Congregation Beth El in Baltimore are doing some-thing. "In the past, if I found a show objectionable, I just turned it off—I didn't watch," said Selma Pollack.

But now, I watch. I watch until I have the names of every single sponsor. And then I write to those sponsors, telling them I won't be buying their products anymore, because of their involvement with the show. And, then, I get 50 of my friends to write too. (Zurawik, 1994)

Boycotts can work, although their strongest effect is on advertisers rather than television networks. For example, a group called Empower America, cochaired by former U.S. Secretary of Education William Bennett and Senator Joseph Lieberman, put pressure on advertisers in the mid-1990s. This pressure resulted in two major advertisers—Proctor & Gamble and Mars—pulling their advertising campaigns off of certain talk shows that contained a good deal of verbal violence (Goff & Mandese, 1995).

Sometimes public pressure works best by going directly to the sellers of products that support violence in the media. For example, public pressure led Wal-Mart to stop selling a wrestler doll named Al Snow, who was one of the stars of the World Wrestling Federation television programs. The doll was modeled after the real-life wrestler, who carries a female mannequin's head into the ring. The doll comes with a woman's head with the words *Help Me* scrawled backward across her forehead ("Wal-mart Pulls Wrestling," 1999).

Another example of how public pressure can force change is in the development of a rating system for video games. Pressure was put on retailers to support the ratings systems. When game manufacturers opposed the ratings system, Toys "R" Us, Wal-Mart, and Babbage's announced that they would not sell unrated video games. Because these three retailers account for 30 to 40% of the video game market, industry opposition to a ratings system largely evaporated, and video game manufacturers began using the ratings system.

Economic pressure works, but in order to be successful, a boycott needs to be initiated and organized by a committed individual who has some credibility. Then that individual must influence other consumers to join the boycott so that it grows in numbers and gains visibility. Although it is difficult to achieve all these characteristics in a campaign, the results of such effort are almost always worthwhile.

Public Action: Organizing Reform Groups

Several women have become almost folk heroes for organizing a reform group and working for years to pressure the industry to provide more responsible programming, especially for children. For example, Terry Rakolta, a mother of four, started Americans for Responsible Television from her suburban Detroit home in 1989 after she watched an episode of *Married . . . With Children* and imagined how such a program would appear to her young children. Her group now has 150,000 members. Another example is Kathryn Montgomery, who started the Center for Media Education in the basement of her house. Her initial annual budget of $15,000 grew to $350,000 within two years. She was able to get grants from organizations such as the John D. and Catherine T. MacArthur Foundation, the Carnegie Foundation, and Baltimore's Abell Foundation (Zurawik, 1994).

By the 1990s there were many such groups, and they were forming coalitions among themselves to share their common goals. For example, in May 1994, a coalition of more than a dozen groups came together to press the FCC to enforce the Children's Television Act of 1991. Member groups ranged from the Consumer Federation of America to the Maryland Campaign for Kids' TV. Then, in June of 1994, the Citizens' Task Force on TV Violence was formed, representing some 400,000 members. Participating groups included the National Parent-Teacher Association, the American Medical Association, the National Council of Churches, the National Education Association, and the American Academy of Pediatrics. Also in 1994, the National Coalition for Non-Violent Programming convened at the Johnson Foundation Wingspread Conference Center in Wisconsin. This alliance represented 500,000 women. Its groups include the Association of Junior Leagues, B'nai B'rith Women, and the National Association of Minority Women in Business.

The combined power of these groups in coalitions was influencing lawmakers. By the mid-1990s, Congress was considering nine different proposals dealing with the issue of violence on television. "There are all kinds of coalitions of citizens making themselves heard, and it's more diverse than ever," said George Gerbner, professor at the University of Pennsylvania and a pioneer in research on media violence (Zurawik, 1994, p. 1A).

Organizing a reform group or organizing a coalition of reform groups requires the most amount of effort of any of the suggestions offered in this chapter. Fortunately, there are people who care enough to undertake these important tasks. Because we are still far from a solution to the problem of media violence, we need more people to become involved at this level.

CONCLUSIONS

Although television has changed little in the amount or context of violence over the five decades, there are more and more reform groups forming and more of our traditional institutions getting involved. As long as this trend continues, there will be a growing concern that will become more visible and influential—perhaps growing to the point when one day it will be strong enough to compel the media businesses to recognize their joint responsibilities to something beyond their short sight on profits.

In the meantime, each of us must protect ourselves from the risks of being affected negatively by all the violence in the fictional stories as well as in news accounts. We need to be more analytically active during our own television exposure and help others become more aware during their exposures. In order to generate a higher level of awareness, we all need to become more media literate. This means we need to be able to tell the difference between con-structive effects and negative effects, between what looks like reality and fantasy, and between fact and myth. We need to understand better the nature of the problem of media violence so that we don't ask for changes that are meaningless or that could actually worsen the current situation. We need good information so we can construct informed opinions. That is our responsibility, and if we do not demonstrate a commitment to meeting our responsibility, how can we be credible in asking the media to accept their responsibility?

⊰ THIRTEEN ⊱

PROGNOSIS FOR IMPROVEMENT

————·•·————

We are currently stuck in an unproductive place on the problem of media violence—and we have been stuck in this place for a long time. The public keeps complaining about media violence. Congress keeps holding hearings and suggesting that the industry change its practices. The industry keeps complaining about government interference, citing the First Amendment. The industry argues that it is in business to provide the public with what it wants. The industry places blame on the public for demanding violence and then complaining about it.

The public keeps believing that the violent content is harmful—but only to other people, especially children, so it asks for ratings of programs. The television industry fights against labeling programs, citing the First Amendment as the right *not* to provide information. The public pressures Congress, which then pressures the television networks to provide ratings, but Congress then allows the industry to develop and administer its own ratings systems with no oversight. The industry develops a ratings system that provides as little information as possible. Few people use the ratings. The industry feels wronged, because it now gives the public what it wants, and the public is not using the ratings. The public says the ratings do not provide useful information.

This surface problem of lack of meaningful change in programming from producers, lack of substantial change in consumption from the public, and lack of ability by policymakers to broker a solution are all traceable to the underlying problem of lack of communication. Everyone has been talking about the problem, but nothing of value has resulted. It is rather as though the different people are paired off in all kinds of conversations in the same room. At first everyone talks softly, but then people must talk louder to make themselves heard over the sound level coming from the other conversations. The sound level continues to escalate until everyone is shouting, but yet no one can be heard. We have reached the point where it is all noise and no communication. The level of misunderstanding and misinformation is high.

The prognosis for moving toward a solution of the surface problem of media violence is not good . . . unless we first address the underlying problem of a lack of understanding about the problem. Working on this underlying problem requires three things. First, we need to get beyond the myths that have been constraining our thinking. We need to replace the worn-out, faulty myths with a set of alternative beliefs that will be more constructive. Second, we need to think of the problem of media violence in a different way—one that will help us see the problem from a fresh perspective. And third, we need to develop a shared sense of responsibility. Metaphorically, we need to begin with a richer soil of understanding, then plant the seeds of a new perspective, and share the caring for its growth.

ALTERNATIVE SET OF BELIEFS

Accepting any of the 11 myths is a sign of misunderstanding the issues inter-woven into the problem of media violence. Although some of the myths have some truth behind them, each one is fundamentally flawed. As long as there is a widespread acceptance of these myths, we will be stuck in the mire of misunderstanding, and the more of these myths we accept, the more walls there are to keep us in a maze of unproductive thinking with no way out.

Instead of the myths, we need an alternative set of beliefs. This alternative set will get us out of the maze of unproductive thinking and move us to new ground where we can begin to perceive a meaningful solution to the problem of media violence. Following is a set of 11 alternative beliefs that need to be accepted in place of the myths.

1. Violence in the media *does* increase the risk of viewers behaving aggressively, but this is only one of several dozen negative effects. If we limit our concern to this one effect, we will greatly underestimate the magnitude of

the problem. Many of the negative effects do not occur immediately after the exposure; they take many weeks or years to manifest themselves. Also, effects can be cognitive, attitudinal, emotional, and physiological; they are not limited to behaviors.

2. Violence in the media affects everyone. No one is immune. We continually experience the process of influence, in that each exposure to media violence affects our levels of risk for a negative effect. Our levels of risk could build for years without a manifestation of an effect. Then one day our behavior changes—not because of that day's exposure, but because of years of increasing risk levels.

3. Violence in the media *does* affect children in negative ways, but it also affects adolescents, adults, and the elderly. Achieving greater age, experience, and cognitive ability does not shield people from negative effects; in fact, these very characteristics may actually make adults more vulnerable to certain effects. If we take a narrow view that the only negative effects are copycat behaviors and nightmares, then children are the most vulnerable group, but there are more than two dozen types of negative effects, and adults are at greater risk than children for experiencing many of these.

4. There *is a great deal* of violence in the media. It appears in all genres, day-parts, and channels of television. The problem with this belief is that the public does not "see" much of this violence, because it is not graphic enough to offend them, so the public is greatly underperceiving the amount of violence to which they are exposed. It is this "unperceived" violence that "comes in under a person's radar" that is responsible for most of the negative effects. Even if programmers removed all the graphic violence that people complain about most, this would do little to ameliorate the problem; in fact, it could make the problem worse by leaving us with only sanitized violence, which could further desensitize viewers.

5. Violence in the media does *not* reflect violence in society. There is a great deal more violence in the media than in real life. Furthermore, the way the violence is portrayed is highly unrealistic. These characteristics lead people to believe that the world is far more violent than it actually is.

6. The media *are* responding to market desires, but the media are not *just* responders to the market. The media also condition us by creating markets

that limit what we can ask for, then reward us when we ask for the limited fare they provide.

7. Violence is *not* an essential element in all fiction. Conflict is an essential element in storytelling, but if the "creatives" who write, produce, and direct these stories want to live up to their name, more of them need to be willing to deviate from the old violence formula.

8. Reducing the amount of violence in the media will *not* solve the problem. The essence of the problem lies more with context than frequency. *How* the violence is portrayed tells us the meaning of the violence. For the past five decades, we have been taught that violence is an acceptable and even desirable means of solving problems, especially for the heroes who are attractive and with whom we identify. It is the repetition of this type of message that is most harmful. If a more prosocial context were used for violence, then the increases in frequency would likely lead to positive—not negative—effects.

9. Media messages are a form of speech and should be protected by the First Amendment, but these messages are also commercial products that are marketed for a profit, so the marketers should bear some responsibility when those products cause harm to their users. It is unfair for message marketers to claim the right of free speech for themselves, charge customers for this "speech," then refuse to acknowledge responsibility for the harmfulness of their words and images.

10. Rating systems *by themselves* will *not* solve the problem. If programs are rated by the same people who are marketing the shows, there is an obvious conflict of interest. The public needs accurate information about the context in addition to the frequency of violence in programs. The television networks provide neither. Instead, networks provide labels with as little information as possible so that potential viewers will not be scared away. It is therefore not surprising that the public does not find the labels useful.

11. There *are many things* you can do to make an effect on reducing the problem. You have already taken the first step by considering the issues presented in this book. The next steps require action. Change your media exposure habits. Help other people become more active discounters of violent portrayals. Get involved with consumer action groups or start your own. Actively support the efforts of educators, religious leaders, and the medical

community to get more involved. Put pressure on advertisers, regulators, and ultimately people in the media industries to think beyond their narrow business interests and consider more their responsibility to society.

NEED FOR PUBLIC HEALTH PERSPECTIVE

Although the alternative set of beliefs just presented will get us out of the maze of unproductive thinking, we need to move to new ground where we can get a different perspective on the problem of media violence. Disseminating more information and dispelling myths can help with the poverty of information, but to generate meaningful action, we need more. We need to change the way we think about this problem. We cannot continue to think that the problem is caused by someone else. We need to believe that we are all affected and that we are all the cause. In short, we are all in this together.

The most useful new view on the problem, I believe, would be from a public health perspective. Looking at the problem from a public health perspective would help change our thinking in four ways. First, we would come to recognize that the problem is widespread throughout society and that we are all at risk. In the early days of the AIDS epidemic in this country, most people thought the problem was confined to a small minority of "other" people—homosexual men and drug users. Now we realize we are all at risk, and knowing this means there is a much wider range of people who feel responsible to reduce that risk.

Second, this new perspective would help us focus less on effects and more on levels of risk and the factors that influence those levels. With heart disease, there are multiple factors that could increase our level of risk—genetics, being overweight, diet, long-term stress, and smoking. The factor of smoking is not a sufficient cause of heart disease, because many smokers never contract the disease. This was the argument used for decades by the tobacco industry to defend itself, but eventually the general public began to understand that although multiple factors influence the risk level for heart disease, smoking was recognized by many people as a very influential one in that set.

Third, this new perspective would convince us that there are things we can do to reduce our risk, but that this task requires a good deal of shared responsibility. Some of the responsibility is ours; we can do things in our own lives to reduce our risk. But some of the responsibility belongs to businesses and institutions. As with the example of smoking, we have the power to make choices that can significantly change our risk levels, but the problem of smoking must also be addressed on a larger scale. When advertisers are permitted to present highly attractive and persuasive messages—especially to children— the risk level throughout society increases. When the rights of nonsmokers to avoid breathing smoke in public buildings are given precedence over the rights of smokers to smoke anywhere, the risk level throughout society decreases.

Fourth, the public health perspective highlights the importance of the common good. Behind this problem of a poverty of responsibility is that individuals focus on their own needs and rarely consider the needs of society. This leads to the question of whether we should do more to protect the rights of individuals who want to maximize their own personal satisfaction or to protect the rights of society and thus maximize the satisfaction of everyone. When the two are in opposition, we cannot satisfy both. There needs to be a negotiation process in which groups subordinate the full pursuit of all their needs and compromise a bit so that a solution can be reached where the common good is maximized. However, there is no adequate forum to do this. The public has the forum of public opinion, but this forum serves only as a stage for criticism. It has no follow-up to ensure that change happens. Producers have created their own forum, but their forum holds the industry's needs preeminent and gives little weight (or even credence) to the needs of the other groups. Policymakers have Congress, but the members of Congress are beholden to campaign money donated by Hollywood, and they are fearful of offending the press. There is no forum superordinate to all these groups where the needs of each group could be kept in balance while the focus is kept primarily on the common good.

If we regard the problem of media violence in terms of a public health issue, we will see the problem in a different manner. To illustrate this, see the analogy in Box 13.1. Notice that changing the industry from the media to pharmaceuticals shows us how different industries are treated by the public and the federal government. It raises the question: Why have the media been treated so differently from the pharmaceutical industry or the tobacco industry? Is it because the rights to free speech apply more to the products of the media industries than the products of other industries? Is it because the public believes that exposure to violence is less harmful than exposure to secondhand smoke? Or is it because we have been slower to apply a public health perspective to the problem of media violence than to the problems of smoking or AIDS? The analogy in Box 13.2 emphasizes the ludicrousness of the

Box 13.1   An Analogy

Let's say the pharmaceutical industry produces a variety of substances to make people feel better. People in the industry believe that a "V-element" is helpful in making people feel good, so they put some of this V-element into most of their products.

After several years, some people in the general public notice that there are some negative side effects of these substances. Researchers outside the pharmaceutical industry begin examining the problem and over time build up a substantial research base of information documenting that the V-element is leading to some serious side effects in a few people each year. Furthermore, the V-element is leading to a wide variety of negative effects in the population at large. The pharmaceutical industry responds that those claims of negative effects are ridiculous. They say that the V-element is a natural substance found in many common places, so there is nothing special about it in their products.

But the public is not satisfied. The public puts pressure on federal regulators to do something. The regulators hold lots of hearings and make lots of speeches. The pharmaceutical industry responds by saying that they are not forcing people to use their products. People use their products voluntarily, and large numbers of people are using the products repeatedly.

The heat is turned up as policymakers consider ways of regulating the products of the pharmaceutical industry. In defense, the industry responds that their product is not illegal and that the research that indicates it harms people is unconvincing.

Policymakers consider regulations to force companies in the industry to label their own products to tell consumers if the product is not appropriate for people of certain ages. The industry uses a First Amendment defense, saying that such a regulation is limiting their right to free speech. They interpret freedom of speech to be the absolute right not to speak if they so choose, and they choose not to speak in the form of labeling their products.

Policymakers offer a compromise. They will deregulate the pharmaceutical industry in substantial ways if the industry agrees to label its products. The industry begrudgingly accepts the compromise. In essence, the industry abandons its argument of total freedom of lack of speech and gets many major business concessions.

The drug companies provide as little information as possible in the labeling of their products for fear that if they say too much, many people might decide not to buy particular drugs. So they put a fancy title on the bottles, assuming that people will know what kind of drug (pain killer, cough medicine, hemorrhoid treatment, eye drops, etc.) it is by the title. Their labeling system then tells consumers whether it is appropriate for the entire family (Drug-G), older children (Drug-PG-7), teenagers (Drug-PG-13), for teenagers under adult supervision (Drug-R), or adults only (Drug-X). Each company labels the drugs it markets with no oversight from anyone else. Also, if they choose not to comply, there is no penalty. Still, the leaders in the industry are upset and feel greatly compromised.

---

assertion that media influence on children can't be *proven* by making the same argument about parents.

Think about what your reaction would be if there were no oversight on quality control or labeling of pharmaceutical products. The companies who make the drugs could make any claims they wanted to advance their own business interests, and we would have to accept those claims. If we were not sure if the drug were appropriate for us or not, we would have to take some and see if we have a negative reaction—one that might not show up for several years.

The medical community is helping guide the way to a public health perspective. Many organizations have made pronouncements about the problem (see Table 13.1). Also, some prominent health organizations are trying to disseminate more health information about the harm of media violence. For example, the American Academy of Pediatrics has a Web site (www.aap.org/advocacy/childhealthmonth/media.htm) that offers tips to parents on how to help their children with their media exposures. Also, the American Medical Association (1996) has published *The AMA's Physician Guide to Media Violence.* These guidelines are for doctors to use in counseling parents

---

Box 13.2 Does This Argument Make Sense to You?

It is often claimed that parents influence the behavior and attitudes of their children, but this is a false notion, unsupported by strong research. Don't be fooled by what academics or critics tell you.

Let's use some common sense here. We have all been exposed to parental messages, yet we do not find ourselves mindlessly following their dictates. Parents do not exert such a powerful effect on us. We all have free will and therefore are not determined by what parents tell us. Many of us can go for years leaving our beds unmade, chewing with our mouths open, or yes, even running with sticks in our hands. That fact alone should be enough to put to rest the notion by the fuzzy-headed academics that parents have an influence on their children.

Supporters of the claim of parental influence say that there have been several thousand studies to support their conclusion, but those studies are flawed. Scholars who interpret this research simply go too far when they make claims that parents have an actual influence on children. For example, much of this research was conducted in laboratory settings and cannot be generalized to the real-world population. Or the research is simply correlational, and therefore no claims for causation can be made. Just because we observe parents giving a particular message to their children and the children acting on that message does not mean that the parents *caused* the subsequent behavior.

The situation of how we are influenced when we are children is just too complex. There are many potential factors involved. Much more research needs to be conducted. Until we know for sure what the influences are, let's stop pointing our fingers at parents.

---

about their children's television and movie choices. The *Guide* gives doctors suggestions on how to talk to parents about their children's viewing habits and how to advise them about making changes. Released in 1996, it was distributed to every state's attorney general and to 60,000 doctors, primarily pediatricians, to help combat the effect television and movie violence has on children.

Table 13.1   Public Health Groups Reject Myth

1976	American Medical Association's House of Delegates declares violence an "environmental hazard."
1984	The American Academy of Pediatrics Task Force on Children and Television releases a report cautioning physicians and parents that television may promote aggressive behavior.
1985	The American Psychological Association Commission on Youth Violence releases a report linking television violence and real-world violence.
1992	The American Psychological Association calls for a federal policy to protect the public from the harms of televised violence.
1993	The American Psychological Association says,

> There is absolutely no doubt that higher levels of viewing violence on television are correlated with increased acceptance of aggressive attitudes and increased aggressive behavior. In addition to increasing violent behaviors toward others, viewing violence on television changes attitudes and behaviors toward violence in significant ways. (p. 33)

1995	The American Academy of Pediatrics, which represents 48,000 pediatricians, says

> the evidence is clear: Violence in entertainment makes some children more aggressive, desensitizes them to real-life violence, and makes them feel they live in a mean and dangerous world. "There's no debate. There is clearly a relationship between media violence and violence in the community," said Vic Strasburger, author of the pediatricians' statement and chief of pediatrics at the University of New Mexico School of Medicine. Dr. Strasburger also said, "We are basically saying the controversy is over. There is clearly a relationship between media violence and violence in society" ("Doctor's Push," 1995, p. A16).

Similar statements were also released by the American Academy of Child and Adolescent Psychiatry, the American Public Health Association, and the National Association of Attorneys General.

1996	The American Medical Association says, "An extensive body of research amply documents a strong correlation between children's exposure to media violence and a number of behavioral and psychological problems, primarily aggressive behavior. The evidence further shows that these problems are caused by the exposure itself" (American Medical Association, 1996).

Another significant event that helped cast the problem in the public health arena occurred in January 2001, when the U.S. Surgeon General, David Satcher, added his voice in support of what researchers had known for decades: Repeated exposure to violent entertainment during early childhood causes more aggressive behavior throughout a child's life. He said, "Exposure to violent media plays an important causal role in this societal problem of youth violence" (Leeds, 2001, p. A1).

SHARED SENSE OF RESPONSIBILITY

Should we continue to protect the satisfaction of individual needs, or should we focus more on the common needs? When the two are in opposition, we cannot satisfy both. Unless we do something about it now, the problem will continue to get worse. This can be illustrated clearly through the economic analyses conducted by Duke University economist James Hamilton (1998). According to Hamilton, the problem of television violence is an example of market failure. He traces the root of the problem to what he calls *negative externalities*. These are the costs that are borne by individuals other than those involved in the production activity.

To illustrate the nature of this problem, Hamilton (1998) uses the analogy of environmental pollution. If a factory generates waste products that are hazardous to the environment, the factory can take the responsibility for restoring the cleanliness of the environment and pass those costs along to consumers; this, of course, would increase the cost of that company's products and might result in lowering the company's sales. Instead, it is in the best interests of the factory to ignore the cleanup costs by regarding them as being outside of—or external to—its decision process. By ignoring these costs, the company can sell its products at an artificially low price, thus enabling it to compete very successfully and amass a large profit. However, the environment is damaged, and the public is left to bear the costs of cleanup itself.

Moving from the manufacturing analogy to the issue of television violence, Hamilton (1998) shows that although all parties are acting rationally to advance their self-interests, society suffers in the form of viewers' being exposed to the constant pollution of violence. Programmers desire most the audiences of men and women ages 18 to 34, because advertisers are willing to pay a premium to get their messages before those high-spending audience members. These two demographics represent the largest audiences for violent programming. Therefore, it is in the best interest of individual programmers to offer violent programs in order to attract these desired audience segments. Other segments of the audience are less desirable, even though the total number of people in these other segments constitutes a majority of all viewers.

Elaborating this example, let's say that Programmer X schedules Program Y at 9 p.m. because this is when the number of viewers from 18 to 34 is largest. Program Y is violent in order to attract this desired audience segment. When there is a large number of this type of viewer watching Program Y, this will attract Advertisers, A, B, and C. Although Program Y does attract large numbers of the desired segments, there are also many children and teens in the audience who are also exposed to the program. However, Programmer X does not care about these children and teens, because Advertisers A, B, and C do not care about these younger audiences. Thus the consideration about whether Program Y will attract children and teens does not enter into the decision to schedule Program Y—this consideration is seen as external to the decision.

Hamilton (1998) says the problem of dealing with the pollution of violence falls to individuals. At the individual level, the costs are very high, and there is very little return. A parent can boycott products advertised on violent programs, but this puts a heavy burden on an individual to monitor those advertisements and then shop around for substitutes. This cost seems especially high when balanced against the effect of a single person's boycott. The costs are also high to parents who want to monitor shows for their children, tape them, and play back only the acceptable ones. Thus "the pursuit of individual self-interest by consumers, producers, and distributors of violent programming leads to undesirable social outcomes, such as the current rates of children's exposure to violent programming" (Hamilton, p. xvii).

Hamilton (1998) conducted a series of analyses revealing that programmers are very aware of the effect of violence on creating the audiences they desire and that they adopt strategies to use violence as a tool to further their own ends. For example, in one analysis, he found that television programmers schedule particular types of violent shows at given days and times so as to build viewer expectations about program content and thus attract more viewers. Programmers also counterprogram violence against popular shows (such as *Seinfeld* and *Monday Night Football*) so as to attract the audience away from those shows. Hamilton observes, "The scheduling of movies during the evening and daytime hours demonstrates how violent content is an externality, for the patterns follow the flow of adults in the viewing audience without a strong regard for the potential exposures of children" (p. 158). He says that the level of violence as well as sexual content is as high at 8 p.m. as it is at 10 p.m.—both when the desired audience segments are viewing in large numbers. But there is also a high concentration of children viewing then, especially in the earlier time period.

In addition, Hamilton (1998) found that the movies scheduled in early afternoons on Saturday contain more violence and nudity than movies scheduled at that time during the weekdays. This clearly shows that programmers realize that there are more desired target people (men and women aged 18-34) watching television on Saturday afternoons than on weekday afternoons. However, there are also many more children viewing at that time, but this information again is treated as external to their decision making.

As for advertising, Hamilton (1998) says that program warnings change the mix of advertisers supporting prime-time movies. Movies with warnings are less likely to attract family-oriented advertisers (food and kitchen products) and more likely to attract advertisers of alcoholic beverages as well as sports and leisure products. Also, on programs with violent warnings, the number of nonprogram minutes is the same as in programs without warnings, but the commercial advertising is a bit less, with the difference being filled in with program promotions. This loss in advertising revenue is a disincentive, so programmers frequently fail to label violent programming. With public criticism of the networks, incentives have shifted to cable channels, where the percentage of shows that contain violence is even higher than on the commercial television broadcast networks. Also, because violent programming is exportable to foreign countries, producers are able to expect more revenue from violent programs and therefore will be more likely to have higher production budgets, leading to higher production values and greater audience attraction.

From an economic point of view, programmers and producers are acting rationally but irresponsibly. It is rational to want to maximize revenue, but the narrow pursuit of revenue, which does not take into consideration the polluting effects of violence on society, is not responsible.

SOME GOOD NEWS FROM THE MEDIA INDUSTRIES

As this book comes to an end, I don't want to leave you with the impression that the people in the media industries are all irresponsible in the way they have shifted blame onto others, hid behind the First Amendment, and refused to acknowledge that there is a problem. There is a growing awareness among people in the media industries that there is a serious problem. Some have even gone so far as to be part of the solution. For some, this means a recognition that there is strong evidence that media violence leads to negative effects. Others take this a step further and recognize that there is a social responsibility attached to artistic products. And others go yet further to effect change in a constructive direction.

Recognition of Influence

A growing number of people in the creative community are recognizing that their shows have all sorts of influences on their viewers and that some of these effects may be negative. For example, a 1994 *U.S. News & World Report* poll found that 78% of Hollywood officials think TV contributes to violence in this country (U.S. News & World Report Online, 1994). Two years later, another *U.S. News & World Report* poll found that 80% of Hollywood executives questioned in a mail survey agreed that there was a link between TV violence and violence in real life.

A group of Hollywood actors, producers, and directors have formed a group calling itself the Creative Coalition. William Baldwin, president of a group, said that there is no question that violence in the media is "contributing or playing a role" in the brutal behavior of some psychologically vulnerable children (Stern, 1999a). Baldwin was joined by other Hollywood insiders (such as Joel Schumacher, Rob Reiner, Mike Farrell, and Gary Ross) in calling for the entertainment industry to acknowledge its influential impact on kids ("Covering the Violence," 1999). The group also suggested that it is time for Hollywood to reexamine its dependence on gunfire to further plotlines (Stern & Petrikin, 1999).

In a speech at Stanford University, the television producer and writer Norman Lear said,

> Who can deny that television is a major influence on our values, our culture, our children? Why else do advertisers spend those billions of dollars a year on commercials if not to influence our consciousness and persuade us to take certain actions, like buy their products? And if our, and our children's, behavior can be influenced to buy products, who can deny that it can be influenced in other directions? The same is true for films, videotapes, radio, recorded music, and now computer software and CD-ROMs. No doubt they, too, shape our attitudes and values and outlook on the world. (quoted in Minow, 1995)

Danny Goldberg, former chairman and CEO of Warner Brothers, said that his views about whether TV images have an impact on people have changed since he witnessed firsthand the impact on his four-year-old daughter when she watched *Power Rangers* (Gardels, 1998).

Chuck D., of the rap group Public Enemy, said music, television, film, and video games "absolutely" affect the world view, growth, and behavior of young people, especially if their parents are ill-equipped to act as filters. "We're living in a time of mass images and if a kid's reality is not being realized, fantasy and reality blur together," the rapper said. "And that can lead to life imitating art." He continued, "Entertainers and media moguls who say their product has no role in youth violence are either 'idiots' or acting out of self-interest" (Harrison, 1999, p. F1).

"Images implant themselves inside people's brains and have a psychological effect upon them," said special effects director Nicholas Brooks, who helped develop some of the technology used in the movie *The Matrix* and was part of the team that won a visual effects Oscar for *What Dreams May Come.* For the latter movie, he helped create a beautiful vision of heaven. But before he got the job, he said, he'd planned to quit the business because the scenes of carnage and violence he was called on to create sickened him. "In every film I worked on in the United States, violence was abundant," said Brooks, who immigrated from England a decade ago. "And there was no balance to the violence, no sense of remorse or showing of the consequences. I just didn't want to do it anymore." The last straw, he said, was *Eraser,* the 1996 Arnold Schwarzenegger action-thriller described in one movie guide as "indefensible on any artistic level, but lots of fun" (Harrison, 1999, p. F1).

Josh Brand, producer of the television shows *St. Elsewhere* and *Northern Exposure,* demonstrates a sophisticated understanding of the media effects research when he says "There are studies [that show] that violent images don't affect people, just as the tobacco industry has studies showing that cigarette smoking doesn't cause cancer." He continues, "I think that there is absolutely no question that the profusion of these kinds of images has a negative effect, not only on children but on human beings in general" (Krasny, 1993).

In a moment of unbridled honesty, Ted Turner of the Turner Broadcasting System said before a congressional subcommittee hearing on media violence, technology, and parental empowerment, "They [network executives] are guilty of murder as far as I can see. We all are. Me too" (Turner, 1994).

Recognition of Responsibility

Others in the creative community are now making statements about their responsibility as artists. "With the privilege of creative freedom there must come responsibility, and not simple lip service," said Ken Wales, a veteran filmmaker and producer of the 1994-1995 CBS series *Christy.* "It must be action, and action means making good choices." Also, Craig Anderson, producer of such CBS TV movies as *The Hallmark Hall of Fame: The Piano* and *The Staircase* said, "When a movie of mine is viewed by 31 million people at one time, I have a responsibility as a person to make sure that the content of that movie is not going to influence people in the wrong way" (Harrison, 1999, p. F1).

Media programs are more than expressions of creative visions; they are also products marketed for profit, and this introduces another type of responsibility. Josh Brand explains,

> If something gets a high rating, say, *The Amy Fisher Story*, then advertisers pay more money. Now, did the networks create the audience for it, or do they pander to what the audience wanted? Is it okay to pollute the emotional and spiritual environment? (quoted in Krasny, 1993)

He continues, "I do believe that some of those ideas are like pollutants" (Krasny, 1993).

Some people in the industry see themselves as conflicted between denial and concern. "It's a very interesting dichotomy," said Warren Littlefield, former entertainment president of NBC and now a producer. "There's a very strong 'don't tread on me' free speech and 'we are not the problem' line of thinking. At the same time, there's 'but we have to be part of the solution'" (Puig, 1999, p. 1D).

Callie Khouri, who won an Academy Award for her screenplay of *Thelma and Louise,* said,

> I have a hard time with violence just to entertain, but I believe it can be very effective in getting a point across. I resorted to it in my film, but there was a conscience to it. Thelma and Louise felt they had done something wrong, and there were big consequences—including psychic consequences. Outlaw movies have always been a catharsis for men, but denied to women. I was extremely frustrated with the literal interpretation of Thelma and Louise. Doesn't anyone read anymore or understand metaphor? The film was supposed to be complex, without easy answers, and with flawed characters. I

thought when Louise shot that guy that there'd be dead silence in the theater. That scene was written carefully: it was an attempted rape, and I wanted to make what she did wrong. And yet people cheered. I was stunned. (quoted in Krasny, 1993)

People in the industry most often pose as businesspeople or artists when talking about the media. However, sometimes we see them as human beings. For example, Brian Grazer, Ron Howard's partner, who has produced more than 20 movies, said,

Most of my films have been sweet-spirited, such as *Parenthood, Splash,* and *My Girl.* I'm proud of them. Others I'm not so proud of. I learned a big lesson with *Kindergarten Cop.* No one objected to the violent confrontation scene, and there was no problem with it in our focus groups. Then I showed it to my five-year-old, and all of a sudden, reflexively, I put my hand over his eyes. I knew at that point that we'd made a mistake. It was too late to cut the scene, but I would cut it now. (quoted in Krasny, 1993)

He continued, "Usually bad movies aren't hits. I don't see Freddy Krueger [*Nightmare on Elm Street*] movies, and I wouldn't want my kids to see them. I don't know why people make such movies. They're sick" (Krasny, 1993).

One actor who is speaking out is Dustin Hoffman, who has starred in some violent movies, such as *Straw Dogs.* Hoffman announced at the 1996 Cannes Film Festival that he is now rejecting films with gratuitous violence. Referring to recent mass murders in Dunblane, Scotland, and in Tasmania, Hoffman asked, "Are you saying film violence doesn't have anything to do with it?" (Cockburn, 1996). Also, Ken Wales, a veteran filmmaker, has also vowed to stop trafficking in violent images.

Vivienne Verdon-Roe, who directed the documentary film *Women For America, For The World,* said,

I can't go to most popular movies without checking them out with friends first, because I can't physically sit through [violent ones]. My body will not allow it. People really ought to think about the effects. They may not faint like I do, but they're getting desensitized to violence, and it contributes to the social violence of gangs and the like.

It's incredibly difficult when there are so few alternatives. Teens go to movies because there's often nothing else for them to do, and if they are gruesome or bad movies, no one in society seems to be saying so. (quoted in Krasny, 1993)

Even MPAA president Jack Valenti has his limits. Valenti said he refused to defend the movie *Scream,* in which a masked figure repeatedly stabbed a bloody and screaming baby-sitter played by Drew Barrymore (Stern & Petrikin, 1999).

Real Change

Although they are too few, there have been some indications of meaningful change. For example, the recording industry seems to be cutting back on violence. During the 1985 season, 61% of music videos contained at least one violent act (Kalis & Neuendorf, 1989). An analysis of music videos in 1994 to 1996 found that only 31% of videos contained at least one violent act (NTVS, 1997). Even accounting for the differences in definition of violence used by the two studies, this still represents a large decrease.

In the music world, when Ice-T's "Cop Killer" caused an uproar in 1992, Time Warner halted its distribution of the song on Sire Records. Then in 1995, Time Warner sold its interest in the label that produced much of the company's "gangsta" rap, Interscope (Harrison, 1999, p. F1). Also, the rap group the Beastie Boys not only rethought their views on violence, they've reworked their past creations to reflect their new attitudes. "When I was younger, I felt like I could say anything and it was funny," Beastie member Adam Yauch told *Rolling Stone Magazine.* "I've started to realize that what I say and do does effect everybody around us" (Harrison, 1999, p. F1).

In the radio industry, Entercom Communications, the United States' sixth-largest radio group, announced a corporate policy to reject any music and advertising that "advocate(s) or condone(s) criminal violence or which contain(s) ultra-violent content in the context of a socially irresponsible message." The policy also includes Entercom personalities. "In the wake of Littleton, we have all sought answers and solutions to this inexplicable tragedy," said David Field, president and CEO of Entercom. "We believe we can make a substantive contribution by voluntarily adopting [this policy]." Managers at Entercom's 42 stations—including Top 40 KDND-FM in Sacramento, California, Album Rocker WAAF-AM in Boston, and Modern Rocker KNDD-FM in Seattle—will have the authority to interpret the policy. "We're not setting up the Entercom standards board," explained Jack Donlevie, Entercom executive vice president. "This is a guideline to assist them in making a decision." No songs have been pulled from Entercom playlists so far. Entercom also said it plans to donate at least $1 million in promotional support to help troubled teens find help (Bachman, 1999). Also, Disney has pulled violent games from its theme parks. Wal-Mart and Montgomery Ward stopped selling violent video games (Grossman & DeGaetano, 1999).

At least one nonmedia company has been trying to address the problem of violence. Smith & Wesson, the nation's largest manufacturer of handguns, was the first major gun manufacturer to decide to adopt tighter controls on the sales of its handguns. Smith & Wesson did not act out of altruism. The company was named in lawsuits in 29 states and wanted to appear to be responsible. In return, 17 of the 29 states agreed to dismiss lawsuits against the company. Immediately after Smith & Wesson made its announcement, the National Rifle Association branded the company as a traitor to the cause of gun ownership rights. Another gun manufacturer, Glock, was considering adopting the controls but decided not to because it feared a consumer boycott (Koszczuk, 2000).

There is other good news about guns. There seem to be fewer instances of handgun violence in movies. The 15 top-grossing movies of 2000 contained a total of two scenes of people getting shot. Also, some Hollywood stars have made public statements against the use of guns. For example, when Drew Barrymore made *Charlie's Angels,* she wanted no guns in the film, saying that gunplay bored her. Also, Bruce Willis in 2000 announced he was on a gun moratorium (Lurie, 2001).

CONCLUSIONS

There is a poverty of responsibility that supports the continuation of the current problems of media violence. This can be seen in the behavior of the five players—the public, entertainment producers, policymakers, researchers, and the press. The people in each of these groups would rather criticize and posture than to confront this serious problem in a responsible fashion. The individual groups are largely unwilling to see the problem from a perspective different from their own.

This is not to say that many of the people in these groups are not sincerely bothered by the problem and want a solution. Instead, the people within each group usually want a solution that places the blame and the burden on *other* groups, so that their own needs and lifestyles are not hindered. Each of these groups has its own set of needs. Often the needs of one group are in direct opposition with the needs of another group, and no one is willing to sacrifice their own pleasures for the greater good. Thus we get back to seeing a poverty of responsibility.

It is time we recognized that we are all responsible for the problem of media violence. Each of us has played our own part in making the problem worse. If we share the responsibility and work together, we can each play a part in making the situation a lot better. It begins with accepting responsibility. Taking a public health perspective will help us all to understand that we are all in this together, and we are all susceptible to risks of harm. When each of us sacrifices a bit of our short-term selfish pleasures, we can together substantially reduce the risk to all of us.

REFERENCES

Albiniak, P. (2000, July 31). Violent media, violent kids? *Broadcasting & Cable*, p. 14.

Alternatives to violence. (1994). *Children Today, 23*(1), 14.

Alton, D. (1994). Our video culture. *Contemporary Review, 264,* 169-172.

American Medical Association. (1996). *Physician guide to media violence.* Chicago: Author.

American Psychological Association. (1993). *Violence and youth: Psychology's response—summary report of the American Psychological Association Commission on Violence and Youth.* Washington, DC: Author.

Anderson, C. A. (1983). Imagination and expectation: The effect of imagining behavioral scripts on personal intentions. *Journal of Personality and Social Psychology, 45,* 293-305.

Andison, F. S. (1977). TV violence and viewer aggression: A cumulation of study results. *Public Opinion Quarterly, 41,* 314-331.

Andrews, E. L. (1995, July 7). FCC, Congress zoom in on broadcast violence. *Daily News,* p. 1.

Atkin, C. (1983). Effects of realistic TV violence vs. fictional violence on aggression. *Journalism Quarterly, 60,* 615-621.

Aversa, J. (1999, May 5). Government employees get no respect on TV. *Tallahassee Democrat,* p. 3A.

Bachman, K. (1999, June 28). Saying "no" to violence. *Mediaweek,* p. 10.

Bagdikian, B. H. (2000). *The media monopoly* (6th ed.). Boston: Beacon.

Baker, R. K., & Ball, S. J. (1969). *Violence and the media.* Washington, DC: Government Printing Office.

Baker, S., & Gore, T. (1989, May 29). Some reasons for "wilding." *Newsweek,* p. 6.

Baldwin, T. F., & Lewis, C. (1972). Violence in television: The industry looks at itself. In G. A. Comstock & E. A. Rubinstein (Eds.), *Television's effects: Media content and control* (Television and Social Behavior, Vol. 1, pp. 290-373). Washington, DC: Government Printing Office.

Ball-Rokeach, S. J. (1972). The legitimation of violence. In J. F. Short Jr. & M. E. Wolfgang (Eds.), *Collective violence* (pp. 100-111). Chicago: Aldine-Atherton.

Bandura, A. (1978). A social learning theory of aggression. *Journal of Communication, 28*(3), 12-29.

Bandura, A. (1979). Psychological mechanisms of aggression. In M. von Cranach, K. Foppa, W. Lepenies, & D. Ploog (Eds.), *Human ethology: Claims and limits of a new discipline* (pp. 316-356). New York: Cambridge University Press.

Bandura, A. (1982). Self efficacy mechanism in human agency. *American Psychologist, 27,* 122-147.

Bandura, A. (1985). *Social foundations of thought and action.* Englewood Cliffs, NJ: Prentice Hall.

Barnhart, A. (1999, May 10). Public "fed up" with TV violence: Summit will focus on effects on youth. *Kansas City Star,* p. A1.

Baron, R. A. (1971a). Aggression as a function of magnitude of victim's pain cues, level of prior anger arousal, and aggressor-victim similarity. *Journal of Personality and Social Psychology, 18,* 48-54.

Baron, R. A. (1971b). Magnitude of victim's pain cues and level of prior anger arousal as determinants of adult aggressive behavior. *Journal of Personality and Social Psychology, 17,* 236-243.

Baron, R. A. (1978). Aggression-inhibiting influence of sexual humor. *Journal of Personality and Social Psychology, 36,* 189-197.

Baron, R. A. (1979). Effects of victim's pain cues, victim's race, and level of prior instigation upon physical aggression. *Journal of Applied Social Psychology, 9,* 103-114.

Bayles, M. (1993). Fake blood: Why nothing gets done about media violence. *Brookings Review, 11*(4), 20-24.

Bennett, W. L. (1988). *News: The politics of illusion.* New York: Longman.

Berger, A. A. (1988). Humor and behavior: Therapeutic aspects of the comedic techniques and other considerations. In B. D. Ruben (Ed.), *Information and behavior* (pp. 226-247). New Brunswick, NJ: Rutgers University Press.

Berkowitz, L. (1962). *Aggression: A social-psychological analysis.* New York: McGraw-Hill.

Berkowitz, L. (1970). Aggressive humors as a stimulus to aggressive responses. *Journal of Personality and Social Psychology, 16,* 710-717.

Berkowitz, L., & Alioto, J. T. (1973). The meaning of an observed event as a determinant of its aggressive consequences. *Journal of Personality and Social Psychology, 28,* 206-217.

Berkowitz, L., & Geen, R. G. (1966). Film violence and the cue properties of available targets. *Journal of Personality and Social Psychology, 3,* 525-530.

Berkowitz, L., & Geen, R. G. (1967). Stimulus qualities of the target of aggression: A further study. *Abnormal and Social Psychology, 65,* 197-202.

Berkowitz, L., & LaPage, A. (1967). Weapons as aggression-eliciting stimuli. *Journal of Personality and Social Psychology, 7,* 202-207.

Besteman, C. (1996). Representing violence and "othering" Somalia. *Cultural Anthropology, 11,* 120-133.

Bianculli, D. (1992). *Teleliteracy: Taking television seriously.* New York: Continuum.

Biddle, F. M. (1996, April 12). Ratings not in the picture, yet despite furor, expect sex and violence as usual on fall TV. *Boston Globe,* p. 59.

Blumer, H. (1933). *Movies and conduct.* New York: Macmillan.

Bok, S. (1998). *Mayhem: Violence as public entertainment.* Reading, MA: Addison-Wesley.

Bower, T. G. R. (1965). Stimulus variables determining space perception in infants. *Science, 149,* 88-89.

Bremner, J. G., & Bryant, P. E. (1977). Place versus response as the basis of spatial errors made by young infants. *Journal of Experimental Child Psychology, 23,* 162-171.

Brennan, P. (1995, January 8). The link between TV and violence. *Washington Post,* p. Y6.

British Broadcasting Corporation. (1972). *Violence on television: Programme content and viewer perceptions.* London: Author.

Brown, R. C., Jr., & Tedeschi, J. T. (1976). Determinants of perceived aggression. *Journal of Social Psychology, 100,* 77-87.

Bryan, J. H., & Schwartz, T. (1971). Effects of film material upon children's behavior. *Psychological Bulletin, 75,* 50-59.

Bryant, J., Carveth, R. A., & Brown, D. (1981). Television viewing and anxiety: An experimental examination. *Journal of Communication, 31*(1), 106-119.

Bryant, P. E., & Kopytynska, H. (1976). Spontaneous measurement by young children. *Nature, 260,* 773-774.

Bureau of Justice Statistics. (1999a). Attitudes toward contributions to violence in society, by demographic characteristics, United States, 1998, Table 2.43. In *Sourcebook of criminal justice statistics, 1998* (p. 122). Washington, DC: Author.

Bureau of Justice Statistics. (1999b). Percent changes in total crime index rates and violent crime rates, United States, 1960-97. In *Sourcebook of criminal justice statistics, 1998* (p. 284). Washington, DC: Author.

Bureau of Justice Statistics. (2001). Prison statistics. Washington, DC: U.S. Department of Justice. Retrieved July 24, 2002, from http://www.ojp.usdoj.gov/bjs/prisons.htm

Butterfield, F. (1996, April 22). Crime may not pay, but it costs America plenty. *Santa Barbara News Press,* p. A1.

Butterworth, G. (Ed.). (1981). *Infancy and epistemology: An evaluation of Piaget's theory.* Brighton, UK: Harvester Press.

Campbell, W. J., & Keogh, R. (1962). *Television and the Australian adolescent.* Sydney, Australia: Angus Robertson.

Cantor, J. (1994). Fright reactions to mass media. In J. Bryant & D. Zillmann (Eds.), *Media effects: Advances in theory and research* (pp. 213-245). Hillsdale, NJ: Lawrence Erlbaum.

Cantor, J. (1998a). *Mommy, I'm scared: How TV and movies frighten children and what we can do to protect them.* New York: Harcourt Brace.

Cantor, J. (1998b). Ratings for program content: The role of research findings. *Annals of the American Academy of Political Social Science, 557,* 54-69.

Cantor, J. (2000). Media violence. *Journal of Adolescent Health, 27*(2S), 30-34.

Cantor, J., & Harrison, K. (1996). Ratings and advisories for television programming. In *National Television Violence Study No. 1* (pp. 267-322). Thousand Oaks, CA: Sage.

Cantor, J., & Hoffner, C. (1990). Children's fear reactions to a televised film as a function of perceived immediacy of depicted threat. *Journal of Broadcasting & Electronic Media, 34,* 421-442.

Cantor, J., & Reilly, S. (1982). Adolescents' fright reactions to television and films. *Journal of Communication, 32*(1), 87-99.

Cantor, J., & Sparks, G. C. (1984). Children's fear responses to mass media: Testing some Piagetian predictions. *Journal of Communication, 34*(2), 90-103.

Cantor, J., Stutman, S., & Duran, V. (1996). *What parents want in a television ratings system: Results of a national survey* (Report released by the National PTA, Institute for Mental Health Initiatives, University of Wisconsin). Madison, WI: National PTA.

Cantor, J., & Wilson, B. J. (1984). Modifying fear responses to mass media in preschool and elementary school children. *Journal of Broadcasting, 28,* 431-443.

Cantor, J., Wilson, B. J., & Hoffner, C. (1986). Emotional responses to a televised nuclear holocaust film. *Communication Research, 13,* 257-277.

Cantril, H. (1940). *The invasion from Mars: A study in the psychology of panic.* Princeton, NJ: Princeton University Press.

Caprara, G. V., D'Imperio, G. D., Gentilomo, A., Mammucari, A., Renzi, P. G., & Travaglia, G. (1984). The eliciting cue value of aggressive slides reconsidered in a personological perspective: The weapons effect and irritability. *European Journal of Social Psychology, 14,* 313-322.

Carlson, M., Marcus-Newhall, A., & Miller, N. (1990). Effects of situational aggression cues: A quantitative review. *Journal of Personality and Social Psychology, 58,* 622-633.

Carveth, R., & Alexander, A. (1985). Soap opera viewing motivations and the cultivation hypothesis. *Journal of Broadcasting & Electronic Media, 29,* 259-273.

Centerwall, B. S. (1989). Exposure to television as a risk factor for violence. *Journal of Epidemiology, 129,* 643-652.

Centerwall, B. S. (1993a). Television and the development of the superego: Pathways to violence. In C. Chiland & J. G. Young (Eds.), *Children and violence* (pp. 178-197). Northvale, NJ: Jason Aronson.

Centerwall, B. S. (1993b). Television and violent crime. *The Public Interest, 111,* 56-71.

Chaffee, S. H. (1972). Television and adolescent aggressiveness (overview). In G. A. Comstock & E. A. Rubinstein (Eds.), *Television and social behavior: Television and adolescent aggressiveness* (Vol. 3, pp. 1-34). Washington, DC: Government Printing Office.

Charters, W. W. (1933). *Motion pictures and youth: A summary.* New York: Macmillan.

Chiricos, T. (1996). Moral panic as ideology: Drugs, violence, race and punishment in America. In *Justice with prejudice: Race and criminal justice in America* (pp. 19-48). New York: Harrow & Heston.

Churnin, N. (1998, December 5). Video values: Does what kids watch affect their morality? *Dallas Morning News,* p. 1G.

City of Renton v. Playtime Theatres, 475 U.S. 41 (1986).

Clark, D. G., & Blankenburg, W. B. (1972). Trends in violent content in selected mass media. In G. Comstock & E. Rubinstein (Eds.), *Media content and control* (Television and Social Behavior, Vol. 1, pp. 188-243). Washington, DC: Government Printing Office.

Clary, M. (2001a, January 25). Defense pulls pro wrestling into murder trial. *Los Angeles Times*, p. A5.

Clary, M. (2001b, January 26). Wrestling defense fails; boy, 13, faces life. *Los Angeles Times*, p. A1.

Cline, V. B., Croft, R. G., & Courier, S. (1973). Desensitization of children to television violence. *Journal of Personality and Social Psychology, 27,* 260-265.

Cockburn, A. (1996, June 3). The war on kids. *Nation*, p. 7.

Collins, W. A. (1973). Effect of temporal separation between motivation, aggression, and consequences: A developmental study. *Developmental Psychology, 8,* 215-221.

Collins, W. A. (1983). Interpretation and inference in children's television viewing. In J. Bryant & D. R. Anderson (Eds.), *Children's understanding of television: Research on attention and comprehension* (pp. 125-150). New York: Academic Press.

Comstock, G. A. (1985). Television and film violence. In S. Apter & A. Goldstein (Eds.), *Youth violence: Programs and prospects*. New York: Pergamon.

Comstock, G. A. (1989). *The evolution of American television*. Newbury Park, CA: Sage.

Comstock, G. A., Chaffee, S., Katzman, N., McCombs, M., & Roberts, D. (1978). *Television and social behavior*. New York: Columbia University Press.

Comstock, G., & Scharrer, E. (1999). *Television: What's on, who's watching, and what it means*. New York: Academic Press.

Comstock, G., & Strasburger, V. C. (1990). Deceptive appearances: Television violence and aggressive behavior. *Journal of Adolescent Health Care, 11*(1), 31-44.

Cooper, C. A. (1996). *Violence on television: Congressional inquiry, public criticism and industry response*. New York: University Press of America.

Covering the violence. (1999, May 31). *Time*.

Cumberbatch, G., Lee, M., Hardy, G., & Jones, I. (1987). *The portrayal of violence on British television*. London: British Broadcasting Corporation.

Dahlburg, J.-T. (2000, August 25). Hollywood unseats French competition. *Los Angeles Times*, p. A5.

Denniston, L. (1993). Chipping away at the First Amendment. *American Journalism Review, 15*(10), 50.

Diamant, A. (1994, October). Media violence. *Parents Magazine, 69*(10), 40.

Diener, E., & De Four, D. (1978). Does television violence enhance programme popularity? *Journal of Personality and Social Psychology, 36,* 333-341.

Diener, E., & Woody, L. W. (1981). TV violence and viewer liking. *Communication Research, 8,* 281-306.

Doctors push for less violence on TV. (1995, June 9). *Houston Chronicle*, p. A16.

Dominick, J. R. (1984). Videogames, television violence, and aggression in teenagers. *Journal of Communication, 34*(2), 136-147.

Donaldson, M. (1978). *Children's minds*. Glasgow: Fontana/Collins.

Donnerstein, E., & Berkowitz, L. (1981). Victim reactions in aggressive erotic films as a factor in violence against women. *Journal of Personality and Social Psychology, 41,* 710-724.

Donnerstein, E., Slaby, R. G., & Eron, L. D. (1994). The mass media and youth aggression. In L. D. Eron, J. H. Gentry, & P. Schlegel (Eds.), *Reason to hope: A psychological perspective on violence and youth* (pp. 219-250). Washington, DC: American Psychological Association.

Doob, A. N., & Climie, R. J. (1972). Delay of measurement and the effects of film violence. *Journal of Experimental Social Psychology, 8,* 136-142.

Dority, B. (1999) The Columbine tragedy: Countering the hysteria. *Humanist, 59*(4), 7.

Dorr, A. (1981). Television and affective development and functioning: Maybe this decade. *Journal of Broadcasting, 25,* 335-345.

Dorr, A. (1986). *Television and children: A special medium for a special audience.* Beverly Hills, CA: Sage.

Douglas, S. (1999, April 5). The devil made me do it: Is *Natural Born Killers* the Ford Pinto of movies? *Nation, 268*(13), 50.

Drabman, R. S., & Thomas, M. H. (1974). Does media violence increase children's toleration of real-life aggression? *Developmental Psychology, 10,* 418-421.

Dysinger, W. S., & Rucknick, C. A. (1933). *The emotional responses of children to the motion picture situation.* New York: Macmillan.

Easterbrook, G. (1996, October). It's unreal: How phony realism in film and literature is corrupting and confusing the American mind. *Washington Monthly, 28*(10), 41.

Eggerton, J. (1995, June 12). Content buck stops with media. *Broadcasting & Cable*, p. 13.

Eller, C. (1999, July 9). Literary manager built career by not following script. *Los Angeles Times*, pp. C1, C5.

Eron, L. D. (1982). Parent-child interaction, television violence, and aggression of children. *American Psychologist, 37,* 197-211.

FCC v. League of Women Voters, 468 U.S. 378 (1984).

FCC v. Pacifica Foundation, 438 U.S. 726 (1978).

Federal Bureau of Investigation. (2001a, May 30). *Crime index trends, preliminary figures 2000* (FBI press release). Washington, DC: Department of Justice.

Federal Bureau of Investigation. (2001b). *Uniform crime report, 1999.* Washington, DC: Author.

Federal Communications Commission. (2000). *FCC commissioner Gloria Tristani urges TV networks to recommit to V-chip education efforts.* Washington, DC: Author. Retrieved July 24, 2002, from http://ftp.fcc.gov/Bureaus/Miscellaneous/News_Releases/2000/nrmc0016.html

Federal Trade Commission. (2000). *FTC releases report on the marketing of violent entertainment to children.* Washington, DC: Author. Retrieved September 11, 2000, from http://www.ftc.gov

Federal Trade Commission. (2001). *Marketing violent entertainment to children: A six month follow-up of industry practices in the motion picture, music recording & electronic game industries.* Washington, DC: Author.

Feshbach, S. (1955). The drive-reducing function of fantasy behavior. *Journal of Abnormal and Social Psychology, 50,* 3-11.

Feshbach, S. (1961). The stimulating versus cathartic effects of a vicarious aggressive activity. *Journal of Abnormal and Social Psychology, 63,* 381-385.

Feshbach, S. (1972). Reality and fantasy in filmed violence. In J. P. Murray, E. A. Rubinstein, & G. A. Comstock (Eds.), *Television and social learning* (Television and Social Behavior, Vol. 2, pp. 318-345). Washington, DC: Government Printing Office.

Feshbach, S. (1976). The role of fantasy in the response to television. *Journal of Social Issues, 32,* 71-89.

Feshbach, S., & Singer, R. D. (1971). *Television and aggression.* San Francisco: Jossey-Bass.

Forgas, J. P., Brown, L. B., & Menyhart, J. (1980). Dimensions of aggression: The perception of aggressive episodes. *British Journal of Social and Clinical Psychology, 19,* 215-227.

Fowles, J. (1999). *The case for television violence.* Thousand Oaks, CA: Sage.

Freedman, J. L. (1984). Effect of television violence on aggressiveness. *Psychological Bulletin, 96,* 227-246.

Freedman, J. L. (1986). Television violence and aggression: A rejoinder. *Psychological Bulletin, 100,* 372-378.

Freedman, J., & Newtson, R. (1975). *The effect of anger on preference for filmed violence.* Paper presented at the annual conference of the American Psychological Association, Chicago, IL.

Freud, S. (1933). *New introductory lectures on psycho-analysis.* New York: Norton.

Freud, S. (1960). *Jokes and their relation to the unconscious* (Std. ed., Vol. 8). London: Hogarth.

Friedrich-Cofer, L., & Huston, A. C. (1986). Television violence and aggression: The debate continues. *Psychological Bulletin, 100,* 364-371.

Furu, T. (1962). *Television and children's life: A before-after study.* Tokyo: NHK Radio and Television Culture Research Institute.

Furu, T. (1971). *The function of television for children and adolescents.* Tokyo: Sophia University Press.

Galloway, S. (1993, July 27). U.S. rating system: Sex before violence. *Hollywood Reporter,* p. 31.

Gardels, N. (1998). Does rock wreck families? *New Perspectives Quarterly, 15*(3), 79-83.

Gardner, H. (1983). *Frames of mind: The theory of multiple intelligences.* New York: Basic Books.

Garvey, M. (2001a, August 2). Study: TV sex less subtle, less often. *Los Angeles Times,* p. A15.

Garvey, M. (2001b, June 21). Washington again taking on Hollywood. *Los Angeles Times,* p. A1.

Garvey, M., & Leeds, J. (2001, April 27). Music industry vigorously defends its rating policies. *Los Angeles Times,* pp. C1, C8.

Geen, R. G. (1975). The meaning of observed violence: Real vs. fictional violence and consequent effects on aggression and emotional arousal. *Journal of Research in Personality, 9,* 270-281.

Geen, R. G. (1994). Television and aggression: Recent developments in research and theory. In D. Zillmann, J. Bryant, & A. C. Huston (Eds.), *Media, children, and the family* (pp. 151-162). Hillsdale, NJ: Lawrence Erlbaum.

Geen, R., & Donnerstein, E. (Eds.). (1998). *Human aggression: Theories, research, and implications for policy.* New York: Academic Press.

Geen, R. G., & Rokosky, J. J. (1973). Interpretations of observed aggression and their effect on GSR. *Journal of Experimental Research in Personality, 6,* 289-292.

Gerbner, G. A. (1994, January). *Highlights of the television violence profile no. 16.* Remarks prepared for the National Association of Television Executives Annual Conference, Miami Beach, FL.

Gerbner, G., Gross, L., Eleey, M. F., Jackson-Beeck, M., Jeffries-Fox, S., & Signorielli, N. (1977). Television violence profile no. 8: The highlights. *Journal of Communication, 27*(2), 171-180.

Gerbner, G. A., Gross, L., Jackson-Beeck, M., Jeffries-Fox, S., & Signorielli, N. (1976). Cultural indicators: Violence profile no. 9. *Journal of Communication, 28(3),* 176-207.

Gerbner, G., Gross, L., Jackson-Beeck, M., Jeffries-Fox, S., & Signorielli, N. (1978). Cultural indicators: Violence profile no. 9. *Journal of Communication, 28*(3), 176-207.

Gerbner, G., Gross, L., Morgan, M., & Signorielli, N. (1980). The "mainstreaming" of America: Violence profile no. 11. *Journal of Communication, 30*(3), 10-29.

Gerbner, G. A., & Signorielli, N. (1990). *Violence profile 1967 to 1988-89: Enduring patterns.* Unpublished manuscript, Annenberg School of Communications, University of Pennsylvania, Philadelphia.

Glassner, B. (1999). *The culture of fear: Why Americans are afraid of the wrong things.* New York: Basic Books.

Goff, L., & Mandese, J. (1995). Bennett group eyes new targets. *Advertising Age, 66*(50), 1, 41.

Goleman, D. (1995). *Emotional intelligence.* New York: Bantam.

Good morning America [Television broadcast]. (1999, June 7). New York: American Broadcasting Company.

Goranson, R. (1969). *Observed violence and aggressive behavior: The effects of negative outcomes to the observed violence.* Unpublished doctoral dissertation, University of Wisconsin, Madison.

Gordon, C. (1999, May 24). Much ado about violence. *Maclean's Magazine*, p. 13.

Greenberg, B. S. (1975). British children and television violence. *Public Opinion Quarterly, 39*, 521-547.

Greenberg, B. S., Edison, N., Korzenny, F., Fernandez-Collado, C., & Atkin, C. K. (1980). Antisocial and prosocial behaviors on television. In B. S. Greenberg (Ed.), *Life on television: Content analysis of U.-S. TV drama* (pp. 99-128). Norwood, NJ: Ablex.

Grossman, D. (1996). *On killing: The psychological cost of learning to kill in war and society.* New York: Little, Brown.

Grossman, D., & DeGaetano, G. (1999). *Stop teaching our kids to kill.* New York: Crown.

Gunter, B. (1980). The cathartic potential of television drama. *Bulletin of the British Psychological Society, 36*, 166-168.

Gunter, B. (1985). *Dimensions of television violence.* Aldershot, UK: Gower.

Gupta, A. (2001, August 10). Warning on suicide copycats. *Los Angeles Times*, p. A26.

Halloran, J. D., Brown, R. L., & Chaney, D. C. (1970). *Television and delinquency.* Leicester, UK: Leicester University Press.

Halloran, J. D., & Croll, P. (1972). Television programmes in Great Britain. In G. A. Comstock & E. A. Rubinstein (Eds.), *Content and control* (Television and Social Behavior, Vol. 1, pp. 415-492). Washington, DC: Government Printing Office.

Hamilton, J. T. (1998). *Channeling violence: The economic market for violent television programming.* Princeton, NJ: Princeton University Press.

Hapkiewicz, W. G. (1979). Children's reactions to cartoon violence. *Journal of Clinical Child Psychology, 8*(1), 30-34.

Harrison, E. (1999, May 1) It's time for a reality check. *Los Angeles Times*, p. F1.

Hashway, R. M., & Duke, L. I. (1992). *Cognitive styles: A primer to the literature.* Lewiston, NY: Edwin Mellen Press.

Hattemer, B. (1994, July). Cause and violent effect: Media and our youth. *The World and I*, pp. 358-369.

Hawkins, R. P. (1977). The dimensional structure of children's perceptions of television reality. *Communication Research, 4*, 299-320.

Hawkins, R. P., & Pingree, S. (1980). Some processes in the cultivation effect. *Communication Research, 7*, 193-226.

Hawkins, R. P., & Pingree, S. (1981a). Uniform messages and habitual viewing: Unnecessary assumptions in social reality effects. *Human Communication Research, 7*, 291-301.

Hawkins, R. P., & Pingree, S. (1981b). Using television to construct social reality. *Journal of Broadcasting, 25*, 347-364.

Hawkins, R. P., & Pingree, S. (1982). Television's influence on social reality. In D. Pearl, L. Bouthilet, & J. Lazar (Eds.), *Television and behavior: Ten years of scientific progress and implications for the eighties* (Vol. 2, pp. 224-247). Rockville, MD: U.S. Department of Health and Human Services.

Healy, J. M. (1990). *Endangered minds: Why children don't think and what we can do about it.* New York: Simon & Schuster.

Hearings on H.R. 1391, Television Violence Act of 1989, before the Subcommittee on Economic and Commercial Law of the House Committee on the Judiciary, 101st Cong., 1st Sess. 34 (1989) (statement of Prof. Cass R. Sunstein).

Hearold, S. (1986). A synthesis of 1043 effects of television on social behavior. In G. Comstock (Ed.), *Public communication and behavior* (Vol. 1, pp. 65-133). San Diego, CA: Academic Press.

Heath, L., Bresolin, L. B., & Rinaldi, R. C. (1989). Effects of media violence on children. *Archives of General Psychiatry, 46,* 376-379.

Hennigan, K. M., Del Rosario, M. L., Heath, L., Cook, T. D., Wharton, J. D., & Calder, B. J. (1982). Impact of the introduction of television on crime in the United States: Empirical findings and theoretical implications. *Journal of Personality and Social Psychology, 42,* 461-477.

Hicks, D. J. (1965). Imitation and retention of film-mediated aggressive peer and adult models. *Journal of Personality and Social Psychology, 2,* 97-100.

Himmelweit, H., Oppenheim, A., & Vince, P. (1958). *Television and the child.* London: Oxford University Press.

Himmelweit, H. T., Swift, B., & Biberian, M. J. (1980). The audience as critic: An approach to the study of entertainment. In P. Tannenbaum (Ed.), *Entertainment functions of television.* Hillsdale, NJ: Lawrence Erlbaum.

Hoffner, C., & Cantor, J. (1985). Developmental differences in responses to a television character's appearance and behavior. *Developmental Psychology, 21,* 1065-1074.

Holland, P. (1994, April 22). Thrills and bills. *New Statesman & Society, 7*(299), 35-36.

Houston knows murder. (1993, July 9). *New York Times,* p. A7.

Howitt, D., & Cumberbatch, G. (1975). *Mass media violence and society.* New York: John Wiley.

Huesmann, L. R., Lagerspetz, K., & Eron, L. D. (1984). Intervening variables in the TV-violence-aggression relation: Evidence from two countries. *Developmental Psychology, 20,* 746-775.

Hutchinson, P. (1993, August 15). *Denver Post,* p. 1A.

Iwao, S., de Sola Pool, I., Hagiwara, S. (1981). Japanese and U.S. media: Some cross-cultural insights into TV violence. *Journal of Communication Disorders, 31*(2), 28-36.

James, M. (2001, May 31). Study finds R-ratings are costly. *Los Angeles Times,* p. C6.

Jo, E., & Berkowitz, L. (1994). A priming effect analysis of media influences: An update. In J. Bryant & D. Zillmann (Eds.), *Media effects: Advances in theory and research* (pp. 43-60). Hillsdale, NJ: Lawrence Erlbaum.

Johnson, S. (2001, August 7). Parents ignore the TV ratings safety net. *Los Angeles Times,* p. F10.

Johnston, D. D. (1995). Adolescents' motivations for viewing graphic horror. *Human Communication Research, 21,* 522-552.

Jones, G. W., Jr. (1971). *The relationship of screen-mediated violence to antisocial behavior* (Doctoral dissertation, Syracuse University). University Microfilms No. 72-60,592.

Jones, T. (1998, May 28). TV ratings frequently a jumble to parents: Nearly half in survey say they really aren't paying much attention. *Chicago Tribune*, p. 1.

Josephson, W. (1987). Television violence and children's aggression: Testing the priming, social script, and disinhibition predictors. *Journal of Personality and Social Psychology, 53,* 882-890.

Kalis, P., & Neuendorf, K. (1989). Aggressive cue prominence and gender participation in MTV. *Journalism Quarterly, 66,* 148-154.

Kane, T., Joseph, J. M., & Tedeschi, J. T. (1976). Personal perception and the Berkowitz paradigm for the study of aggression. *Journal of Personality and Social Psychology, 33,* 663-673.

Kaplan, R. M., & Singer, R. D. (1976). Psychological effects of television violence: A review and methodological critique. *Journal of Social Issues, 34,* 176-188.

Kapoor, S., Kang, J. G., Kim, W. Y., & Kim, S. K. (1994). Televised violence and viewers' perceptions of social reality: The Korean case. *Communication Research Reports, 11,* 189-200.

Kellner, M. (1999, June 14). Taking on Tinseltown: Parents of slain classmates say media are to blame. *Christianity Today.* Retrieved July 27, 2002, from http://www.christianitytoday.com/ct/9t7/9t7016.html

Kennedy, J. P., II. (1996, February 5). *Congressional Record.*

Kent, S. L. (1997, May 18). *Seattle Times*, p. C1.

King, P. M. (1986). Formal reasoning in adults: A review and critique. In R. A. Mines & K. S. Kitchenor (Eds.), *Adult cognitive development: Methods and models* (pp. 1-21). New York: Praeger.

Kitchenor, K. S. (1983). Cognition, metacognition and epistemic cognition: A three-level model of cognitive processing. *Human Development, 4,* 222-232.

Kleiner, C. (1999, September 6). When "ready to rock" becomes ready to riot. *U.S. News & World Report*, p. 59.

Kniveton, B. H. (1976). Social learning and imitation in relation to TV. In R. Brown (Ed.), *Children and television* (pp. 237-266). Beverly Hills, CA: Sage.

Kohlberg, L. (1966). Moral education in the schools: A developmental view. *School Review, 74,* 1-30.

Kohlberg, L. (1981). *The philosophy of moral development: Moral stages and the idea of justice.* New York: Harper & Row.

Koszczuk, J. (2000, March 26). Gun lobby taking aim at straying gun maker. *Tallahassee Democrat,* pp. 1B, 3B.

Krasny, M. (1993, January). Passing the buck in Tinseltown. *Mother Jones.* Retrieved July 27, 2002, from http://www.mojones.com/mother_jones/JA93/krasny.html

Kunkel, D., Maynard Farinola, W. J., Cope, K. M., Donnerstein, E., Biely, E., & Zwarun, L. (1998). *An assessment of the television industry's use of V-chip ratings.* Menlo Park, CA: Henry J. Kaiser Family Foundation.

Lacayo, R. (1995, June 12). Are music and movies killing America's soul? *Time*, pp. 24-30.

Lazarus, R. S., Opton, E. M., Nomikos, M. S., & Rankin, N. O. (1965). The principle of short-circuiting of threat: Further evidence. *Journal of Personality, 33*, 622-635.

Leeds, J. (2001, January 17). Surgeon gen. links TV, real violence. *Los Angeles Times*, p. A1.

Leland, J. (1995, December 11). Violence, reel to real. *Newsweek*, p. 16.

Leo, J. (1999a, May 24). The devil with Ms. Jones. *U.S. News & World Report*, p. 30.

Leo, J. (1999b, May 10). Gunning for Hollywood. *U.S. News & World Report*, p. 16.

Lesser, H. (1977). *Television and the preschool child*. New York: Academic Press.

Levine, M. (1998). *See no evil: A guide to protecting our children from media violence*. San Francisco: Jossey-Bass.

Leyens, J. -P., & Picus, S. (1973). Identification with the winner of a fight and name mediation: Their differential effects upon subsequent aggressive behaviour. *British Journal of Social Clinical Psychology, 12*, 374-377.

Liebert, R. M. (1972). Television and social learning: Some relationships between viewing violence and behaving aggressively (overview). In J. P. Murray, E. A. Rubinstein, & G. A. Comstock (Eds.), *Television and social learning* (Television and Social Behavior, Vol. 2, pp. 1-42). Washington, DC: Government Printing Office.

Liebert, R. M., Neale, J. M., & Davidson, E. A. (1973). *The early window: Effects of television on children and youth*. Elmsford, NY: Pergamon.

Liebert, R. M., & Poulos, R. W. (1975). Television and personality development: The socializing effects of an entertainment medium. In A. Davids (Ed.), *Child personality and psychopathology: Current topics* (Vol. 2, pp. 61-97). New York: Wiley.

Liebert, R. M., & Schwartzberg, N. S. (1977). Effects of mass media. *Annual Review of Psychology, 28*, 141-173.

Liebert, R. M., Sobol, M. P., & Davidson, E. S. (1972). Catharsis of aggression among institutionalized boys: Fact or artifact? In G. A. Comstock, E. A. Rubinstein, & J. P. Murray (Eds.), *Television's effects: Further explorations* (Television and Social Behavior, Vol. 5, pp. 351-359). Washington, DC: Government Printing Office.

Leifer, A. D., & Roberts, D. F. (1972). Children's responses to television violence. In J. P. Murray, E. A. Rubinstein, & G. A. Comstock (Eds.), *Television and social learning* (Television and Social Behavior, Vol. 2, pp. 43-180). Washington, DC: Government Printing Office.

Linne, O. (1971). The viewer's aggression as a function of variously edited TV films. *Communications, 2*(1), 101-111.

Liss, M. B., Reinhardt, L. C., & Fredriksen, S. (1983). TV heroes: The impact of rhetoric and deeds. *Journal of Applied Developmental Psychology, 4*, 175-187.

Lorenz, K. Z. (1963). *On aggression*. New York: Harcourt, Brace & World.

Lowry, B. (1997, September 21). TV on decline but few back U.S. regulation. *Los Angeles Times*, pp. A1, A40, A41.

Lowry, S. A., & DeFleur, M. L. (1995). *Milestones in mass communication research: Media effects* (3rd ed.). White Plains, NY: Longman.

Lurie, B. D. (2001, May 28). Not yet farewell to arms, but films have fewer guns. *Los Angeles Times,* p. F4.

Lutterbeck, D. (1995). Prime time politics. *Common Cause Magazine, 21*(1), 24-27.

Maccoby, E. E. (1964). Effects of the mass media. In M. L. Hoffman & L. W. Hoffman (Eds.), *Review of child development research* (pp. 323-348). New York: Russell Sage Foundation.

Maguire, K., Pastore, A. N., & Flanagan, T. J. (Eds.). (1993). *Bureau of Justice statistics sourcebook of criminal justice statistics—1992.* Washington, DC: U.S. Department of Justice.

Malcolm, T. (1999, May 28). Teen violence: Does violent media make violent kids? *National Catholic Reporter, 35*(30), 14.

Males, M. (1993). School-age pregnancy: Why hasn't prevention worked? *Journal of School Health, 63,* 429-432.

Males, M. A. (1996). *Scapegoat generation: America's war on adolescents.* Monroe, ME: Common Courage Press.

Martin, A. -L. (1998, June). Everybody's in this. *Sources, 102,* 5-7.

Masters, K., McDowell, J., & Ressner, J. (1999, June 28). Bullets over Hollywood. *Time.*

McArthur, D. L., Peek-Asa, C., Webb, T., Fisher, K., Cook, B., Brown, N., & Kraus, J. (2000). Violence and its injury consequences in American movies: A public health perspective. *Western Journal of Medicine, 173,* 164-169.

McAvoy, K., & Coe, S. (1993). TV rocked by Reno ultimatum. *Broadcasting and Cable, 123*(43), 6, 14.

McCain, R. (1998, December 21). Television's bloody hands. *Insight on the News, 14*(47), 31.

McCann, T. E., & Sheehan, P. W. (1985).Violent content in Australian television. *Australian Psychologist, 20*(1), 33-42.

McGarrigle, J., & Donaldson, M. (1975). Conservation accidents. *Cognition, 3,* 341-350.

McHan, E. J. (1985). Imitation of aggression by Lebanese children. *The Journal of Social Psychology, 125,* 613-617.

McLeod, J. M., Atkin, C. K., & Chaffee, S. H. (1972). Adolescents, parents, and television use: Adolescent self-report measures from Maryland and Wisconsin samples. In G. A. Comstock & E. A. Rubinstein (Eds.), *Television and social behavior: Television and adolescent aggressiveness* (Vol. 3, pp. 173-238). Washington, DC: Government Printing Office.

McLeod, J. J., & Chaffee, S. H. (1973). Interpersonal approaches to communication research. *American Behavioral Scientist, 16,* 469-499.

Medved, M. (1992). *Hollywood vs. America: Popular culture and the war on traditional values.* New York: HarperCollins.

Mees, U. (1990). Constitutive elements of the concept of human aggression. *Aggressive Behavior, 16,* 285-295.

Messner, S. F. (1986). Television violence and violent crime: An aggregate analysis. *Social Problems, 33,* 218-235.

Meyer, T. P. (1972). Effects of viewing justified and unjustified real film violence on aggressive behavior. *Journal of Personality and Social Psychology, 23,* 21-29.

Mifflin, L. (1998, November 9). Media: "Springer" returns to its antics. *New York Times*, p. C7.

Mikami, S. (1993). A cross-national comparison of the U.S.-Japanese TV drama: International cultural indicators. *KEIO Communication Review, 15,* 29-44.

Mines, R. A., & Kitchenor, K. S. (1986). *Adult cognitive development: Methods and models.* New York: Praeger.

Minow, N. (1995). *Television's values and the values of our children.* Washington, DC: Annenberg Washington Program.

Minow, N. N., & LeMay, C. L. (1995). *Abandoned in the wasteland: Children, television, and the First Amendment.* New York: Hill & Wang.

Molitor, F., & Hirsch, K. W. (1994). Children's toleration of real life aggression after exposure to media violence: A replication of the Drabman and Thomas studies. *Child Study Journal, 24*(3), 191-207.

Moore, C., & Fry, D. (1986). The effect of the experimenter's intention on the child's understanding of conservation. *Cognition, 22,* 283-298.

Morgan, M. (1983). Symbolic victimization and real world fear. *Human Communication Research, 9,* 146-157.

Morgan, M. (1986). Television and the erosion of regional diversity. *Journal of Broadcasting & Electronic Media, 30,* 123-139.

Morris, H. J. (2000, June 5). G isn't what it used to be. *U.S. News & World Report*, p. 91.

Morris, H. J., & Silver, M. (1999, September 20). G, why R ratings so confusing? *U.S. News & World Report*, pp. 68, 70.

Morrison, D. E. (1993). The idea of violence. In A. M. Hargrave (Ed.), *Violence in factual television, annual review 1993* (pp. 124-129). London: John Libbey.

Most believe TV violence begets crime. (1993, December 19). *Houston Post*, p. 26.

Munakata, K., & Kashiwagi, A. (1991). Effect of viewing TV programs with violence on children and their families: Five years later. *Hoso Bunka Foundation Research Report, 14,* 275-278.

Mundy, A. (1995, July 24). The unifying effect of smut. *Mediaweek*, p. 16.

Mustonen, A., & Pulkkinen, L. (1993). Aggression in television programs in Finland. *Aggressive Behavior, 19,* 175-183.

National Foundation to Improve Television. (1996). *Mission statement.* Boston, MA: Author.

National Institute of Mental Health. (1982). *Television and behavior: Ten years of scientific progress and implications for the eighties.* Washington, DC: Government Printing Office.

National Television Violence Study. (1996). *Technical report* (Vol. 1). Thousand Oaks, CA: Sage.

National Television Violence Study. (1997). *Technical report* (Vol. 2). Thousand Oaks, CA: Sage.

National Television Violence Study. (1998). *Technical report* (Vol. 3). Thousand Oaks, CA: Sage.

National Television Violence Study. (1999). *Technical report* (Vol. 3). Thousand Oaks, CA: Sage.

Neimark, E. D. (1979). Current status of formal operations research. *Human Development, 22,* 60-67.

Neuman, S. B. (1991). *Literacy in the television age: The myth of the TV effect.* Norwood, NJ: Ablex.

The new right's TV hit list. (1981, June 15). *Newsweek,* p. 101.

New York City plans to sue gun industry. (2000, June 20). *USA Today,* p. 4A.

Nielsen Media Research. (1998). *1998 report on television.* New York: Author.

O'Donnell, P. (1992, Summer). Killing the golden goose: Hollywood's death wish. *Beverly Hills Bar Journal,* p. 103.

Ogles, R. M., & Hoffner, C. (1987). Film violence and perceptions of crime: The cultivation effect. In M. L. McLaughlin (Ed.), *Communication Yearbook 10* (pp. 384-394). Thousand Oaks, CA: Sage.

Oldenburg, A., & Snider, M. (1999, May 4). Entertainment in the cross hairs. *USA Today,* p. 1D.

Oliver, M. B. (1994). Portrayals of crime, race, and aggression in "reality based" police shows: A content analysis. *Journal of Broadcasting & Electronic Media, 38,* 179-192.

Oliver, M. B., & Armstrong, B. (1995). Predictors of viewing and enjoyment of reality-based and fictional crime shows. *Journalism & Mass Communication Quarterly, 72,* 559-570.

Osborn, D. K., & Endsley, R. C. (1971). Emotional reactions of young children to TV violence. *Child Development, 42,* 321-331.

Paik, H., & Comstock, G. (1994). The effects of television violence on antisocial behavior: A meta-analysis. *Communication Research, 21,* 516-546.

Parley, H. (1985, November 5). Church study deplores industry profit motive. *Dallas Morning News.*

Paul Kagan and Associates. (1994, February 27). From 1984 to 1993, R-rated movies grossed less than PG. *Washington Post.*

Pearl, D., Bouthilet, L., & Lazar J. (Eds.). (1982). *Television and behavior: Ten years of scientific progress and implications for the eighties: Vol. 2. Technical reviews.* Rockville, MD: U.S. Department of Health and Human Services.

Perry, D. G., & Perry, L. C. (1976). Identification with film characters, covert aggressive verbalization, and reactions to film violence. *Journal of Research in Personality, 10,* 399-409.

Philips, C. (2001, January 25). Murder case spotlights marketing of violent lyrics. *Los Angeles Times,* pp. C1, C7.

Phillips, D. P., & Hensley, J. E. (1984). When violence is rewarded or punished: The impact of mass media stories on homicide. *Journal of Communication, 34*(3), 101-116.

Piaget, J., & Inhelder, B. (1969). *The psychology of the child.* London: Routledge.

Potter, W. J. (1986). Perceived reality in the cultivation hypothesis. *Journal of Broadcasting & Electronic Media, 30*, 159-174.

Potter, W. J. (1988). Perceived reality in television effects research. *Journal of Broadcasting & Electronic Media, 32*, 23-41.

Potter, W. J. (1991). The relationships between first and second order measures of cultivation. *Human Communication Research, 18*, 92-113.

Potter, W. J. (1994). A methodological critique of cultivation research. *Journalism Monographs.*

Potter, W. J. (1999). *On media violence.* Thousand Oaks, CA: Sage.

Potter, W. J. (2001). *Media literacy* (2nd ed.). Thousand Oaks, CA: Sage.

Potter, W. J., & Berry, M. (1998, May). *Constructions of judgments of violence.* Paper presented to the Annual Meeting of the International Communication Association, San Francisco, CA.

Potter, W. J., & Chang, I. K. (1990). Television exposure measures and the cultivation hypothesis. *Journal of Broadcasting & Electronic Media, 34*, 313-333.

Potter, W. J., Pekurny, R., Pashupati, K., Hoffman, E., & Davis, K. (2000, April). *Viewers' interpretations of violence on television.* Paper presented at the Annual Meeting of the Broadcast Education Association, Las Vegas, NV.

Potter, W. J., & Vaughan, M. (1997). Aggression in television entertainment: Profiles and trends. *Communication Research Reports, 14*, 116-124.

Potter, W. J., Vaughan, M., Warren, R., Howley, K., Land, A., & Hagemeyer, J. (1995). How real is the portrayal of aggression in television entertainment programming? *Journal of Broadcasting & Electronic Media, 39*, 496-516.

Potter, W. J., & Ware, W. (1987). An analysis of the contexts of antisocial acts on prime-time television. *Communication Research, 14*, 664-686.

Potter, W. J., & Warren, R. (1996). Considering policies to protect children from TV violence. *Journal of Communication, 46*(4), 116-138.

Potter, W. J., Warren, R., Vaughan, M., Howley, K., Land, A., & Hagemeyer, J. (1997). Antisocial acts in reality programming on television. *Journal of Broadcasting & Electronic Media, 41*, 69-89.

Preston, M. I. (1941). Children's reactions to movie horrors and radio crime. *Journal of Pediatrics, 19*, 147-168.

Puig, C. (1999, June 7). Hollywood examines its soul. *USA Today*, p. 1D.

Reimer, B., & Rosengren, K. E. (1990). Cultivated viewers and readers: A life-style perspective. In N. Signorielli & M. Morgan (Eds.), *Cultivation analysis: New directions in media effects research* (pp. 181-206). Newbury Park, CA: Sage.

Reitman, V. (2001, June 9). School slayings horrify Japan. *Los Angeles Times*, pp. A1, A8.

Resnick, P. (1997). Filtering information on the Internet. *Scientific American, 276*(3), 62-64.

Rich, F. (1997, November 22). The Baptist pratfall. *New York Times*, p. A15.

Rich, F. (1998, May 2). Coming to you dead from L.A. *New York Times.*

Robb, C. (1991, July 8). Are we hooked on media violence? *Boston Globe*, p. 27.

Roberts, D. F., & Maccoby, N. (1985). Effects of mass communication. In G. Lindzey & E. Aronson (Eds.), *Handbook of social psychology: Vol. 2. Special fields and applications* (3rd ed., pp. 539-598). New York: Random House.

Roberts, D. F., & Schramm, W. (1971). Children's learning from the mass media. In W. Schramm & D. F. Roberts (Eds.), *The process and effects of mass communication* (Rev. ed., pp. 596-611). Urbana: University of Illinois Press.

Ross, J. (1999). *Child care survey: Rage & anger outbursts in children.* Fort Worth, TX: Campfire Boys and Girls.

Rouner, D. (1984). Active television viewing and the cultivation hypothesis. *Journalism Quarterly, 61,* 168-174.

Rubin, A. M., Perse, E. M., & Taylor, D. S. (1988). A methodological examination of cultivation. *Communication Research, 15,* 107-133.

Rule, B. G., & Ferguson, T. J. (1986). The effects of media violence on attitudes, emotions, and cognitions. *Journal of Social Issues, 42,* 29-50.

Salovey, P., & Mayer, J. D. (1990). Emotional intelligence. *Imagination, Cognition, and Personality, 9,* 185-211.

Salvoza, M. F. (1997, May 16-18). *USA Weekend,* p. 20.

Sanders, B. (1994). *A is for ox: Violence, electronic media, and the silencing of the written word.* New York: Pantheon.

Sanders, E. (2001, May 27). Corporate free speech is escalating. *Los Angeles Times,* pp. C1, C14.

Sanders, G. S., & Baron, R. S. (1975). Pain cues and uncertainty as determinants of aggression in a situation involving repeated instigation. *Journal of Personality and Social Psychology, 32,* 495-502.

Sapolsky, B. S., & Zillmann, D. (1978). Experience and empathy: Affective reactions to witnessing childbirth. *Journal of Social Psychology, 105,* 131-144.

Satellite Network Committee, National Cable Television Association. (1994). *Voices against violence: A cable television industry initiative.* Washington, DC: Author.

Schwartz, S. (1984, Winter). Send help before it's too late. *Parent's Choice,* p. 2.

Scream 3 director says he didn't hold back. (1999, November 2). *Tallahassee Democrat,* p. 2B.

Sherman, B. L., & Dominick, J. R. (1986). Violence and sex in music videos: TV and rock 'n' roll. *Journal of Communication, 36*(1), 79-93.

Shirley, K. W. (1973). *Television and children: A modeling analysis review essay.* Unpublished doctoral dissertation, University of Kansas, Lawrence.

Siegel, A. E. (1958). The influence of violence in the mass media upon children's role expectations. *Child Development, 29,* 35-56.

Signorielli, N. (1990). Television's mean and dangerous world: A continuation of the cultural indicators perspective. In N. Signorielli & M. Morgan (Eds.), *Cultivation analysis: New directions in media effects research* (pp. 85-106). Newbury Park, CA: Sage.

Silverblatt, A. (1995). *Media literacy: Keys to interpreting media messages.* Westport, CT: Praeger.

Simon, S. (2001, April 11). Armed and potentially dangerous. *Los Angeles Times,* p. A5.

Singer, J. L. (1971). The influence of violence portrayed in television or motion pictures upon overt aggressive behavior. In J. L. Singer (Ed.), *The control of aggression and violence: Cognitive and physiological factors.* New York: Academic Press.

Slaby, R. G., Quarfoth, G. R., & McConnachie, G. A. (1976). Television violence and its sponsors. *Journal of Communication, 26*(1), 88-96.

Smith, P. K., & Cowie, H. (1988). *Understanding children's development.* Oxford, UK: Basil Blackwell.

Sparks, G. G. (1986). Developing a scale to assess cognitive responses to frightening films. *Journal of Broadcasting & Electronic Media, 30,* 65-73.

Sparks, G. G., & Cantor, J. (1986). Developmental differences in fright responses to a television program depicting a character transformation. *Journal of Broadcasting & Electronic Media, 30,* 309-323.

Stanley, T. L. (2001, June 2). UPN goes without standards executive. *Los Angeles Times,* pp. F1, F8.

Stein, A. H., & Friedrich, L. K. (1975). Television content and young children's behavior. In J. P. Murray, E. A. Rubinstein, & G. A. Comstock (Eds.), *Television and social learning* (Television and Social Behavior, Vol. 2). Washington, DC: Government Printing Office.

Stein, B. (1981). Norman Lear vs. The Moral Majority: The war to clean up TV. *Saturday Review,* p. 23.

Stern, C. (1999a, May 10). Biz, violence, and pols: D.C. youth-rage confab opens. *Variety.*

Stern, C. (1999b, May 24). Valenti corrals H'wood CEOs to buck backlash. *Variety, 375*(2), 4.

Stern, C., & Petrikin, C. (1999, June 7). Gunfight at DC corral. *Variety, 375*(4), 1.

Sternberg, R. J., & Berg, C. A. (1987). What are theories of adult intellectual development theories of? In C. Schooler & K. W. Schaie (Eds.), *Cognitive functioning and social structure over the life course* (pp. 3-23). Norwood, NJ: Ablex.

Sullivan, B. (1998, May 17). [Review of the book *On Killing: The Psychological Cost of Learning to Kill in War and Society*]. *The [Memphis, TN] Commercial Appeal,* p. B1.

Summary of bills to regulate violence on TV. (1993). *News Media & the Law, 18*(1), 40-41.

Surbeck, E. (1975). Young children's emotional reactions to T.V. violence: The effects of children's perceptions of reality. *Dissertation Abstracts International, 35,* 5139A.

Surette, R. (1998). *Media, crime, and criminal justice: Images and realities* (2nd ed.). Belmont, CA: Wadsworth.

Surgeon General's Scientific Advisory Committee on Television and Social Behavior. (1972). *Television and growing up: The impact of televised violence.* Washington, DC: Author.

Tan, A. S. (1981). *Mass communication theories and research.* Columbus, OH: Grid.

Tangney, J. P. (1988). Aspects of the family and children's television viewing content preferences. *Child Development, 59,* 1070-1079.

Tangney, J. P., & Feshbach, S. (1988). Children's television viewing frequency: Individual differences and demographic correlates. *Aggressive Behavior, 14,* 145-158.

Tannenbaum, P., & Gaer, E. P. (1965). Mood changes as a function of stress of protagonist and degree of identification in film-viewing situation. *Journal of Personality and Social Psychology, 2,* 612-616.

Tannenbaum, P. H., & Zillmann, D. (1975). Emotional arousal in the facilitation of aggression through communication. In L. Berkowitz (Ed.), *Advances in experimental social psychology* (Vol. 8, pp. 149-192). New York: Academic Press.

Teinowitz, I. (1999, May 10). Ad Council responds to first lady's ad call. *Ad Age,* p. 61.

Texeira, E. (2001, April 10). Coverage of youth crime promotes fear, study says. *Los Angeles Times,* p. B3.

Thomas, M. H., & Drabman, R. S. (1975). Toleration of real life aggression as a function of exposure to televised violence and age of subject. *Merrill-Palmer Quarterly, 21*(3), 227-232.

Thomas, M. H., & Drabman, R. S. (1978). Effects of television violence on expectations of other's aggression. *Personality and Social Psychology Bulletin, 4,* 73-76.

Thomas, M. H., Horton, R. W., Lippincott, E. C., & Drabman, R. S. (1977). Desensitization to portrayals of real-life aggression as a function of exposure to television violence. *Journal of Personality and Social Psychology, 35,* 450-458.

Thomas, M. H., & Tell, P. M. (1974). Effects of viewing real versus fantasy violence upon interpersonal aggression. *Journal of Research in Personality, 8,* 153-160.

Turkle, S. (2000, October). Remarks from the Panel on Social/Emotional Development. Presented at the Digital Childhood Conference, Washington, DC.

Turner, C. W., & Berkowitz, L. (1972). Identification with film aggressor (covert role taking) and reactions to film violence. *Journal of Personality and Social Psychology, 21,* 256-264.

Turner, T. E. (1994). Testimony. In *Violence on television: Hearings before the Subcommittee on Telecommunications and Finance, House of Representatives: May 12, June 25, July 1 and 29, September 15, 1993* (pp. 105-121). Washington, DC: Government Printing Office.

U.S. Department of Justice, Federal Bureau of Investigation. (1999, October 17). *Crime in the United States 1998: Uniform crime statistics.* Washington, DC: Author.

U.S. News & World Report Online. (1994). *Culture & ideas: Special report* [Online]. Retrieved from Webmaster@usnews.com

Van der Voort, T. H. A. (1986). *Television violence: A child's-eye view.* Amsterdam: North-Holland.

Van Horne, H. (1981). The "Moral Majority" and us. *Television Quarterly, 18*(1), 65-66.

Violence on television. (1993). *Congressional Digest, 72*(12), 290-300.

von Feilitzen, C. (1975). Findings of Scandinavian research on child and television in the process of socialization. *Fernsehen und Bildung, 9,* 54-84.

Wald, M. L. (1997, July 18). "Violent aggressive" motorists account for 28,000 deaths. *Santa Barbara New-Press,* p. B6.

Wallace, A., & Fiore, F. (1999, May 25). Hollywood surprised by Clinton's violence inquiry. *Los Angeles Times*, p. B1.

Wal-mart pulls wrestling doll from shelves. (1999, November 3). *Tallahassee Democrat*, p. 7E.

Walters, R. H., & Willows, D. C. (1968). Imitative behavior of disturbed and nondisturbed children following exposure to aggressive and nonaggressive models. *Child Development, 39,* 79-89.

Wartella, E., Olivarez, A., & Jennings, N. (1998). Children and television violence in the United States. In U. Carlsson & C. von Feilitzen (Eds.), *Children and media violence* (pp. 55-62). Goteborg, Sweden: UNESCO International Clearinghouse on Children and Violence on the Screen.

Weaver, J., & Wakshlag, J. (1986). Perceived vulnerability to crime, criminal victimization experience, and television viewing. *Journal of Broadcasting & Electronic Media, 30,* 141-158.

Wells, W. D. (1973). *Television and aggression: Replication of an experimental field study.* Unpublished manuscript, Graduate School of Business, University of Chicago.

Wertham, F. (1954). *Seduction of the innocent.* New York: Rinehart.

Whitman, D. (1996, December 16). I'm OK, you're not. *U.S. News & World Report,* pp. 24-30.

Williams, A. (1999, June 6). Extra! Extra! Family-friendly films make money for Hollywood. *Eastside Journal,* P. B4.

Williams, T. M. (Ed.). (1986). *The impact of television.* Orlando, FL: Academic Press.

Williams, T. M., Zabrack, M. L., & Joy, L. A. (1982). The portrayal of aggression on North American television. *Journal of Applied Social Psychology, 12,* 360-380.

Wilson, B. J., & Cantor, J. (1985). Developmental difference in empathy with a television protagonist's fear. *Journal of Experimental Child Psychology, 39,* 284-299.

Wilson, B. J., Hoffner, C., & Cantor, J. (1987). Children's perceptions of the effectiveness of techniques to reduce fear from mass media. *Journal of Applied Developmental Psychology, 8,* 39-52.

Wober, J. M. (1978). Televised violence and paranoid perception: The view from Great Britain. *Public Opinion Quarterly, 42,* 315-321.

Wood, W., Wong, F. Y., & Chachere, J. G. (1991). Effects of media violence on viewers' aggression in unconstrained social interaction. *Psychological Bulletin, 109,* 371-383.

Yokota, F., & Thompson, K. M. (2000). Violence in G-rated animated films. *Journal of the American Medical Association, 283*(20), 2716-2720.

Zillmann, D. (1971). Excitation transfer in communication-mediated aggressive behavior. *Journal of Experimental Social Psychology, 7,* 419-434.

Zillmann, D. (1978). Attribution and misattribution of excitatory reactions. In J. H. Harvey, W. Ickes, & R. F. Kidd (Eds.), *New directions in attribution research* (Vol. 2, pp. 335-368). Hillsdale, NJ: Lawrence Erlbaum.

Zillmann, D. (1979). *Hostility and aggression.* Hillsdale, NJ: Lawrence Erlbaum.

Zillmann, D. (1982). Television viewing and arousal. In D. Pearl, L. Bouthilet, & J. Lazar (Eds.), *Television and behavior: Ten years of scientific progress and implications for the eighties* (Technical Reviews, Vol. 2, pp. 53-67). Rockville, MD: U.S. Department of Health and Human Services.

Zillmann, D. (1991). Television viewing physiological arousal. In J. Bryant & D. Zillmann (Eds.), *Responding to the screen* (pp. 103-133). Hillsdale, NJ: Lawrence Erlbaum.

Zillmann, D. (1998). The psychology of appeal of portrayals of violence. In J. H. Goldstein (Ed.), *Why we watch: The attractiveness of violent entertainment* (pp. 179-211). New York: Oxford University Press.

Zillmann, D., & Wakshlag, J. (1985). Fear of victimization and the appeal of crime drama. In D. Zillmann & J. Bryant (Eds.), *Selective exposure to communication* (pp. 141-156). Hillsdale, NJ: Lawrence Erlbaum.

Zillmann, D., Weaver, J. B., III, Mundorf, N., & Aust, C. F. (1986). Effects of an opposite-gender companion's affect to horror on distress, delight, and attraction. *Journal of Personality and Social Psychology, 51,* 586-594.

Zurawik, D. (1994, January 1). *The Baltimore Sun,* p. 1A.

INDEX

ABOUT THE AUTHOR

W. James Potter earned a Ph.D. in media theory and another Ph.D. in instructional technology and has tested his media literacy ideas in his teaching at Stanford University, UCLA, Indiana University, Florida State University, and especially at the University of California at Santa Barbara, where he is currently a professor in the Department of Communication. He has served on the editorial boards of six journals, been a reviewer for a dozen more, and was editor of the *Journal of Broadcasting & Electronic Media.* He has published six books in the fields of qualitative methodologies, media violence, theory, and literacy.